Mometrix TEST PREPARATION

I0866806

OSAT®

Superintendent (248) Secrets Study Guide

DEAR FUTURE EXAM SUCCESS STORY

First of all, **THANK YOU** for purchasing Mometrix study materials!

Second, congratulations! You are one of the few determined test-takers who are committed to doing whatever it takes to excel on your exam. **You have come to the right place.** We developed these study materials with one goal in mind: to deliver you the information you need in a format that's concise and easy to use.

In addition to optimizing your guide for the content of the test, we've outlined our recommended steps for breaking down the preparation process into small, attainable goals so you can make sure you stay on track.

We've also analyzed the entire test-taking process, identifying the most common pitfalls and showing how you can overcome them and be ready for any curveball the test throws you.

Standardized testing is one of the biggest obstacles on your road to success, which only increases the importance of doing well in the high-pressure, high-stakes environment of test day. Your results on this test could have a significant impact on your future, and this guide provides the information and practical advice to help you achieve your full potential on test day.

Your success is our success

We would love to hear from you! If you would like to share the story of your exam success or if you have any questions or comments in regard to our products, please contact us at **800-673-8175** or **support@mometrix.com**.

Thanks again for your business and we wish you continued success!

Sincerely,
The Mometrix Test Preparation Team

Need more help? Check out our flashcards at:
http://MometrixFlashcards.com/CEOE

Written and edited by the Mometrix Exam Secrets Test Prep Team
Printed in the United States of America

TABLE OF CONTENTS

Introduction

Thank you for purchasing this resource! You have made the choice to prepare yourself for a test that could have a huge impact on your future, and this guide is designed to help you be fully ready for test day. Obviously, it's important to have a solid understanding of the test material, but you also need to be prepared for the unique environment and stressors of the test, so that you can perform to the best of your abilities.

For this purpose, the first section that appears in this guide is the **Secret Keys**. We've devoted countless hours to meticulously researching what works and what doesn't, and we've boiled down our findings to the five most impactful steps you can take to improve your performance on the test. We start at the beginning with study planning and move through the preparation process, all the way to the testing strategies that will help you get the most out of what you know when you're finally sitting in front of the test.

We recommend that you start preparing for your test as far in advance as possible. However, if you've bought this guide as a last-minute study resource and only have a few days before your test, we recommend that you skip over the first two Secret Keys since they address a long-term study plan.

If you struggle with **test anxiety**, we strongly encourage you to check out our recommendations for how you can overcome it. Test anxiety is a formidable foe, but it can be beaten, and we want to make sure you have the tools you need to defeat it.

Secret Key #1 – Plan Big, Study Small

There's a lot riding on your performance. If you want to ace this test, you're going to need to keep your skills sharp and the material fresh in your mind. You need a plan that lets you review everything you need to know while still fitting in your schedule. We'll break this strategy down into three categories.

Information Organization

Start with the information you already have: the official test outline. From this, you can make a complete list of all the concepts you need to cover before the test. Organize these concepts into groups that can be studied together, and create a list of any related vocabulary you need to learn so you can brush up on any difficult terms. You'll want to keep this vocabulary list handy once you actually start studying since you may need to add to it along the way.

Time Management

Once you have your set of study concepts, decide how to spread them out over the time you have left before the test. Break your study plan into small, clear goals so you have a manageable task for each day and know exactly what you're doing. Then just focus on one small step at a time. When you manage your time this way, you don't need to spend hours at a time studying. Studying a small block of content for a short period each day helps you retain information better and avoid stressing over how much you have left to do. You can relax knowing that you have a plan to cover everything in time. In order for this strategy to be effective though, you have to start studying early and stick to your schedule. Avoid the exhaustion and futility that comes from last-minute cramming!

Study Environment

The environment you study in has a big impact on your learning. Studying in a coffee shop, while probably more enjoyable, is not likely to be as fruitful as studying in a quiet room. It's important to keep distractions to a minimum. You're only planning to study for a short block of time, so make the most of it. Don't pause to check your phone or get up to find a snack. It's also important to **avoid multitasking**. Research has consistently shown that multitasking will make your studying dramatically less effective. Your study area should also be comfortable and well-lit so you don't have the distraction of straining your eyes or sitting on an uncomfortable chair.

The time of day you study is also important. You want to be rested and alert. Don't wait until just before bedtime. Study when you'll be most likely to comprehend and remember. Even better, if you know what time of day your test will be, set that time aside for study. That way your brain will be used to working on that subject at that specific time and you'll have a better chance of recalling information.

Finally, it can be helpful to team up with others who are studying for the same test. Your actual studying should be done in as isolated an environment as possible, but the work of organizing the information and setting up the study plan can be divided up. In between study sessions, you can discuss with your teammates the concepts that you're all studying and quiz each other on the details. Just be sure that your teammates are as serious about the test as you are. If you find that your study time is being replaced with social time, you might need to find a new team.

Secret Key #2 – Make Your Studying Count

You're devoting a lot of time and effort to preparing for this test, so you want to be absolutely certain it will pay off. This means doing more than just reading the content and hoping you can remember it on test day. It's important to make every minute of study count. There are two main areas you can focus on to make your studying count.

Retention

It doesn't matter how much time you study if you can't remember the material. You need to make sure you are retaining the concepts. To check your retention of the information you're learning, try recalling it at later times with minimal prompting. Try carrying around flashcards and glance at one or two from time to time or ask a friend who's also studying for the test to quiz you.

To enhance your retention, look for ways to put the information into practice so that you can apply it rather than simply recalling it. If you're using the information in practical ways, it will be much easier to remember. Similarly, it helps to solidify a concept in your mind if you're not only reading it to yourself but also explaining it to someone else. Ask a friend to let you teach them about a concept you're a little shaky on (or speak aloud to an imaginary audience if necessary). As you try to summarize, define, give examples, and answer your friend's questions, you'll understand the concepts better and they will stay with you longer. Finally, step back for a big picture view and ask yourself how each piece of information fits with the whole subject. When you link the different concepts together and see them working together as a whole, it's easier to remember the individual components.

Finally, practice showing your work on any multi-step problems, even if you're just studying. Writing out each step you take to solve a problem will help solidify the process in your mind, and you'll be more likely to remember it during the test.

Modality

Modality simply refers to the means or method by which you study. Choosing a study modality that fits your own individual learning style is crucial. No two people learn best in exactly the same way, so it's important to know your strengths and use them to your advantage.

For example, if you learn best by visualization, focus on visualizing a concept in your mind and draw an image or a diagram. Try color-coding your notes, illustrating them, or creating symbols that will trigger your mind to recall a learned concept. If you learn best by hearing or discussing information, find a study partner who learns the same way or read aloud to yourself. Think about how to put the information in your own words. Imagine that you are giving a lecture on the topic and record yourself so you can listen to it later.

For any learning style, flashcards can be helpful. Organize the information so you can take advantage of spare moments to review. Underline key words or phrases. Use different colors for different categories. Mnemonic devices (such as creating a short list in which every item starts with the same letter) can also help with retention. Find what works best for you and use it to store the information in your mind most effectively and easily.

Secret Key #3 – Practice the Right Way

Your success on test day depends not only on how many hours you put into preparing, but also on whether you prepared the right way. It's good to check along the way to see if your studying is paying off. One of the most effective ways to do this is by taking practice tests to evaluate your progress. Practice tests are useful because they show exactly where you need to improve. Every time you take a practice test, pay special attention to these three groups of questions:

- The questions you got wrong
- The questions you had to guess on, even if you guessed right
- The questions you found difficult or slow to work through

This will show you exactly what your weak areas are, and where you need to devote more study time. Ask yourself why each of these questions gave you trouble. Was it because you didn't understand the material? Was it because you didn't remember the vocabulary? Do you need more repetitions on this type of question to build speed and confidence? Dig into those questions and figure out how you can strengthen your weak areas as you go back to review the material.

Additionally, many practice tests have a section explaining the answer choices. It can be tempting to read the explanation and think that you now have a good understanding of the concept. However, an explanation likely only covers part of the question's broader context. Even if the explanation makes perfect sense, **go back and investigate** every concept related to the question until you're positive you have a thorough understanding.

As you go along, keep in mind that the practice test is just that: practice. Memorizing these questions and answers will not be very helpful on the actual test because it is unlikely to have any of the same exact questions. If you only know the right answers to the sample questions, you won't be prepared for the real thing. **Study the concepts** until you understand them fully, and then you'll be able to answer any question that shows up on the test.

It's important to wait on the practice tests until you're ready. If you take a test on your first day of study, you may be overwhelmed by the amount of material covered and how much you need to learn. Work up to it gradually.

On test day, you'll need to be prepared for answering questions, managing your time, and using the test-taking strategies you've learned. It's a lot to balance, like a mental marathon that will have a big impact on your future. Like training for a marathon, you'll need to start slowly and work your way up. When test day arrives, you'll be ready.

Start with the strategies you've read in the first two Secret Keys—plan your course and study in the way that works best for you. If you have time, consider using multiple study resources to get different approaches to the same concepts. It can be helpful to see difficult concepts from more than one angle. Then find a good source for practice tests. Many times, the test website will suggest potential study resources or provide sample tests.

Practice Test Strategy

If you're able to find at least three practice tests, we recommend this strategy:

Untimed and Open-Book Practice

Take the first test with no time constraints and with your notes and study guide handy. Take your time and focus on applying the strategies you've learned.

Timed and Open-Book Practice

Take the second practice test open-book as well, but set a timer and practice pacing yourself to finish in time.

Timed and Closed-Book Practice

Take any other practice tests as if it were test day. Set a timer and put away your study materials. Sit at a table or desk in a quiet room, imagine yourself at the testing center, and answer questions as quickly and accurately as possible.

Keep repeating timed and closed-book tests on a regular basis until you run out of practice tests or it's time for the actual test. Your mind will be ready for the schedule and stress of test day, and you'll be able to focus on recalling the material you've learned.

Secret Key #4 – Pace Yourself

Once you're fully prepared for the material on the test, your biggest challenge on test day will be managing your time. Just knowing that the clock is ticking can make you panic even if you have plenty of time left. Work on pacing yourself so you can build confidence against the time constraints of the exam. Pacing is a difficult skill to master, especially in a high-pressure environment, so **practice is vital**.

Set time expectations for your pace based on how much time is available. For example, if a section has 60 questions and the time limit is 30 minutes, you know you have to average 30 seconds or less per question in order to answer them all. Although 30 seconds is the hard limit, set 25 seconds per question as your goal, so you reserve extra time to spend on harder questions. When you budget extra time for the harder questions, you no longer have any reason to stress when those questions take longer to answer.

Don't let this time expectation distract you from working through the test at a calm, steady pace, but keep it in mind so you don't spend too much time on any one question. Recognize that taking extra time on one question you don't understand may keep you from answering two that you do understand later in the test. If your time limit for a question is up and you're still not sure of the answer, mark it and move on, and come back to it later if the time and the test format allow. If the testing format doesn't allow you to return to earlier questions, just make an educated guess; then put it out of your mind and move on.

On the easier questions, be careful not to rush. It may seem wise to hurry through them so you have more time for the challenging ones, but it's not worth missing one if you know the concept and just didn't take the time to read the question fully. Work efficiently but make sure you understand the question and have looked at all of the answer choices, since more than one may seem right at first.

Even if you're paying attention to the time, you may find yourself a little behind at some point. You should speed up to get back on track, but do so wisely. Don't panic; just take a few seconds less on each question until you're caught up. Don't guess without thinking, but do look through the answer choices and eliminate any you know are wrong. If you can get down to two choices, it is often worthwhile to guess from those. Once you've chosen an answer, move on and don't dwell on any that you skipped or had to hurry through. If a question was taking too long, chances are it was one of the harder ones, so you weren't as likely to get it right anyway.

On the other hand, if you find yourself getting ahead of schedule, it may be beneficial to slow down a little. The more quickly you work, the more likely you are to make a careless mistake that will affect your score. You've budgeted time for each question, so don't be afraid to spend that time. Practice an efficient but careful pace to get the most out of the time you have.

Secret Key #5 – Have a Plan for Guessing

When you're taking the test, you may find yourself stuck on a question. Some of the answer choices seem better than others, but you don't see the one answer choice that is obviously correct. What do you do?

The scenario described above is very common, yet most test takers have not effectively prepared for it. Developing and practicing a plan for guessing may be one of the single most effective uses of your time as you get ready for the exam.

In developing your plan for guessing, there are three questions to address:

- When should you start the guessing process?
- How should you narrow down the choices?
- Which answer should you choose?

When to Start the Guessing Process

Unless your plan for guessing is to select C every time (which, despite its merits, is not what we recommend), you need to leave yourself enough time to apply your answer elimination strategies. Since you have a limited amount of time for each question, that means that if you're going to give yourself the best shot at guessing correctly, you have to decide quickly whether or not you will guess.

Of course, the best-case scenario is that you don't have to guess at all, so first, see if you can answer the question based on your knowledge of the subject and basic reasoning skills. Focus on the key words in the question and try to jog your memory of related topics. Give yourself a chance to bring the knowledge to mind, but once you realize that you don't have (or you can't access) the knowledge you need to answer the question, it's time to start the guessing process.

It's almost always better to start the guessing process too early than too late. It only takes a few seconds to remember something and answer the question from knowledge. Carefully eliminating wrong answer choices takes longer. Plus, going through the process of eliminating answer choices can actually help jog your memory.

Summary: Start the guessing process as soon as you decide that you can't answer the question based on your knowledge.

How to Narrow Down the Choices

The next chapter in this book (**Test-Taking Strategies**) includes a wide range of strategies for how to approach questions and how to look for answer choices to eliminate. You will definitely want to read those carefully, practice them, and figure out which ones work best for you. Here though, we're going to address a mindset rather than a particular strategy.

Your odds of guessing an answer correctly depend on how many options you are choosing from.

Number of options left	5	4	3	2	1
Odds of guessing correctly	20%	25%	33%	50%	100%

You can see from this chart just how valuable it is to be able to eliminate incorrect answers and make an educated guess, but there are two things that many test takers do that cause them to miss out on the benefits of guessing:

- Accidentally eliminating the correct answer
- Selecting an answer based on an impression

We'll look at the first one here, and the second one in the next section.

To avoid accidentally eliminating the correct answer, we recommend a thought exercise called **the $5 challenge**. In this challenge, you only eliminate an answer choice from contention if you are willing to bet $5 on it being wrong. Why $5? Five dollars is a small but not insignificant amount of money. It's an amount you could afford to lose but wouldn't want to throw away. And while losing $5 once might not hurt too much, doing it twenty times will set you back $100. In the same way, each small decision you make—eliminating a choice here, guessing on a question there—won't by itself impact your score very much, but when you put them all together, they can make a big difference. By holding each answer choice elimination decision to a higher standard, you can reduce the risk of accidentally eliminating the correct answer.

The $5 challenge can also be applied in a positive sense: If you are willing to bet $5 that an answer choice *is* correct, go ahead and mark it as correct.

Summary: Only eliminate an answer choice if you are willing to bet $5 that it is wrong.

Which Answer to Choose

You're taking the test. You've run into a hard question and decided you'll have to guess. You've eliminated all the answer choices you're willing to bet $5 on. Now you have to pick an answer. Why do we even need to talk about this? Why can't you just pick whichever one you feel like when the time comes?

The answer to these questions is that if you don't come into the test with a plan, you'll rely on your impression to select an answer choice, and if you do that, you risk falling into a trap. The test writers know that everyone who takes their test will be guessing on some of the questions, so they intentionally write wrong answer choices to seem plausible. You still have to pick an answer though, and if the wrong answer choices are designed to look right, how can you ever be sure that you're not falling for their trap? The best solution we've found to this dilemma is to take the decision out of your hands entirely. Here is the process we recommend:

Once you've eliminated any choices that you are confident (willing to bet $5) are wrong, select the first remaining choice as your answer.

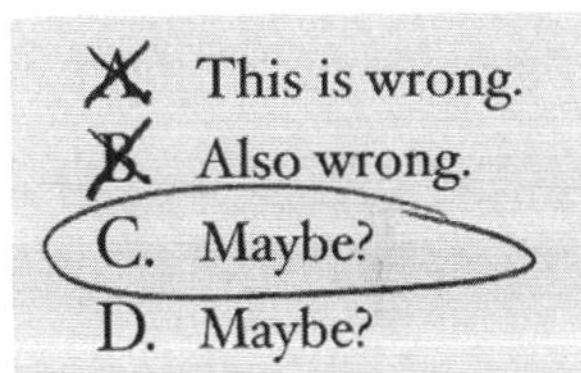

Whether you choose to select the first remaining choice, the second, or the last, the important thing is that you use some preselected standard. Using this approach guarantees that you will not be enticed into selecting an answer choice that looks right, because you are not basing your decision on how the answer choices look.

This is not meant to make you question your knowledge. Instead, it is to help you recognize the difference between your knowledge and your impressions. There's a huge difference between thinking an answer is right because of what you know, and thinking an answer is right because it looks or sounds like it should be right.

Summary: To ensure that your selection is appropriately random, make a predetermined selection from among all answer choices you have not eliminated.

Test-Taking Strategies

This section contains a list of test-taking strategies that you may find helpful as you work through the test. By taking what you know and applying logical thought, you can maximize your chances of answering any question correctly!

It is very important to realize that every question is different and every person is different: no single strategy will work on every question, and no single strategy will work for every person. That's why we've included all of them here, so you can try them out and determine which ones work best for different types of questions and which ones work best for you.

Question Strategies

✓ Read Carefully

Read the question and the answer choices carefully. Don't miss the question because you misread the terms. You have plenty of time to read each question thoroughly and make sure you understand what is being asked. Yet a happy medium must be attained, so don't waste too much time. You must read carefully and efficiently.

✓ Contextual Clues

Look for contextual clues. If the question includes a word you are not familiar with, look at the immediate context for some indication of what the word might mean. Contextual clues can often give you all the information you need to decipher the meaning of an unfamiliar word. Even if you can't determine the meaning, you may be able to narrow down the possibilities enough to make a solid guess at the answer to the question.

✓ Prefixes

If you're having trouble with a word in the question or answer choices, try dissecting it. Take advantage of every clue that the word might include. Prefixes can be a huge help. Usually, they allow you to determine a basic meaning. *Pre-* means before, *post-* means after, *pro-* is positive, *de-* is negative. From prefixes, you can get an idea of the general meaning of the word and try to put it into context.

✓ Hedge Words

Watch out for critical hedge words, such as *likely, may, can, often, almost, mostly, usually, generally, rarely,* and *sometimes.* Question writers insert these hedge phrases to cover every possibility. Often an answer choice will be wrong simply because it leaves no room for exception. Be on guard for answer choices that have definitive words such as *exactly* and *always.*

✓ Switchback Words

Stay alert for *switchbacks.* These are the words and phrases frequently used to alert you to shifts in thought. The most common switchback words are *but, although,* and *however.* Others include *nevertheless, on the other hand, even though, while, in spite of, despite,* and *regardless of.* Switchback words are important to catch because they can change the direction of the question or an answer choice.

✓ Face Value

When in doubt, use common sense. Accept the situation in the problem at face value. Don't read too much into it. These problems will not require you to make wild assumptions. If you have to go beyond creativity and warp time or space in order to have an answer choice fit the question, then you should move on and consider the other answer choices. These are normal problems rooted in reality. The applicable relationship or explanation may not be readily apparent, but it is there for you to figure out. Use your common sense to interpret anything that isn't clear.

Answer Choice Strategies

✓ Answer Selection

The most thorough way to pick an answer choice is to identify and eliminate wrong answers until only one is left, then confirm it is the correct answer. Sometimes an answer choice may immediately seem right, but be careful. The test writers will usually put more than one reasonable answer choice on each question, so take a second to read all of them and make sure that the other choices are not equally obvious. As long as you have time left, it is better to read every answer choice than to pick the first one that looks right without checking the others.

✓ Answer Choice Families

An answer choice family consists of two (in rare cases, three) answer choices that are very similar in construction and cannot all be true at the same time. If you see two answer choices that are direct opposites or parallels, one of them is usually the correct answer. For instance, if one answer choice says that quantity *x* increases and another either says that quantity *x* decreases (opposite) or says that quantity *y* increases (parallel), then those answer choices would fall into the same family. An answer choice that doesn't match the construction of the answer choice family is more likely to be incorrect. Most questions will not have answer choice families, but when they do appear, you should be prepared to recognize them.

✓ Eliminate Answers

Eliminate answer choices as soon as you realize they are wrong, but make sure you consider all possibilities. If you are eliminating answer choices and realize that the last one you are left with is also wrong, don't panic. Start over and consider each choice again. There may be something you missed the first time that you will realize on the second pass.

✓ Avoid Fact Traps

Don't be distracted by an answer choice that is factually true but doesn't answer the question. You are looking for the choice that answers the question. Stay focused on what the question is asking for so you don't accidentally pick an answer that is true but incorrect. Always go back to the question and make sure the answer choice you've selected actually answers the question and is not merely a true statement.

✓ Extreme Statements

In general, you should avoid answers that put forth extreme actions as standard practice or proclaim controversial ideas as established fact. An answer choice that states the "process should be used in certain situations, if…" is much more likely to be correct than one that states the "process should be discontinued completely." The first is a calm rational statement and doesn't even make a definitive, uncompromising stance, using a hedge word *if* to provide wiggle room, whereas the second choice is far more extreme.

✓ Benchmark

As you read through the answer choices and you come across one that seems to answer the question well, mentally select that answer choice. This is not your final answer, but it's the one that will help you evaluate the other answer choices. The one that you selected is your benchmark or standard for judging each of the other answer choices. Every other answer choice must be compared to your benchmark. That choice is correct until proven otherwise by another answer choice beating it. If you find a better answer, then that one becomes your new benchmark. Once you've decided that no other choice answers the question as well as your benchmark, you have your final answer.

⊘ Predict the Answer

Before you even start looking at the answer choices, it is often best to try to predict the answer. When you come up with the answer on your own, it is easier to avoid distractions and traps because you will know exactly what to look for. The right answer choice is unlikely to be word-for-word what you came up with, but it should be a close match. Even if you are confident that you have the right answer, you should still take the time to read each option before moving on.

General Strategies

⊘ Tough Questions

If you are stumped on a problem or it appears too hard or too difficult, don't waste time. Move on! Remember though, if you can quickly check for obviously incorrect answer choices, your chances of guessing correctly are greatly improved. Before you completely give up, at least try to knock out a couple of possible answers. Eliminate what you can and then guess at the remaining answer choices before moving on.

⊘ Check Your Work

Since you will probably not know every term listed and the answer to every question, it is important that you get credit for the ones that you do know. Don't miss any questions through careless mistakes. If at all possible, try to take a second to look back over your answer selection and make sure you've selected the correct answer choice and haven't made a costly careless mistake (such as marking an answer choice that you didn't mean to mark). This quick double check should more than pay for itself in caught mistakes for the time it costs.

⊘ Pace Yourself

It's easy to be overwhelmed when you're looking at a page full of questions; your mind is confused and full of random thoughts, and the clock is ticking down faster than you would like. Calm down and maintain the pace that you have set for yourself. Especially as you get down to the last few minutes of the test, don't let the small numbers on the clock make you panic. As long as you are on track by monitoring your pace, you are guaranteed to have time for each question.

⊘ Don't Rush

It is very easy to make errors when you are in a hurry. Maintaining a fast pace in answering questions is pointless if it makes you miss questions that you would have gotten right otherwise. Test writers like to include distracting information and wrong answers that seem right. Taking a little extra time to avoid careless mistakes can make all the difference in your test score. Find a pace that allows you to be confident in the answers that you select.

⊘ Keep Moving

Panicking will not help you pass the test, so do your best to stay calm and keep moving. Taking deep breaths and going through the answer elimination steps you practiced can help to break through a stress barrier and keep your pace.

Final Notes

The combination of a solid foundation of content knowledge and the confidence that comes from practicing your plan for applying that knowledge is the key to maximizing your performance on test day. As your foundation of content knowledge is built up and strengthened, you'll find that the strategies included in this chapter become more and more effective in helping you quickly sift through the distractions and traps of the test to isolate the correct answer.

Now that you're preparing to move forward into the test content chapters of this book, be sure to keep your goal in mind. As you read, think about how you will be able to apply this information on the test. If you've already seen sample questions for the test and you have an idea of the question format and style, try to come up with questions of your own that you can answer based on what you're reading. This will give you valuable practice applying your knowledge in the same ways you can expect to on test day.

Good luck and good studying!

Visionary Leadership and Continuous District Improvement

Culture of Learning

It is the leader's goal to develop a culture of learning on the district campuses. The leader must incorporate this goal into the school vision and goals. As a result, when there is **evidence of a culture of learning** on the campuses, this is also evidence that the leader's vision and goals are being implemented. In a culture of learning, both adults and students work toward **learning goals** and are self-motivated to achieve these goals. They also have access to the necessary **resources** to support and drive engagement in the learning process. Evidence of the culture of learning includes **students and staff** who are goal-oriented and self-motivated to learn and engage in the learning process, motivation to perform at the highest levels academically, and skilled use of available resources to engage in the learning process. When these are present, it will be evident that the vision and goals can be accomplished.

Creating a Culture of Learning

A culture of learning is an environment with an emphasis on learning and a high expectation for academic achievement. It involves intellectual stimulation for students, staff, and leadership. Evidence of a **culture of learning** includes implementing effective classroom instructional strategies for student learning, implementing processes of continuous improvement to increase student learning and academic performance, participating in professional development for teachers and staff collectively and individually, and the acquiring and sharing of knowledge by leadership. When a culture of learning is present, district leaders seek ways to support the learning needs of all students so all can be **academically successful**. District leaders also seek ways to support the learning needs of **teachers and staff** to assist them in their professional growth.

Developing a Culture of Learning

To develop a culture of learning on each campus, a district leader must consider this culture in all decision-making. First, the schools in the district should be **designed** in a way that facilitates a culture of learning. This means that there are sufficient **learning spaces** to accommodate a variety of learning strategies, along with furniture and resources that support learning in those spaces. For example, each school should have a library resource center with appropriate shelving, books, and technology resources. A district leader must also hire and train **staff** in a way that supports a culture of learning. Candidates for hire that do not support a culture of learning should not be selected. The leader must also communicate **expectations** for a culture of learning to staff, students, parents, and community stakeholders to ensure that everyone is aware of the expectations. When possible, the leader can support the district's culture by encouraging **families** to develop their own culture of learning and providing the resources and support for them to do so. For example, the leader may give books to families to encourage reading in the home.

District Vision and Goals

District Vision

The district vision serves as a guide and a foundation for all strategic planning and communicates the **purpose** and **focus** of the district to all stakeholders. One of the goals of a district leader is to create a **culture of learning** on the campuses. Including this concept in the district vision can help to communicate the importance of cultivating a culture of learning to all stakeholders. Also, the district vision will help to guide creation of **goals** that lead to the development of this culture. A vision that includes this focus will ensure that district goals are aligned with a culture of learning and will help to establish and maintain the culture. When the district vision clearly incorporates a culture of learning, it will be apparent to all stakeholders that this is a key part of the district's purpose and focus.

DISTRICT GOALS

District goals help to determine where to devote energy and resources. When leaders set goals, they identify the necessary **resources** for achieving them. Goals must be aligned with the **characteristics** and **outcomes** of a culture of learning to ensure that the available resources, such as staff, funds, and time, are used to develop and maintain this culture. Rather than diverting resources to various competing goals, this will maximize the use of resources and effort. When a leader uses district goals to support a culture of learning, the culture will be strengthened as these goals are attained. The various aspects of a culture of learning can be incorporated into the district goals. For example, district goals can include high expectations for academic performance, goals related to college and career readiness for students, and implementation of student-centered instructional strategies for teachers.

STUDENT-CENTERED DISTRICT GOALS

A leader can employ several strategies to ensure that district goals are student-centered. First, goals should be designed with **student outcomes** as a focus. These can include any outcome that is measured in terms of student-related data, such as academic performance or attendance. For example, a district leader may develop a goal of increasing the district attendance rate to 99% for the school year. This goal is directly related to a student outcome and the strategies that would be implemented to achieve this goal would directly benefit students. Second, all district goals should directly **impact students**. When developing goals, it is appropriate to ask how accomplishing the goal would impact students, as well as how students would be affected if the goal were not accomplished. If there is no impact to students, the goal is likely not student-centered. Third, goals should be developed with the purpose of **benefitting all students**. Student-centered goals do not marginalize or omit groups of students but benefit all students. For example, a district leader might set a district goal to increase test performance in reading for all students, not just those who have demonstrated deficiencies in prior performance.

PURPOSE OF DISTRICT VISION

The purpose of a district vision is to convey the **direction** of the district to all stakeholders. A vision is a message or statement that describes how a leader envisions the school in the future. Through the district vision, the district's **focus** and **priorities** can be conveyed to all stakeholders, including staff, students, and the community. The vision should inspire and motivate teachers and staff to pursue the district's goals. The district vision also provides direction for the teachers and staff in decision-making processes. All **strategic planning** should be guided by the district vision so that all goals and plans are designed with the purpose of achieving this vision. An example of a district vision is as follows: Our vision at XYZ School District is to equip and prepare students to be college and career ready, life-long learners, and responsible global citizens who are exemplary examples of the core values of respect, integrity, and perseverance.

Data-Informed Goals and Vision

TYPES OF DATA USED TO DEVELOP DISTRICT VISION

The majority of data that an education leader will have access to and be expected to analyze is **quantitative data**. This includes student academic performance data, attendance data, demographics, and many other key data points. Quantitative data can be analyzed using mathematical processes and can be represented in numerical form. For example, a district leader may calculate that the district attendance rate is 96.8% annually or that 1 out of every 10 students receives special education services. Quantitative data can provide answers to "what" or "who" questions, but it cannot provide answers regarding "why" or "how." To understand why the data appears as it does, it is important for leaders to gather **qualitative data** from students, staff, and stakeholders. Qualitative data reflects opinions, perceptions, feelings, and assumptions. For example, a district leader may receive student concern about bullying on a campus, or parents and community members may communicate to the district leader that the staff do not seem friendly. Quantitative and qualitative data should be used together to develop the vision for the district.

Sources of Data

There are many sources of quantitative and qualitative data that a leader can use to develop a district vision. Sources of **quantitative data** include student academic performance data, attendance data, demographics, and other key data points. **Student academic performance data** is frequently used in developing a vision. Leaders can obtain this data from historical standardized test performance data, beginning-of-the year assessments in a variety of academic areas, teacher-assigned grades for classroom performance, and benchmark assessments. **Qualitative data** can be obtained from observations of teachers and students, feedback from teachers and students, focus groups, anonymous surveys, and other information from stakeholders. This type of information tells the education leader about school culture, values, attitudes, and beliefs. It should be used as a frame for understanding the quantitative data in order to gain a complete picture of the district's status.

Aligning the District Goals with the District Vision

The district vision describes how the leadership envisions the district in the future, and the district goals are the ways that the district will accomplish that vision. Each **district goal** should clearly demonstrate that by accomplishing the goal, the campus will be closer to realizing its **vision**. For example, a district may state in its vision that it will be a premier STEM (Science, Technology, Engineering, and Math) district. District leaders should work toward that vision by setting ambitious goals in the areas of science, technology, engineering, and math. **Aligned goals** could include the academic performance of students in these subject areas, increasing STEM course offerings, recruiting students for the STEM program, or earning awards and recognition in STEM competitions. An **unaligned goal** could be expanding the fine arts program. Aligning district goals with the district vision will ensure that all resources and energies are devoted to realizing the vision.

Using Data from Multiple Sources

It is important to use data from multiple sources to develop the district vision and goals because one source may portray a **limited** or **skewed** picture of the district. Using multiple sources can confirm the **validity** of data and provide a more complete picture of the complex dynamics of each campus. For example, a district leader may obtain past academic data showing that fifth grade students have consistently performed at an advanced level. However, additional data may demonstrate that these students were already performing at an advanced level prior to fifth grade and were not growing academically. Additionally, using multiple sources of data can help a leader identify specific areas for **improvement** so that goals are targeted. For example, a leader may find that ninth-grade students are consistently performing below standard in math. However, investigating which middle schools these students attended may reveal that the struggling students all attended the same middle school. Instead of assuming that math was an area of deficit for the entire ninth-grade class, this additional data could lead to a more specific goal to guide which resources are targeted.

Involving Stakeholders in Developing Vision

Types of Stakeholders

Stakeholders include anyone who has an interest in or is vested in the school district. The **primary stakeholders** in districts are the **children** because they are most directly impacted by the decisions made regarding the district, so they should be engaged in the development of the district vision. Another significant group of stakeholders includes the **faculty and staff** because they are also directly impacted by the decisions. Other stakeholders include parents, district personnel, school board members, community members, and community business partners. A leader can involve these stakeholders in the development of the district vision by soliciting their **opinions and feedback**. This can be done through one-on-one interviews, focus groups, and community meetings, among other methods, to obtain their perspectives. Stakeholders can be motivated to engage in the development of the district vision when the district leader communicates a desire for their involvement and demonstrates respect for their input and opinions. This requires the district leader to devote time and opportunity to meet with various stakeholders and to engage in conversation regarding the school vision.

Using a Variety of Perspectives

It is important to involve stakeholders in the **development of the district vision** in order to incorporate a variety of perspectives and increase buy-in for the vision. Often, district leaders who are in the process of developing a vision for the district are new to the position, so they cannot be expected to know every aspect of the district's dynamics or all the nuances of each campus. It is important to involve stakeholders in the process of developing the vision so that the leader can have as much information as possible. Also, including stakeholders in the process creates **buy-in**. If stakeholders believe that their feelings and opinions have been heard and incorporated into the creation of the vision, it can lead to greater engagement with the goals aligned to that. A leader wants all stakeholders to be **advocates** of the district vision, so stakeholders must be included in the development of the vision.

Reaching Consensus Among Stakeholders

When engaging stakeholders in the development of the district vision and goals, it can be a challenge to reach **consensus**, especially when viewpoints seem to conflict. It is important for a district leader to clearly communicate how consensus will be fairly achieved. Stakeholders who are aware of the process for providing input before participating will know what to expect and are more likely to be receptive to **compromise** in the event of dissension. Additionally, the leader must be **respectful** of all input and must acknowledge opinions and perspectives, even if they are not aligned with the majority or his or her own opinions. Incorporating **voting processes**, such as an anonymous ballot or online survey, can facilitate the use of the majority's viewpoints without identifying dissenters. Finally, the district leader must convey that, although the stakeholders' input is valued and will be considered, he or she still retains the ultimate **responsibility** for decision-making.

Goals that Meet Diverse Needs

Addressing Equity Issues

When developing the district vision and goals, a district leader must ensure that all students—regardless of race, religion, academic background, or education access—will be **successful**. When collecting data to inform the development of the district vision and goals, a district leader should determine whether any groups of students have been **disenfranchised** in the past and, if so, how the district vision and goals can be designed to prevent that disenfranchisement from happening in the future. For example, a district leader may find that historically students who are of limited English proficiency (LEP) have not performed as well as their peers in math on standardized tests. This may necessitate the design of additional goals to support the improvement of LEP students in math. Equity does not mean equality. **Equity** means that some groups of students may need additional resources and support in order for them to meet performance standards. The district vision and goals must take into account the strengths and needs of all students so that all can receive an equitable education and be successful.

IDENTIFYING DIVERSE NEEDS OF STUDENTS

Students have diverse needs and not all of these needs can be predicted based on the students' demographic groups. For example, not all students in poverty have the same needs, nor do all students who speak limited English. The district leader should make an effort to **identify student needs** so they can be addressed in the development of the district's vision and goals. A leader can identify these needs by speaking directly to **students**. This gives students the opportunity to articulate their own needs. Also, the leader can speak with **families** to identify additional student needs. This is particularly helpful when students are young and cannot accurately identify their own needs. Finally, the district leader can observe students in the schools and identify **deficit areas** of each school's program. For example, the district leader may notice that many students arrive late to school and are tired and hungry when they arrive. The district leader can then use this observation data to inform the development of the district goals and vision.

Implementing Vision and Goals

DEVELOPING AN IMPLEMENTATION PLAN

To achieve a district vision and goals, a plan must be in place. A well-constructed plan serves as a **guide** for how the goals will be accomplished. Having a plan conveys to stakeholders that the vision and goals are feasible, and it instills confidence in the district administration. A plan also serves as a **framework** for directing the actions of a leadership team and campus faculty and staff. A leader cannot be everywhere all the time, so having a plan in place ensures that **progress** can be made, even in the leader's absence. Finally, having a plan helps to keep the efforts of leadership and staff **focused**. Many aspects of a district can become distractions to the primary goals and these distractions can cause leaders to divert resources and efforts to the wrong areas. A plan keeps efforts and resources focused and purposeful, which increases the plan's chance of being effective.

COMPONENTS OF AN EFFECTIVE PLAN

An effective plan should include action steps, persons responsible, time frames, milestones, resources needed, and evidence of implementation. The **action steps** in a plan should clearly outline what needs to be done to accomplish the plan. These steps should be broken down so that someone who did not participate in developing the plan can understand what needs to be done. An effective plan also identifies the **persons responsible** for each aspect of the plan. If no one is held accountable for the actions to accomplish the plan, they likely will not get done. The plan should also be **time bound**. This will help to identify whether the plan is on track for completion. **Milestones** serve as checkpoints that help to determine the progress of the plan. The plan will include the **resources needed** to accomplish it so that these resources are planned for and obtained. This will prevent delay in accomplishing the plan. Finally, the **evidence of implementation** should be included in the plan so that ongoing monitoring can take place. Evidence of implementation could include documents, visible indicators, or regular meetings, depending on the specific needs of the plan.

POTENTIAL BARRIERS TO IMPLEMENTING VISION AND GOALS

Both expected and unexpected barriers may arise when implementing the vision and goals. It can be **expected** that stakeholders who did not wholeheartedly agree with the creation of the vision and goals may be reluctant to implement the plan to achieve them. This can be a barrier because a lack of support for or direct opposition to the vision and goals can delay progress. Many **unexpected barriers** may also arise. These may include changes in district policy and procedure, changes in state law, shortfalls in school budgets, and staff changes, among others. For example, standardized test performance expectations or adoption of a new test can affect goals. Additionally, the loss of a teacher or the promotion of a leadership team member could also affect the successful implementation of the vision and goals. Some school districts have experienced unexpected loss of instructional time due to inclement weather conditions, creating a barrier to accomplishing school goals.

Types of Barriers to Implementing Vision and Goals

When planning the implementation of the district vision and goals, the district leader may encounter barriers that will slow the planning process. One barrier is attempting to **analyze too much data**. Data is valuable to the planning process, but an abundance of data can become overwhelming and delay progress. The district leader must identify what data is needed and what can be put aside. Another barrier is the **lack of consensus** from other stakeholders who are providing input to the development of the plan. Stakeholders such as community members, parents, and staff may have conflicting ideas and suggestions related to the development of the vision and goals. The leader must determine which feedback to incorporate in the plan, as not all ideas are sound or can be prioritized. Finally, a barrier that can be difficult to overcome is **garnering support** for the implementation of change in the district schools. In most instances, a district leader will be appointed in the place of a predecessor who already had a district vision and goals in place. Stakeholders may be resistant to drastic changes in the vision and goals, so the leader must overcome these objections to do what is best for the students.

Overcoming Potential Barriers

A leader can employ various strategies to overcome potential barriers to implementing the vision and goals effectively. To **overcome lack of support** of the vision and goals, the leader can include as many stakeholders as possible in the development of the vision and goals. This will increase buy-in and communicate the vision and goals often so that stakeholders are reminded of the district's focus. A leader can also include **strategies** in the action plan to address potential barriers, such as loss of staff. For example, a leader can designate teams, rather than individuals, to work on components of the plan. Therefore, if a staff member is lost, other team members can continue implementation of a goal. The leader can also consider **actions or contingency plans** to enact if barriers arise. For example, if a goal requires a designated number of new computers, a leader may consider what to do if a budget shortfall allows for the purchase of only half of the computers.

Leading by Example

Leading by example can support the implementation of the district vision and goals by inspiring others, conveying priorities, and garnering support from stakeholders. When a leader sets an **example of expected behavior**, staff and students will be inspired to participate and to follow the leader's example, **implementing** the vision and goals in the same way as their leader. This increases the effort devoted to accomplishing the vision and goals. When the leader engages in behaviors that implement the vision and goals, this conveys to stakeholders that the vision and goals are **priorities** because this is where the leader chooses to devote time. When a leader's priorities are clear to stakeholders, it is easier for the leader to encourage them to participate in those prioritized activities and to implement action plans related to those priorities. For example, if a leader makes it evident through his or her own actions that reading instruction is a priority for the campuses, then stakeholders will expect and support further initiatives relating to reading instruction. In contrast, when a leader's actions do not match the goals and vision, this results in a mixed message to stakeholders.

Aligning Human, Fiscal, and Material Resources

The strategies and initiatives for implementing the vision and goals require **resources**, so a leader must ensure that all human, fiscal, and material resources are aligned to the vision and goals. **Aligning resources to the vision and goals** will ensure fewer barriers to implementation. In contrast, when resources are not aligned to the vision and goals, not only will leaders find it difficult to implement the mission and vision, they will also find that their efforts are being diverted to the other areas that the resources have been devoted to. This results in a less significant **impact** of those resources for the benefit of students and the district as a whole. For example, if the vision for the district is to have state-of-the-art technology for classroom instruction, the leader must ensure that there are qualified staff members who are able to utilize the technology, funds for the purchase of technology hardware and software, and additional resources such as storage and server space for the additional technology. If any aspect of the resources is **misaligned**, there is a greater possibility that the goal or vision will not be obtained.

Delegating Responsibility

A leader cannot do an effective job without support. In order to balance the duties and responsibilities of being a district leader, an effective leader must identify tasks and activities that can be **delegated** to other leadership team members or administrative staff. If a leader does not delegate tasks and responsibilities, he or she may be overwhelmed and unable to meet all of the demands necessary to implement the mission and vision. When a leader designs an **action plan** for accomplishing the vision and goals, he or she must also identify the **staff members** who can complete those actions. For example, another member of the leadership team can be assigned a specific project, such as hosting the quarterly community literacy nights for the school year. Also, a clerical staff person can assist the leader in designing and formatting documents related to a project. The role of the leader is to lead and manage a team that can implement the vision, not to implement the vision independently and individually. Delegation is also important when the leader is not available. This ensures that the work of accomplishing the vision and goals will continue even in the leader's absence.

Role of Delegation

The superintendent cannot monitor progress for all district goals alone, but instead must **delegate** responsibility and authority to other staff to successfully implement the accountability model. Depending on the size of the district, the superintendent may delegate authority to a single person or to a team or department. These staff persons then report progress to the superintendent according to the **timelines** set in the accountability model. For example, the superintendent may set an academic performance goal for third-grade students in mathematics as determined by a standardized assessment. Performance indicators for this goal may include student academic performance and teacher performance in third-grade math. As a result, the superintendent can delegate the responsibility of monitoring progress to a curriculum and instruction department. This department would then have the responsibility and authority to develop assessments or evaluations to collect actionable data, collaborate with other departments, and provide resources and support for third-grade math classrooms. The leader of the curriculum and instruction department would be responsible for **reporting progress** to the superintendent according to the timeline set in the accountability model. The process of establishing goals, delegating responsibility, and monitoring progress would be implemented for all district goals.

Expectations of Goals

Measurable Expectations

Using Data to Support Measurable Expectations

Data can support the setting and tracking of measurable expectations. When a leader uses data to communicate **expectations** to faculty and staff, it increases the staff's ability to meet those expectations and helps staff to determine if they are meeting expectations. For example, a leader can set the expectation that teachers and staff maintain a 98% attendance rate at work. Setting this measurable expectation makes it easier for staff to self-regulate and also helps leaders to address failure to meet expectations. By using data, a leader can determine if expectations are being met, which can help determine whether the school is on track to **meet or exceed goals**. For example, a leader may expect 90% of students to meet performance standards in reading. If 93% of students meet performance standards, the leader will know that the expectation is being exceeded and it is likely that the district will meet their goal. In contrast, when data is not used to support expectations, it can be difficult to determine progress toward meeting expectations, identify potential areas of weakness, or address failures to meet expectations.

Identifying Trends and Patterns

The identification of trends and patterns in district performance can be valuable in forming action plans so that decision-making can be targeted and strategic. When expectations are measurable, the data that is collected and analyzed can reveal **patterns and trends**. For example, if a leader were to review student reading progress using data from the last three assessments, it may be revealed that a particular demographic group is consistently underperforming. This trend can help the leader provide **targeted resources and interventions** to meet the reading performance expectation. Similarly, an analysis of student attendance data may reveal a pattern of poor attendance on rainy days. Identifying this pattern can help the leader to **address the barriers** that rainy days create for student attendance so that students can meet attendance expectations.

Monitoring Progress Towards Goals

A leader must monitor progress toward goals to increase the likelihood of meeting those goals. Leaders should check the **progress** of goals in regular intervals throughout the school year based on these measurable expectations. This allows the leader to determine if the district is **on track** to meet a goal and, if not, allows time to make changes to the action plan. For example, a leader may set an annual goal for 90% of students to meet academic performance expectations in math on standardized tests. This goal could be broken down into measurable expectations, such as performance on particular math standards, which are reviewed at regular intervals, like every three weeks. If a leader were to determine that at least 90% of students were not successful on a particular math standard, this could indicate a danger of not meeting the annual goal. However, because this data was obtained before the administration of the standardized test, the leader has time to develop and implement **interventions** such as math tutorials, increasing the likelihood of meeting the goal.

Supporting High-Performance Expectations

Measurable expectations support high performance because they clearly define the expectations for students and staff, as well as the standard used to measure the expectation. A measurable expectation can lead to **higher expectations of performance** because it is clear and facilitates monitoring. When expectations are not measurable, the result is ambiguity or confusion. It can be difficult for a person to know if he or she is meeting expectations and this ambiguity can convey that he or she will not be monitored. In contrast, when expectations are measurable, a leader can clearly convey how students and staff can meet those expectations and how they will be **monitored**. For example, if a leader sets a general expectation for high student performance in math, teachers may be confused about the performance indicators and subsequently have varying expectations for math performance and how students can demonstrate that performance, such as classwork, homework, and exams. In contrast, a leader could set an expectation that all students will maintain a passing grade in math classes and pass all math exams. The leader can then monitor the expectation by reviewing class and exam grades so that those who are not meeting expectations can be addressed.

Accountability Model to Systematically Monitor Progress

Role of Data Collection

In order to monitor progress in a systematic way, the superintendent must develop processes for collecting **accurate and actionable data**. For example, the superintendent may set an academic performance goal for third-grade students in mathematics as determined by a standardized assessment. In order to monitor the progress of third-grade students toward this goal, the superintendent may develop several **indicators** of student progress and performance in this area. These indicators may include student performance on math benchmark assessments, student math class grades, third-grade student attendance rates, or evaluation of third-grade math teacher performance. The **accountability model** involves setting checkpoints and milestones for each of these data points and having a plan of action if checkpoints and milestones are not met. For example, the accountability model may include monitoring student performance on a math benchmark exam every three weeks. After the math benchmark exam is administered, the data would be aggregated and analyzed to determine if third-grade students are on track to meet the performance goal. If they are not on track, then an intervention plan would be implemented to address the areas of weakness and to increase the likelihood the students will meet the goal.

MEASURABLE VS. NON-MEASURABLE GOALS

Measurable goals can be **quantified** and non-measurable goals cannot be quantified. An example of a measurable goal is: 95% of eighth-grade students will earn a score of 70% or above on the math benchmark exam. This goal is **measurable** because it can be determined whether or not it was met by calculating the percentage of students who demonstrated the defined proficiency on the exam. It also identifies what **performance** is expected of the students in order to reach the goal. When goals are measurable, it is easy to determine whether or not they have been met. In contrast, a non-measurable goal may be ambiguous, and it may be difficult to determine whether or not it has been met. An example of a **non-measurable goal** is: eighth-grade students will be successful on the math benchmark exam. This goal is not measurable because it does not state how students demonstrate success on the benchmark exam, nor how many students must be successful to meet the goal.

CONVERTING NON-MEASURABLE GOALS INTO MEASURABLE GOALS

Non-measurable goals can be converted into measurable goals by making them **quantifiable**. To make goals quantifiable, the leader must determine how **success** is measured for each behavior identified in the goal and how to know that success has been achieved. When a goal involves a **performance standard or assessment**, it should be clearly identified. For example, rather than using the phrase "demonstrate proficiency" in a goal, the leader should identify what constitutes proficiency, such as earning a particular score. Some goals involve behaviors that are not easily quantifiable, such as goals related to culture or attitudes. In these instances, a leader must determine how these behaviors will be measured, such as by **observations or surveys**. For example, a leader may wish all staff to be perceived as courteous. The leader can survey students and parents regarding the courtesy of staff and set a goal of an average rating of 4 out of 5 or greater in the area of courtesy. Alternatively, the leader may use observations to measure the goal, such as requiring front office personal to greet all visitors immediately upon entry 100% of the time.

INEFFECTIVENESS OF NON-MEASURABLE GOALS

Non-measurable goals can often be ineffective because they do not clearly convey how to **achieve the goal** or how one knows when the goal has been achieved. When there is no measure of what constitutes **success**, then those working toward the goal will be guided by their own perception of success, which may not be in line with the leader's expectations. For example, if the goal is for all fifth-grade students to be successful on a test, a leader may expect students to earn scores of 90% or greater but the teacher may expect scores of 70% or greater. In order to ensure clarity of goals and to help develop strategies to reach those goals, the goals must be **measurable**. This ensures that all involved parties know the exact target that they are trying to reach and can determine if and when they have reached the target.

Communication and Implementing Vision and Goals

IMPORTANCE OF THE CLEAR COMMUNICATION OF THE VISION AND GOALS

It is important to communicate the district vision and goals clearly so that stakeholders can **understand and support** them. If the vision and goals are unclear, stakeholders may have difficulty determining if they support the vision and goals or what to expect on the campuses when the vision and goals are implemented. To communicate clearly, a leader should avoid **technical terms and jargon** that may not be easily understood by stakeholders. For example, a leader can communicate to stakeholders that the district goal is to increase reading performance, rather than referring to a specific reading program or strategy that may not be familiar to them. Clear communication of district vision and goals helps to garner **support from stakeholders** for district initiatives. When communication is clear, the vision and goals can be easily aligned with outside support and resources from the community, state, and federal programs.

Communicating the Vision and Goals to Stakeholders

When the vision and goals are communicated effectively to stakeholders, they can in turn support the culture of learning. When stakeholders know and understand the vision, they can identify how to **support** it and help to **develop the culture of learning**. For example, if a business stakeholder in the community becomes aware of the school's vision to implement technology in the classroom to develop a culture of learning, he or she may decide to donate computers for a computer lab. Had the stakeholder not known that the school could benefit from the donation, he or she may not have taken that action. All stakeholders may not be in a position to give to the school, but they can support the culture of learning through their **participation** in school and community events and by **advocating** for the district and its needs to school and government representatives. Communicating the vision and goals to stakeholders increases the number of people who can offer their support in implementation.

Ensuring Clear Communication

A leader will know if the communication of vision and goals to stakeholders is clear and effective by observing the **stakeholders' behavior**. When the vision and goals are clear, stakeholders are more likely to **buy in** to the leader's vision and assist in achieving it. Stakeholders who understand the vision and goals can articulate them in their own words. They will be able to **communicate** the vision and goals to other stakeholders and to the leader. Their behavior will be **aligned** to the vision and goals as well. Also, stakeholders who understand the vision will propose ideas and actions that are aligned to the vision, avoiding those that are opposed or a distraction to the vision. When the communication of the vision and goals is clear and effective, all stakeholders will **understand** the vision and goals and how they can participate in achieving them.

Hierarchical Communication

Hierarchical communication refers to communicating up and down the chain of command. Leaders **communicate up** by communicating with superiors, such as district office staff or the superintendent. Leaders **communicate down** by communicating with faculty and staff. Communicating with various members of the hierarchy often takes different communication skills. For example, communicating with a superior may involve responding to specific requests or demands or demonstrating alignment of district vision and goals with local, state, or federal requirements. Communicating up in this manner may occur via emails and memorandums, meetings, or visits. In contrast, communicating with faculty and staff requires communicating in a way that inspires them to perform as a team in order to achieve the district vision and goals. This type of communication also involves holding district team members accountable for their performance. This communication down may occur via emails or memorandums, faculty meetings, or in professional learning communities. Leaders must **recognize their audience** when communicating so that they can use the most effective communication strategy.

Communicating Implementation of the Vision and Goals

A leader must ensure that stakeholders are aware of how the various district initiatives and actions align to the vision and goals. A leader can do this by frequently and clearly **identifying this alignment**. This can be communicated in writing or verbally. District plans for the implementation of the vision and goals should **identify** the planned initiatives and activities. For example, if the district's vision is to achieve excellence in literacy, the leader could indicate in the district plan that one or more of the schools will host literacy nights. At the literacy nights, the leader should clearly explain to participants that it is a strategy for achieving the goal of excellence in literacy. The leader could also include the district's vision statement on the agenda for the literacy night. A leader cannot assume that all stakeholders understand the connection between the day-to-day campus activities and the vision and goals that have been set. Therefore, the leader needs to **verbally explain the connection** at every opportunity.

Communicating the Vision and Goals Through Others

A district leader can utilize other persons to help communicate the vision and goals. Members of the leadership team can help. Often, these **other leaders** come into contact with staff and parents more frequently than the superintendent and therefore have more opportunities to convey the vision and goals. Additionally, parents can be instrumental. **Parent leaders**, such as those who lead parent organizations or are influential in the community, can help to spread the word about the district vision and goals. Also, in diverse communities, **staff members** who speak multiple languages may be utilized to communicate the district vision and goals to parents and community members of a variety of backgrounds. When **stakeholders** hear the vision and goals from persons other than the leader, they will perceive that the vision and goals are supported, and they are more likely to support them as well. In order for this type of communication to be effective, the district leader must ensure that everyone has a sound understanding of the district vision and goals before sharing them with others.

Aspects of Clear Communication

Verbal and Nonverbal Communication

Leaders can clearly communicate the district vision and goals to stakeholders using verbal, written, and nonverbal communication. Leaders can **communicate verbally** by formally hosting meetings and events that help to share the vision and goals for the district. Leaders can host community meetings and invite parents, community members, and other stakeholders to attend. These meetings are opportunities for the leader to clarify and elaborate on the vision and goals. Leaders can also hold staff meetings and student assemblies on the campuses. Additionally, the vision and goals should be verbalized at every opportunity. A leader can use **written communication** to communicate the vision and goals, such as in formal reports, emails, and memorandums. For example, some leaders incorporate the district's vision in the footer of formal written documents so that it is always visible. All written communication should align to the vision and reinforce the goals for the district. Finally, the leader's behavior can serve as a **nonverbal communication** of the vision and goals. For example, if the vision of the district is to cultivate students who are life-long learners, then the leader can model this behavior by reading, participating in training, and taking classes.

Timely Communication

Timely communication requires proper planning. The **calendar of events** for the school year should be outlined in advance. The leader needs to identify the types of communication to share at various **periods** throughout the year, such as the beginning of the school year, school holidays, testing periods, and others. A leader must also provide **advance notice** so that staff and families can properly prepare and plan for school events and activities. Leaders can provide this advance notice using calendars, announcements, flyers, and phone calls. Communicating in **multiple ways** ensures that the communication is received in a timely manner. There can be an abundance of information about events, activities, and other aspects of the school that needs to be shared with staff, families, and students, so the leader should delegate the aggregation and dissemination of this information to other staff as necessary. The leader can set expectations for how these staff members communicate to families and students. For example, if a school department hosts an event, the event should be placed on the school calendar and parents should be informed with sufficient time to prepare for and support the event.

Two-Way Communication

The act of communication involves a sender and a receiver. If communication is sent but not received, it is not effective. A leader can increase the possibility of effective communication by using a **variety of mediums**. These may include phone calls, meetings, emails, memorandums, and formal letters or documents. Additionally, a leader can survey stakeholders to determine the **preferred mode of communication**. For communication to be deemed effective, leaders must confirm that it has been received. Leaders can request a response or feedback on the communication so that it is acknowledged and the leader can be sure that the message was received in the intended way. Effective communication also means that the leader can be the **receiver** of communication, not just the sender. Leaders should be open to taking phone calls, responding to emails, or participating in meetings that allow others to communicate with them. When the leader acts as the receiver, he or she should acknowledge that the message was received so the sender is aware that the communication was effective.

Handling Miscommunication

If the leader becomes aware of a miscommunication, he or she should act immediately to correct it. Failing to correct a miscommunication can lead to confusion, conflict, and lack of engagement in and support of the school program. First, the leader should **identify the miscommunication**. Then the leader should make an effort to **correct** it by acknowledging that the message was not sent properly and providing the correct message. For example, a district leader could notify parents that the school's art program would not be part of the vision for the upcoming school year, and the parents might infer that the art program would be eliminated. The district leader should inform parents that the art program will not be eliminated and then explain how it will be affected in the upcoming school year. The district leader should also assume **responsibility** for the initial ineffective communication.

Adjusting and Revising Goals

Adjusting Vision, Goals, Implementation, and Communication Strategies

Continuous Improvement

The process of continuous improvement is the ongoing act of assessing performance and adjusting efforts to improve that performance. With a process of **continuous improvement**, parts of the work process can be addressed before they begin to fail. Low-performing processes are improved as well as performance that is considered acceptable. All aspects of the work process are examined to determine where improvements can be made to reach **excellence**. To implement a process of continuous improvement, **procedures of evaluation** must be developed and implemented at regular checkpoints. Based on these evaluations, the leadership team can identify areas of improvement and initiate **interventions and actions** based on these areas. In schools, the regular evaluation of process toward the district vision and goals can be developed into a process of continuous improvement. However, district leaders must focus on both the strengths and weaknesses of the district in this process. Deficient areas can be improved to perform to standard and areas performing at standard can be innovated for improvement.

Effectively Monitoring Progress

A leader can effectively monitor progress by planning regular checkpoints, analyzing data, and actively engaging in the work. The leader must plan in advance when to check progress on the projects and tasks that are being implemented in the school district. This monitoring should include the projects that the leader is working on as well as those that have been delegated to others. These **checkpoints** should occur with enough frequency that adjustments can be made in a timely manner. The leader must also **analyze data** on a regular basis. All goals should have measurable metrics, which means that data points can demonstrate whether the goal is on track to be achieved. Therefore, a leader must be skilled at analyzing data and making decisions based on it. Finally, a leader can effectively monitor progress by viewing the work and **engaging** in it firsthand. For example, if a district goal is to reduce the number of students who are tardy, the district leader may engage in morning duty to monitor the arrival and attendance tracking of students. This engagement can add context to the data and help the leader to identify areas of improvement.

Facilitating Self-Directed Change and Improvement

Self-directed change and improvement can help achieve the district vision and goals. Staff members who can make changes and improvement to their practice on their own do not require as much **intervention** of district leaders and coaches as other staff members, freeing those resources to be utilized in other areas. To succeed on their own, staff members must be fully aware of the **district visions and goals** and the **expectations** placed on them in pursuit of those goals. A leader can facilitate self-directed change and improvement by providing **adequate staff resources**, such as instructional resources and professional development opportunities. The leader must also provide staff members with **access to data** for monitoring progress and performance. Finally, the leader must develop a **culture and climate of self-improvement** in which staff are comfortable revealing weaknesses and taking risks to improve their practice.

Self-Reflection

Self-reflection is the process of examining one's self in relation to a desired expectation of performance. This process can help with **adjusting the vision and goals** when it is completed by those responsible for carrying out tasks and projects related to the vision and goals. Self-reflection can help to determine whether the goals should be **revised** or if persons striving toward the goals need **improvement**. For example, if a district goal is to improve reading instruction, reading teachers could engage in self-reflection to determine if they are implementing the action plan with fidelity and are teaching to their best ability. If not, the teachers would engage in **self-directed change** to meet the goal. In contrast, if the reading teachers were faithfully implementing the action plan and performing to the best of their ability, this could indicate that the goal itself and its associated strategies may require revision to meet the students' needs. When all staff members engage in self-reflection, it becomes easier for the district as a whole to make changes and improve.

Systematically Reviewing and Revising Goals

Goals are not concrete and should be reviewed and revised periodically. A leader can examine goals to determine whether a district is likely to **achieve or exceed** them. A leader can also determine whether goals are in complete **alignment** with the vision of the schools. Just as a leader regularly monitors the activities implemented for the completion of the goal, the leader will need to examine the goals themselves. Since a goal is measurable, the leader can determine if the **current data** shows that the campus is on track for meeting it. The leader may observe unexpected **barriers** to achieving the goal that require a revision or the setting of an additional goal. For example, if the district sets a goal for reading performance, the leader may notice that students receiving special education services are not performing as well as students who do not receive these services, and that their reading performance is contributing to a low overall reading performance goal. The leader may then create a new goal that specifically addresses the needs of this student population with its own set of strategies and interventions.

Adjusting Communication Strategies

Communication of the vision and goals to all stakeholders is critical to the successful achievement of the vision and goals. The leader will know that communication strategies need to be adjusted if staff members have difficulty **articulating** or **implementing** the goals and vision. All staff members should be able to discuss the district goals and vision among themselves and with other stakeholders. If they are unable to do this, it is possible that communication was not effective initially or that subsequent communication of changes and adjustments to the vision and goals was ineffective. Another indication that communication strategies need adjustment is difficulty for staff members in **implementing the action plans** related to the vision and goals. If they are unclear about what is expected of them or what steps they need to take to meet expectations, these aspects of the action plan may not have been conveyed clearly. Communicating effectively removes **barriers to implementation**.

Gathering Data and Identifying Strong and Weak Areas

Identifying Strengths and Weaknesses of District Performance

The district leader can use quantitative, anecdotal, and observational data to identify the strengths and weaknesses of district performance. This involves regular reporting of **student performance data** and other data points related to key areas such as attendance and discipline. This data is usually analyzed in relation to setting and reviewing goals, so leaders can actively identify the **strengths and weaknesses** of the district when this data is reviewed. Also, other team members or district office personnel might convey areas of strength or weakness to the leaders based on their campus experiences. These persons may share how a particular teacher or department is performing or provide feedback regarding a system or process on one of the campuses. Also, a leader may make **observations on campus** to help identify areas of strength or areas that need improvement. For example, a leader may participate in lunch duty in the cafeteria and observe processes that need to be improved. A leader should refer to **multiple sources of data and evidence** to develop a holistic view of the strengths and weaknesses of district performance.

Addressing Identified Strengths

A leader should address identified strengths in the district by using them as opportunities for praise and reinforcement, as well as leverage for improvement. Effective leaders encourage staff by praising and celebrating **achievements** and recognizing **strengths**. This motivates staff members to continue the effective performance. For strengths to remain as strengths, a leader must recognize them and **reinforce** the actions and attitudes that led to their achievement. The leader can also use these strengths as **leverage** for making improvements. For example, if the third-grade reading teachers in a particular school have consistently achieved high performance in reading, this can be recognized and praised. Then the strategies that these teachers implement in the third-grade classroom can be analyzed for application to other third-grade classrooms or the other grade levels. Reinforcing and praising strengths builds confidence in team members, helping them to address needed improvements in the district. Similarly, the skills that are effective in building the strengths can also be applied to areas of weakness.

Addressing Identified Weaknesses

Weaknesses identified in the district must be addressed to improve them. However, this should be done strategically to avoid demoralizing team members. If a leader identifies multiple weaknesses, they should be **prioritized** rather than attempting to address all of the weaknesses at once. Attempting to address everything at one time can be overwhelming to team members. When developing plans to address weaknesses, the leader needs to identify how the **strengths** of the campus and the individual team members can be used to improve the areas of weakness. For example, a campus may be having difficulty with classroom management, but certain teachers may be effective classroom managers. These teachers can be used to develop a district-wide strategy for addressing this area of weakness. Similarly, the district may demonstrate weakness in math performance, but strength in reading performance. The district leader can identify the strategies that make reading performance effective and implement them in math instruction.

District Accountability Measures

The purpose of district accountability measures is to ensure that all students are learning and performing according to predetermined standards. These **measures of accountability** are standardized and the state and federal governments provide **assessments** of schools based on these accountability standards. District leaders can use these school reports to identify areas of strength and weakness in the district programming as measured by performance on state-mandated assessments. For example, the district leader may review the district's accountability ratings and find that the third-grade class in one of the schools did not perform according to expectations in reading. Based on that information, the leader can identify which teachers taught third-grade reading, what curriculum was used, and what other factors may have impacted students' scores. That information can then be used to determine what aspects of the third-grade reading program are strong and which are weak and need improvement. District accountability measures are a critical means of determining a school's strengths and weaknesses.

Implementing Changes

Professional Development

To implement change, identifying areas for improvement is not enough. Staff members need to know what they can do to improve their practice. As a result, **professional development** can help a leader implement change. When leaders participate in professional development themselves, they can learn how to be better leaders and how to implement new or better instructional practices on the campuses. When teachers and other staff participate in professional development, they can also learn how to grow as professionals and implement **improved instructional strategies** in the classroom. Leaders should tailor professional development to meet the needs of the staff and to address district weaknesses. Leaders should also offer opportunities for **staff members** to participate in individualized and group professional development, organized by content area, grade level, or shared strengths or weaknesses. Additionally, leaders should implement professional development in innovative ways, such as coaching, modeling, book talks, and other professional development strategies.

Study of Research-Based and Proven Best Practices

Areas of deficit or weakness in the district often result from a lack of knowledge rather than a lack of capability. Leaders and team members must continually learn about their practice and how they can improve, and should search for successful strategies that can be implemented in their district. To address weak areas, it is better to implement strategies that are backed by **research** and have been **proven** to obtain good results. This can save the district the time, effort, and resources that could be wasted if untested, unproven strategies are implemented unsuccessfully. When a leader is looking for strategies to foster change in the district, using research-based, proven best practices is beneficial because there will be **clear direction** for successfully implementing the strategy as well as an idea of the expected results. When untested strategies are implemented, the outcome is less sure. Untested strategies also often take more research and a process of trial and error to implement, also known as a learning curve, which can delay the proper implementation of change.

Enlisting Support

A leader cannot bring about district change alone. To make changes happen, the leader must enlist support. Fostering change as a **change agent** requires leaders to be strategic in how they communicate the change and how they garner supporters for it. First, the leader needs to **communicate** the change effectively. Many people are unwilling to support changes because they fear the unknown. The leader should not only communicate what is to be changed, but also how it will affect the various staff members and how they are aligned to the vision and goals. Next, the leader needs to gather other leaders within the team and **persuade** them to support the change. Leaders in the district may carry official titles of leadership or simply have influence over other staff members. Enlisting the support of these persons will positively affect the perceptions of the remaining staff. Lastly, the leader needs to be a constant **advocate** of change and a **participant** in it. Staff members will watch the leader to see if the desire for change is authentic and long-lasting. They will be more likely to support it when they observe that the leader is serious about change.

Anticipating and Preparing for Implementing Change

When implementing change, a district leader should anticipate and prepare for **varying levels of support**, as well as direct **opposition** to the change. Some team members will be as **enthusiastic** about the change as the leader. The leader should be prepared to leverage these team members by encouraging them, providing them with resources necessary to implement the changes, and using them to influence the other team members. Some team members will be **indecisive** about the change and not quite ready to support it. The leader should be prepared to spend more time and resources on this group to help encourage them to support the change. This group may require additional communication strategies and support to bring them on board. The district leader should also anticipate a third group of staff members who are **opposed** to the change and may even be vocal in their opposition. The district leader should be prepared to defend the change and offer rebuttals to arguments against it, both publicly and privately. The majority of the leader's focus should be on the first two groups; however, the oppositional group can be detrimental to the progress of the first two groups if it is not addressed appropriately.

Modeling Openness to Change

The leader is a model in the district and team members will imitate his or her attitudes. If a leader would like the staff to be open to proposed change, he or she must also be a **model of openness to change**. There are many ways to accomplish a goal, and just because something is working does not mean that it cannot be improved. Changes may be proposed by team members other than the leader, or from the state or other regulatory agency. In these instances, the leader should model openness to change. The leader can be **receptive** to the proposed change and **optimistic** as to how the change can positively affect the district. The leader can also demonstrate a **positive attitude** during the change, should it be implemented. The leader can expect a similar response from staff if change is proposed in the district, so leadership should model the qualities and attitudes they desire from staff. In contrast, if the leader is not open to change, staff will likely imitate that attitude and be opposed to changes proposed by the leader.

Change Process Model

It is likely that the school district superintendent will be responsible for implementing many significant changes within the school system, which requires a deliberate process for effectively implementing and managing change. There are many **change process models** that have been developed and implemented in school systems and organizations in a variety of fields. These models include the McKinsey 7-S Model, Lewin's Change Management Model, and Kotter's 8 Step Change Model, among many others. It is critical for a superintendent to determine which change process model is appropriate based on their leadership style, the organizational dynamics, the magnitude of the change, and the timeline for the change. Change process models break the process for change into **steps** so that implementing change becomes systematic and manageable. Some models have more steps than others or vary in the rationale for how change is broken down. Although each change process model will have its unique terminology and philosophy, most change processes determine how to foster support for the change among employees and stakeholders, how to overcome resistance to change, how to implement the change, and how to make the change sustainable.

Using an Accountability Model to Systematically Monitor Progress

An effective superintendent is able to monitor and evaluate progress toward district goals and objectives in order to **sustain continuous improvement**. There are various models that the leader can use as a guide or structure for monitoring. Some of these models are unique to the field of education and may be provided through state education agencies or other education support centers. The **key elements of an accountability model** include identifying the specific goals and objectives to be met, designating milestones or checkpoints for monitoring progress toward the goals and objectives, and determining appropriate actions based on whether the organization is on track to meet those goals and objectives. The superintendent will also need to be effective in **delegating** authority and accountability to others to help systematically monitor progress. The superintendent must also be able to **collect and analyze data** effectively to determine progress toward goals and be able to effectively implement action planning to adjust programs and practices based on progress monitoring.

Chapter Quiz

Ready to see how well you retained what you just read? Scan the QR code to go directly to the chapter quiz interface for this study guide. If you're using a computer, simply visit the online resources page at **mometrix.com/resources719/osatsuper248** and click the Chapter Quizzes link.

Instructional Leadership, District Culture and Learning Environment, and Staff Development

Leadership Models and Styles

Leader's Personal Values and Beliefs and the Effectiveness of Leadership

A leader's personal values and beliefs shape his or her behavior, as well as expectations from staff and students. One's personal beliefs will dictate what is **prioritized** as a leader and as a district team. If the leader's values and beliefs reflect positive attributes, these can have a positive impact on the effectiveness of leadership. In contrast, if the leader's beliefs and values are contrary to district and community norms, these can make it difficult to lead effectively. Additionally, if **staff members** have values and beliefs that are contrary to the leader's, they may find it difficult to follow the leader. For example, if the leader values reading and believes that everyone should be an avid reader, he or she would likely emphasize and prioritize reading initiatives and be effective in promoting reading on the campuses. On the other hand, if a leader did not personally value a characteristic such as punctuality in staff and students, that leader may have difficult effectively enforcing promptness among staff and students. The leader's values and beliefs are often demonstrated in the school mission and vision, as well as through the leader's words and actions.

Acting as a Role Model

People observe the leader's behavior for **alignment** between his or her words and actions. This alignment is necessary for a leader to be viewed as genuine and authentic. The leader serves as a **role model** for both staff and students. For **staff**, the leader should exemplify the mission and vision of the district through behavior and words. The leader should also set the example in adhering to district policy, like those described in the employee handbook. Additionally, the leader should set the example for **district culture**, such as how staff members treat one another and students. For **students**, the leader is a role model in dress, conduct, speech, and other areas. Many people in the community may look up to the leader as well as an example to follow. As a role model, the leader's behavior can influence the behavior of others as he or she comes into contact with them.

Servant Leader

A servant leader is a person who leads by **serving others first**. A servant leader identifies the team's needs by assessing the team or listening to team members and then meets those needs. Meeting the team's needs helps to equip them to get their job done effectively and efficiently. A servant leader shares power through **empowering** others to be effective and by providing them with the tools and resources to be effective. This is in contrast to a leader who exerts authority over others in a "top-down" approach. A servant leader is often found **participating** in the work with the team, both to support the team and to experience the team members' jobs. A faculty with a servant leader is more likely to feel more confident in their ability to do their job because their leader has empowered and equipped them and does not micromanage their work. Servant leaders are often described as caring, compassionate, thoughtful, and humble.

Transactional and Transformational Leadership Styles

Transactional and transformational leadership styles are very different and produce different results from team members. **Transactional leaders** are most concerned about how to effectively implement and perform under the current rules, policies, and procedures, whereas transformational leaders are focused on change and improvement. Transactional leaders emphasize compliance and monitor progress toward goals using systems of rewards and punishment. These leaders can be task-oriented or focused on results only. These types of leaders can also become micromanagers. In contrast, **transformational leaders** focus on the staff behaviors that lead to success. They focus on organizational values and implementation of the mission and vision in order to meet goals. These types of leaders focus on growing staff members in order to meet goals and solicit staff buy-in in the decision-making process. There are pros and cons of each leadership style and many leaders alternate between these leadership styles or blend them together in order to lead effectively.

SHARED LEADERSHIP

Shared leadership is the **delegation** of authority and responsibility to other team members. This type of leadership is the opposite of **authoritarian leadership** or micromanaging. Instead, a leader will appoint persons with particular leadership responsibilities and grant them the authority to fulfill those responsibilities. For example, the district leader may ask a skilled teacher to lead a curriculum revision process and supervise a group of other teachers on the task. When sharing leadership, responsibility can be delegated to any staff persons who are capable of fulfilling the role. It is not dependent on job titles. Shared leadership also involves including team members in the leader's **decision-making processes**. This means that the district leader may solicit opinions, ideas, and feedback from staff members before making a decision. This can be accomplished through focus groups, appointing advisors, or taking votes during meetings.

Distributing Responsibility through Roles and Delegation

ROLES THAT CAN HELP ACCOMPLISH THE VISION

Many roles are performed on campuses to ensure that day-to-day activities are carried out. Each of these roles can contribute to accomplishing the **school vision**. Some of the roles include the administrative team, school counselors, teacher leaders, and support staff. The **administrative team** is essential in accomplishing the vision because projects and assignments that directly impact the vision and school goals can be delegated to them. These administrators have the authority and training to support the leader in leading the district to success. **School counselors** can help accomplish the vision by supporting the psychosocial needs of students so that they can be their best, academically and socially. School counselors are often part of the team that handles student scheduling and post-graduation plans, so they can help students meet the expectations associated with district goals. **Teacher leaders** can help to accomplish the vision by leading, encouraging, and supporting their fellow teachers. Finally, **support staff** can help accomplish the vision by ensuring that the logistics of a plan are appropriate, communication is timely and effective, and staff and stakeholders feel supported and equipped to implement the vision.

IDENTIFYING POSITION AND BOUNDARY LIMITATIONS

A superintendent must understand the roles, functions, and expectations of their role as superintendent as well as the roles, functions, and expectations of the board of education. Identifying **position and boundary limitations** can help with managing and meeting expectations. For example, the only employee of the board of education is the superintendent. The board of education does not have the authority to hire or fire any other employees of the district. It is the superintendent's responsibility to **hire, manage, and lead** an effective team. Understanding this responsibility can help the superintendent in determining actions to take in regard to district employees. As the board of education's employee, the superintendent must ensure that **performance expectations** for the superintendent role are met or exceeded. If those expectations are not met, the superintendent must understand that the board of education has the ability to take action regarding the superintendent's employment status. Additionally, understanding the roles and the limitations of those roles can prevent either party from placing unfair or unreasonable expectations on the other.

Statutory Roles

Statutory roles or roles as dictated by education law must be identified and communicated by the superintendent to the school board. These roles include that of the superintendent, principal, teachers, counselors, librarians, specialists, and others. Education law also dictates the role of the school board. Many of these roles require **certification** from the state for a person to be employed in a school under that title. State statute determines what **qualifications** must be met for persons to obtain certification and how persons are to fulfill these roles. The **functions** of these roles are also outlined by statute. It is important for the superintendent to understand and communicate statutory roles to manage hiring, expectations for performance, and evaluations of performance. This information impacts staffing decisions, budgeting decisions, and programming decisions. For example, understanding the statute regarding the hiring and placement of certified teachers can affect staff recruitment efforts, budget decisions, and other aspects of district operations. Additionally, statute serves as the basis for developing job descriptions and performance evaluations for staff.

Separating Roles

A superintendent should separate roles to provide **clarity** in job functions and **manage expectations** for performance and evaluation. One of the primary ways that a superintendent can separate roles is to develop an **organizational chart**. This chart is a visual representation of the roles that staff play, including the board of education, and how these roles relate to one another. Another strategy to separate roles is to **write job or role descriptions**, include these descriptions in policy documents, and make these available to all parties. Finally, a superintendent should be careful not to **act outside his or her roles** or advise others to act outside of their roles. For example, it would not be appropriate to allow a board member or group of board members to dictate who the superintendent should hire. Although board members may make suggestions for hire, the superintendent would not want to give the impression that the board members as individuals or as a collective have any authority in relation to the hiring of employees.

Addressing Individual Board Member Issues

A superintendent can develop and apply **protocols** to address **individual board member issues**. These protocols will ensure that all issues held by board members are dealt with fairly. Without protocols, individual board members can feel that their issues are not addressed as quickly as other members or that the superintendent exhibits favoritism toward certain members. Establishing protocols promotes **fairness and equity** in addressing board member issues and promotes **accountability**. Protocols may include acceptable methods for communicating issues, the timeline for the superintendent's response to issues, and procedures for how to proceed if the issue cannot be resolved. For example, the superintendent may request that issues be communicated in writing via email using a certain format and that board members allow three business days for a written response. The protocols should be transparent and adhered to in order to effectively communicate and collaborate with board members and to prevent discord among board members or between the board members and the superintendent.

Interactions with Board Members

The superintendent's interactions with board members have the potential of **strengthening** or **weakening** the relationship between the superintendent and the board. When the superintendent treats members of the board fairly, equally, and with respect, and communicates with the board as a collective on a regular basis, the relationship is strengthened. These **positive interactions** build trust between both parties and instills confidence in the board that the superintendent can fulfill his or her duties. In contrast, if the superintendent prioritizes certain board members over others, fails to communicate effectively or consistently, or has **negative interactions** with board members, this can cause a lack of confidence in the superintendent's ability to perform his or her job adequately as perceived by the board. For example, sharing information with only two board members rather than communicating with all of the board members can have a negative impact on the superintendent's relationship with the board members with whom the superintendent failed to communicate. The superintendent's interactions with the board, both public and private, are impactful and should be done with forethought and care.

Distributing Responsibility and the Role of Shared Vision

Goal Implementation with a Shared Vision

A vision can be shared in two ways. In the **development** of a vision, the leader can solicit the **opinions and feedback** of stakeholders so that a variety of perspectives, opinions, and beliefs can be incorporated into the vision. When the vision is developed in this manner, participants can see their contribution to the vision by the way that it is articulated and implemented. A vision is also shared when a leader effectively **communicates** the vision, the rationale for the vision, and the plans for implementing the vision to stakeholders. When a vision is shared, this can assist with **goal implementation** because of buy-in from stakeholders. People are more willing to agree with and participate in plans that they helped to develop. Additionally, having a shared vision means that stakeholders will understand it well enough to work toward goal implementation, even without direct supervision from the leader. They will be able to take action to advance toward the district goals.

Delegating Tasks and Responsibilities

Leading a district is a great responsibility that cannot be done alone. To lead effectively, a leader must **delegate** tasks and responsibilities. Delegation is important because a leader does not have the time or resources to perform all responsibilities on their own. Most initiatives require a **team** of people to get the job done in a timely and efficient manner. Delegation is also important because a leader will not have all of the **skills** necessary to perform every task. For example, a project may require computer networking expertise which the leader may not have. In order for projects to be completely effective, tasks and responsibilities should be delegated according to **skillsets**. Delegation is also important because there are tasks and responsibilities that only the leader can perform, so his or her time should **prioritize** these types of activities. Other activities that can be accomplished by other team members should be delegated whenever possible. Delegation also ensures that the district will run efficiently in the **absence** of the leader, such as during a meeting or other event.

Delegation and Accountability

For delegation to be effective, a leader must hold team members **accountable**. A leader cannot delegate tasks and responsibilities without checking on the progress, or he or she may discover too late that the job was not done or did not meet expectations. Instead, a leader can incorporate accountability into delegation. This can be done by setting regular **check-in dates** with team members to meet about task progress, providing the leader with an opportunity to give feedback. The leader can also set certain **milestones** that must be accomplished to demonstrate progress. The leader should emphasize to the team member that **completion** of the project is his or her responsibility and that the completion is a reflection of job performance. When a leader includes accountability through regular check-ins, pre-established milestones, and communication of responsibility, the team member will be clear about expectations and able to perform the delegated task, and the leader will be reassured that the job is being completed to satisfaction.

Delegation and Authority

For effective delegation of tasks and responsibilities, those responsible must have the appropriate **authority** to accomplish the tasks. Often, the projects that need to be delegated are not ones that can be done independently. They require the **coordination** of other people and resources. It may be necessary for the district leader to expressly communicate to the person to whom the task is delegated as well as those assisting that the project leader has the authority to implement the project. This will help those leading the project to have **confidence** in their ability to get the job done. For example, if a project requires the scheduling of a community meeting, the project leader would need the authority to secure the venue, make purchases, and gather volunteers for the event. Providing team members with authority enables them to accomplish their delegated tasks with little to no dependence on the district leader. In contrast, when a project leader does not have the appropriate authority to get the project done, the project could be delayed or remain incomplete, waiting on assistance from the district leader.

Group Processes

Group processes refers to the way members of a group interact with one another in order to accomplish tasks and projects individually and collectively. Members of an organization may work together **consistently**, such as in a department of an organization, or may work together **temporarily** such as on a short-term project or collaboration. Group processes involve ways of communicating, problem-solving, assigning and performing roles, and decision-making. **Communication** involves the mode, frequency, style, and efficacy of communication between members within the group. This communication may include patterns of communication when a group meets or works in person, as well as how group members communicate remotely. **Problem-solving** within a group involves methods, styles, and strategies for addressing foreseen and unforeseen problems or challenges that may arise as the group works toward accomplishing a goal. **Roles** in group processes describes how group members fulfill both official roles such as titles or job descriptions and unofficial roles such as taking the lead on projects, managing time, improving relationships within the group, and resolving conflict. **Decision-making** in group processes describes the method in which decisions are made, such as voting.

Leadership Efficacy

A leader must **understand group processes** in order to effectively **manage teams**. Group processes affect how team members work together, communicate, solve problems, and accomplish tasks and projects. When a leader understands the dynamics of teams, the leader can strategize as to how to best **communicate** with the team, support the team, and lead the team. For example, a leader may determine that in-person communication with a particular department as a whole is more effective than communicating via email or with the team leader alone. A leader may also determine that the composition of a certain team or department is ineffective and needs to be reorganized. Additionally, group processes affect the school leader's **relationship** and **management** of other groups such as school boards, community organizations, or other coalitions. Understanding group processes can help the leader to garner support, launch initiatives, and build consensus. If a leader does not understand how group processes work, that leader may miss opportunities to **improve organization efficiency and productivity** or gain support from stakeholders.

Goal Progress Monitoring and Communication

Effectively Monitoring Goal Progress

A leader effectively monitors goal progress by implementing clear checkpoints and milestones in goal activities. Each goal should be broken down into smaller goals, or **milestones**, that can be reviewed in regular intervals. This allows the leader to analyze progress toward the goal in a timely manner so that, if progress is insufficient, there is time to intervene and make changes to the action steps. For example, if the campus goal is to achieve a 90% passing rate on reading assessments for third-grade students, the campus leader would want established milestones to monitor reading progress throughout the school year. The leader may review reading data every three weeks to determine if third-grade students are reaching and maintaining a 90% passing rate in reading. If not, the leader could implement additional strategies to increase the support for reading instruction. **Checkpoints** for goals are often aligned with grading periods, as identified on the school academic calendar.

Effectively Communicating Goal Progress

Goal progress should be communicated effectively and in a timely manner, especially to those who are instrumental in achieving the goal. First, the district leader should **monitor goal progress** closely so that related communication can occur promptly. Communicating goal progress is pointless if it is done with no time left to make adjustments. The district leader should **communicate progress consistently**, whether positive or negative. Communicating **positive goal progress** encourages others and reassures them that their actions are appropriate. This can serve as positive reinforcement that may even increase staff performance. In contrast, communicating **negative goal progress** is necessary so that corrections can be made. When communicating goal progress, conducting **in-person** conversations or meetings is beneficial because it allows for two-way communication. During these conversations, the district leader may discover unexpected barriers and challenges that need to be addressed.

Culture of High Standards and Expectations

Equity and Equality

All students are expected to meet the standards outlined by the state and federal governments. District leaders are responsible for providing students with the instruction, resources, and support necessary to meet these standards. **Equality** refers to providing all students with the same amount of resources and support, regardless of their needs. **Equity** refers to providing students with the resources and support that meet their individual needs. An example of equality would be that all students receive ninety minutes of reading instruction each day. An example of equity would be that students who have shown deficiencies in reading receive an extra thirty minutes of reading instruction each day. When leaders implement equity in schools, this may mean that some students receive more **resources and support** than others, or different support and resources. Leaders must be aware of what students need so that the right resources and support can be used to support these students. This need may be due to a lack of educational opportunity, physical or intellectual disabilities, or other circumstances. All students need resources and support to enrich their education, but practicing equity means that students will receive the appropriate amount of resources based on their identified needs.

Review Video: Equality vs Equity
Visit mometrix.com/academy and enter code: 685648

Creating a Culture of High Expectations

A culture of high expectations means that staff and students strive toward high goals and excellence. A leader can create a **culture of high expectations** by setting district goals **above minimum standards**. For example, if the required student attendance rate is 90%, the leader can set a goal for a 95% attendance rate for the campus. The leader can also **reward** student and staff performance that exceeds expectations. For example, the leader may publicly celebrate students who achieve Honor Roll. Another strategy for creating a culture of high expectations is to provide **models of excellence** for students and staff. These models can be effective programs in other districts, role models in the community, or exemplary staff and students on campus. To create a culture of high expectations, a leader must also **address performance that does not meet expectations** in an effective manner. It must be clear to staff and students that performing below expectations is not acceptable. The leader must also **provide the resources necessary** for staff and students to meet the high expectations that have been set.

Evidence of a Culture of High Expectations on School Campuses

It is evident that a district has a culture of high expectations by what is seen and heard on the campuses. The culture of high expectations is first evidenced by the **appearance of a campus**, including its cleanliness, organization, and posted materials. Bulletin boards and other visual aids in the hallways and in classrooms should demonstrate high expectations for academic achievement, character, and behavior. For example, a school may post college pennants and posters in the hallways to demonstrate an expectation that students are college-ready. Similarly, the **instruction** that is observed in the classroom should be evidence of high expectations for students and their ability to perform academically. The culture of high expectations is also evidenced by how **students and staff speak**. When there are high expectations, teachers and students speak positively about learning and meeting goals. There is little to no negative talk in regard to learning and performance. Instead there is problem-solving, brainstorming, and action-planning to meet academic goals. Finally, a culture of high expectations is evidenced by **performance**, which is indicated by goal attainment and student performance data.

Evidence of a Culture of High Expectations in Classrooms

Within the classroom, a culture of high expectations is evident by the **appearance** of the classroom and the **behavior** of teacher and students. First, the classroom will be neat, organized, and conducive to learning. Posted materials will be academically relevant, positive, and encouraging. In a classroom with a culture of high expectations, the teacher begins class on time and is prepared for the lesson. Materials and technology are ready for the start of class and there is a clear objective for the day's lesson. The teacher makes an effort to engage all students and uses a variety of instructional strategies to do so. In this classroom, students are eager to participate and remain engaged in the lesson throughout its entirety. Students demonstrate engagement in and mastery of the content by engaging in discussion with the teacher and their peers. There are few, if any, behavioral problems in this type of classroom, and if they do arise the teacher addresses them quickly and appropriately. There is evidence in the classroom of a good relationship and rapport between the teacher and the students. Students are not allowed to disengage from the lesson.

Identifying and Responding to Achievement Gaps

Achievement Gaps

The term "achievement gap" refers to the disparity in educational performance of students of low socioeconomic status, minority students, and female students. **Educational performance** is measured by many indicators such as course grades, pass/fail rates and promotion, standardized test performance, course selection, graduation rates, college enrollment rates, and many other indicators. The achievement gap exists as a national phenomenon but is also observed at the state level, district level, and even within campuses. Achievement gap was identified as an issue over fifty years ago and continues today. There is an abundance of research regarding why it exists and how to address it at all educational levels, but so far there has not been great success in eliminating it. As a result, leaders should be prepared to **identify and address** achievement gaps on their campuses.

Performance Indicators

The best way to determine the existence of an achievement gap in a district is to analyze **student performance indicators**. Leaders can use a variety of performance indicators to identify if an achievement gap exists in their district and, if so, for whom. Leaders can analyze performance data for **standardized tests** administered over the past 2–3 years to identify any disparities. The data should be compared based on socioeconomic status, race and ethnicity, gender, special education status, limited English proficiency status, and any other subgroups that are relevant to the campus. If an achievement gap exists, students in a particular **subgroup** will consistently perform at a lower rate when compared to the other groups of students. This method of analysis should be repeated for other performance indicators such as grades, pass/fail rates, promotion and retention, graduation, and any others that are relevant to the district goals.

Comparing Performance with Outside Standards

A district leader may evaluate data on the campuses and determine that all students, regardless of demographics, are performing academically at **comparable rates**. This is often the case in districts with little to no diversity. However, a lack of evidence of an achievement gap within a campus does not mean that students are not affected by it. The district leader should **compare** the performance of students in his or her district to other schools in the surrounding area. The leader may then find that his or her students are not performing at the same level as students in other schools. For example, a district leader may find that the majority of students in his or her district are demonstrating a proficiency of 76% in math, while students in other districts are demonstrating a proficiency of 88%. Consequently, the district leader may realize that students in his or her schools need to improve in math to remain on pace with their academic peers.

Reducing the Achievement Gap

To reduce the achievement gap in the district, leaders should **assess** the needs of the underperforming groups of students and **align resources and support** in an equitable manner. Leaders can provide **targeted interventions** to these students based on their identified needs. For example, the leader may schedule math and reading tutorials for a particular subgroup of students who have demonstrated deficiencies in that area. A leader should also set **district goals** that specifically address the performance of underperforming groups of students. This will ensure that there is an action plan for addressing the needs of these students, as well as specific resources dedicated to their performance. Finally, a leader should **track data** for the performance indicators that show the achievement gap. This data should be collected and analyzed at regular intervals so that additional interventions, resources, and support can be implemented, if necessary. In order to reduce the achievement gap, the leader should target these students with resources and support and monitor their progress on a regular basis.

Addressing the Achievement Gap Through Goal Setting and Data Monitoring

Goal Setting

Goal-setting can help to address the achievement gap because it focuses attention on the groups of students who need extra support and helps to target resources in those areas. Areas in which district leaders create goals receive **attention and targeted resources**. When goals are developed that specifically address areas of the school programming with evidence of an achievement gap, the district leader can turn the focus of students, staff, and the community to these areas. Additionally, when goals are created, there is a **determination** to accomplish those goals, so if a goal is related to the achievement gap, it is more likely that the gap will be addressed. For example, if the district leader has seen evidence in the data that Hispanic students with limited English proficiency are lagging behind their peers in reading performance, the district leader can develop a district goal that specifically addresses the reading performance of Hispanic students with limited English proficiency. As a result, there would be an increased focus on all Hispanic students with limited English proficiency, including the dedication of time, effort, and resources.

Data Monitoring

Data monitoring can be used to address the achievement gap because it can help to **identify** areas of the district program where the gap exists and to **monitor changes** in the achievement gap in the district. First, data should be used to identify where an achievement gap is present. The achievement gap is typically present in **reading and math content areas**, but can vary among other subject areas, as well as by groups of students. For example, a district leader may find that there is a gap in math performance between African American students and their peers, but that the gap is largest among African American males. Additionally, the data can show the district leader where the gap may be **narrowing** due to the instructional strategies and changes in school programming, or where the gap has **shifted** to another group of students. Therefore, data monitoring is key in identifying the achievement gap, determining the efficacy of strategies implemented to address the achievement gap, and assessing changes in the achievement gap among other student populations.

Staff Evaluations and Performance

Evaluating Staff Members

For a district to reach its goals and achieve its vision, all staff members must perform to expectations. It is essential that staff members be **evaluated** to ensure that expectations are being met. Evaluations of staff members provide an opportunity for leaders to identify areas of **strength and weakness** among the staff and to provide constructive **feedback** to staff members so that they can grow professionally. Leaders can use these evaluations to determine what additional **support and resources** are needed to improve staff member performance. For example, a leader may discover through evaluation that the science department on one campus demonstrates deficiencies in providing hands-on instruction to students. The leader can then identify professional development and coaching to assist the science teachers in improving this area. Evaluations are also used to determine whether staff members will have continued employment. Staff members who consistently perform below expectations may have to be removed from their position and assigned to a different position or campus.

Standardized Evaluation

State law requires that teachers be evaluated with a **standardized evaluation system**. The state may recommend a certain teacher evaluation system, but school districts can often choose which system to implement. Whether the school district adopts the recommended evaluation tool or develops its own, the standards for evaluation must meet or exceed the expectations outlined by the state. For teachers to be evaluated, the **evaluator** (often the district leader) must be trained in using the tool. Additionally, **teachers** must be trained on the tool that will be used to evaluate them. Evaluation often includes regular observations by the evaluator, collection of artifacts or data related to their practice, and conferences with the evaluator to discuss feedback. Teacher evaluation is usually based on **performance** in relation to the standards outlined in the evaluation tool, as well as **growth or progress**. Teacher performance standards are often related to instructional practice and strategies, professionalism, growth and professional development, and student performance. The evaluation process occurs throughout the school year and teachers normally receive a final evaluation rating at the conclusion of the school year.

Observing Staff Performance

Leaders should use as many opportunities as possible to **observe staff performance** so they will have a well-rounded view of the performance. The opportunities may include various days of the week or times of day, as well as varied circumstances. Teachers can be observed while engaging in their instructional practice in the **classroom**. They can also be observed while they are engaged in collaboration as they participate in **professional learning communities**. Additionally, teachers can be observed while they are fulfilling **duty assignments** such as arrival, dismissal, cafeteria, or hall duty. Other staff members can also be observed at different times, whether performing normal duties or engaging in special events such as community events, student events, or district events. A leader should be intentional and deliberate about seeking out different opportunities to observe staff at a variety of times, in a variety of circumstances, to obtain a fair and holistic view of staff performance.

Observing Staff in Varied Scenarios

It is important to observe staff in a variety of scenarios and at different times to get an accurate impression of staff performance. If a leader observes a staff member infrequently or always at the same time, this may lead to an inaccurate perception of that person's performance. For teachers, **class dynamics** may vary throughout the day. When a leader does not vary the time of day for observing a teacher, he or she will not know how that teacher responds to varied classroom dynamics or how instruction is practiced in all of the assigned courses. For example, a teacher may have a small class in the afternoon with fewer challenges than other classes. If a leader observes the teacher only during that class, he or she may not see all of the **instructional and classroom management skills** that the teacher demonstrates throughout the school day. If a leader consistently observes a teacher at the same time, it can also lead to predictability. A staff person could prepare for observation, so that it is not an authentic reflection of that person's regular work performance.

Improving Staff Performance

Conducting observations can help to improve staff performance by providing opportunity for **feedback and growth**. Observations allow a leader to see a staff member in action. When a leader observes a teacher or other staff member, he or she will note **strengths and weaknesses** in that employee's performance in relation to campus and district expectations. The leader can specifically reference what was observed as evidence of those strengths and weaknesses. This data will then help the leader to provide feedback regarding performance. The leader can also provide suggestions for improvement or give access to professional development and resources that will help the staff member to improve. Observations can also illustrate staff members' strengths so that they can build on them and continue to grow in those areas. Feedback and recommendations can also be used immediately to improve performance.

Professional Development and Staff Performance Standards

Calibrating Standards

One district may include multiple people who evaluate the performance of teachers and staff. The process of **calibration** is the training of all evaluators to maintain and look for the same **standards of performance**. When a team is not calibrated, different evaluators may have different perceptions of excellence, which can lead to confusion and inconsistency in staff performance. To calibrate staff evaluators, the team of evaluators should observe a staff person **together** at the same time. They each conduct an observation as if they were conducting it alone. After the observation is complete, the team of evaluators meets to discuss what they observed and how they would evaluate the staff person. The leader helps the team identify where their evaluations are **aligned or misaligned** in regard to the performance expectations. For example, a leader may believe that the observed teacher did a poor job implementing collaborative learning, while another evaluator believes that the teacher implemented collaborative learning in an acceptable manner. The leader would then refer to the performance standards and discuss the observed evidence to reach a consensus. This process would be repeated until all evaluators are able to independently assess staff members in like manner.

Supporting Teachers' Growth with Evaluations

Teacher evaluations support their growth because evaluations help to identify **areas of needed improvement** and hold teachers accountable for addressing those areas. Evaluations are based on a set of **performance standards** and will reveal if a teacher is not adequately meeting any of those standards. A teacher who needs to improve will know exactly where to focus improvement efforts, based on the evaluation results. The evaluation will also help the leader know how to best support the teacher in **growing professionally**. Additionally, evaluations hold teachers **accountable** for improving their practice. The accountability comes from the process of conducting evaluations, including timelines and deadlines, self-reflection, and conversations with the evaluator regarding areas of growth. When professional growth or efforts to achieve growth are not observed in the teacher, the teacher is at risk for receiving a negative evaluation at the end of the school year. A negative evaluation could result in outcomes such as probation or termination. The process of evaluating teachers ensures that they are growing professionally to become the best teachers they can be.

Selecting Professional Development

A leader needs to be deliberate in selecting professional development for staff members so that it is purposeful in helping staff achieve the district goals and vision. One strategy a leader can use includes analyzing how the professional development **aligns** with the district vision and goals. For example, if the district goal is to increase reading performance, then selecting a professional development session on implementing effective reading instructional practices would be appropriate. Another strategy that a leader can use to select professional development is to **identify weak areas** of staff based on observations and evaluations. A leader may observe that several teachers are having difficulty implementing effective classroom management strategies, so that leader may seek out professional development that addresses classroom management. Also, a leader must ensure that staff members participate in professional development that is **mandated by the district or the state**, such as something related to special populations of students or law and policy.

Supporting Teacher Growth with Coaching

A coach is a professional who helps a teacher to develop the skills necessary to work effectively. This coach is a staff person who does not supervise or evaluate the person being coached. This helps to foster a **relationship of trust** between the coach and the teacher. A coach will identify a teacher's areas of **strengths and weakness** based on a predetermined rubric or set of expectations. Then the coach will provide one-on-one support to help the teacher **improve targeted areas**. The coach may provide books and resources or recommend professional development sessions. The coach may also **model** effective teaching, **observe** the teacher in practice to provide real-time feedback, **assist** in the lesson planning process, and **guide** the teacher in self-reflection and critical analysis processes. A coach provides **individualized, targeted support** to teachers, which helps them to grow, usually in a shorter period of time than other forms of professional development support.

Utilizing High-Performing Teachers to Support the Growth of Others

High-performing teachers in the district can support the growth of other teachers by becoming leaders, serving as models, and coaching. High-performing teachers may exceed performance expectations in many areas or only a few, but their strengths can be **leveraged** to benefit the other teachers in the district. A leader may utilize high-performing teachers as leaders in the district in several ways. These teachers may be promoted to lead departments or be tasked with **leading collaborative meetings**, such as professional learning communities. Leaders may also direct these teachers to lead **on-campus professional development sessions** relating to their areas of strength. These teachers can also serve as **models** to the other teachers. Teachers who need to improve in certain areas may be asked to observe a high-performing teacher to see how a particular skill or strategy is implemented in the classroom. A high-performing teacher can also have a coaching role for other teachers to provide one-one-one support in certain performance areas.

Addressing the Needs of Veteran Staff

The needs of veteran staff can vary greatly due to their different experience levels and years of service. As a result, the superintendent must develop a means of **assessing** the needs of these staff in order to inform development of **strategies** to address those needs. Their needs may be assessed through personnel evaluations, surveys, focus groups, or other methods. The superintendent must have the means to collect this data, aggregate it, and utilize it in addressing the varying needs of the veteran staff. Many districts employ **instructional coaches** at the campus or district level that can personalize support for veteran staff. These coaches spend time with the teacher to identify their strengths and weaknesses, then they spend time with the individual teacher to help them to improve. Also, the superintendent may offer varied **professional development sessions** throughout the year to address these needs or designate funding for staff attendance at trainings delivered by outside agencies or other educational support organizations. Finally, the superintendent may purchase **resources and materials** that support professional development.

Addressing the Needs of Novice Staff

It is expected that novice staff will need training and support in order to be successful educators. Novice teachers often have similar needs, so the superintendent can plan in advance to meet these needs. The superintendent can develop a plan of **professional development, training, and support** that can address the needs of novice teachers and staff. This may include providing systematic training and professional development sessions prior to these new staff persons beginning their job. Many districts offer **induction programs, in-services, and boot camps** prior to the start of the school year for new teachers and staff only. These trainings focus on common needs that the teachers may have as novice staff and key information related to working in their school district. Additionally, novice teacher support may include **meetings and training** scheduled throughout the year to provide support for common areas of need such as lesson planning, delivering effective instruction, and classroom management. These novice staff persons may also be provided with **coaches or mentors** for assistance and support. Mentors are often veteran teachers on the novice teacher's campus or in another location in the district.

Superintendent as an Instructional Leader

The superintendent should act as the instructional leader in the district. This is important because it helps the leader to focus on instruction on the campuses, helps to support teachers, and establishes credibility with the faculty. When a superintendent is an instructional leader, **instruction** is prioritized. This impacts all school operations, including scheduling, alignment of resources, and support. Also, instructional leaders are able to support teachers in improving their skills related to **teaching and learning**. A superintendent who is experienced in and familiar with instruction will be a better evaluator of instruction and can offer expertise in improving instructional practice. Also, acting as an instructional leader gives **validity** to the superintendent's feedback relating to instruction. Teachers will be more receptive to feedback and advice regarding their instructional practice if the leader has demonstrated that he or she prioritizes instruction and has knowledge and expertise in that area. The superintendent should be prepared and willing to take the lead instructionally in the district in a variety of forms, such as providing feedback, demonstrating or modeling expectations, and collaborating and problem-solving with teaching staff.

Superintendent's Participation in Professional Development

A superintendent should participate in professional development for his or her own growth and development and to demonstrate solidarity with staff members. When possible, a leader should participate in **professional development** with the staff so that he or she can learn as well. When the leader participates in the professional development, this helps to identify the actions and behaviors he or she can expect from **staff** that also participate in the session. For example, if teachers participated in a professional development session regarding collaborative learning strategies, the leader would need to know what effective implementation of those strategies would look like in the classroom and how to support teachers as they implement them. Also, when the leader participates in professional development with staff, this demonstrates to the team that the leader values the opportunity for professional development and views it as a **priority**. This will increase **buy-in** from the staff and help them to be more receptive of the information and training that they receive at the professional development session.

Collaborative Teaching and Learning

Collaborative Teaching and Learning

Collaborative teaching involves two or more teachers engaging in instruction together. Collaborative teaching can take many forms, such as team teaching, co-teaching, and others. For example, one teacher may act as a **lead teacher** and present instruction to students while the other teacher acts as a **support**, helping to manage student behavior and reinforce concepts with struggling students. In another model, a teacher may present **new instruction** to students while another teacher in the room provides **remedial or intervention instruction** to a small group of students. Other team teaching models involve students being divided into **groups** and receiving new instruction from a teacher within their groups. In a team teaching model in which both teachers act as lead teachers, there are often **student rotations** or **instructional stations** involved. Collaborative teaching requires **co-planning** on the part of the team teachers and a good **working relationship** between them. Collaborative teaching allows for more flexibility within the classroom and exposes students to differentiated instruction and a wider variety of teaching styles.

Professional Learning Communities

Professional learning communities can be structured in a variety of ways to support collaboration among educators in the district. Most often, these **professional learning communities** are organized in a way that allows staff with shared roles or responsibilities to collaborate together under the leadership of one person who is designated to **lead** the community and is often trained to do so. For example, a professional learning community structured by **grade level** may consist of all eighth-grade teachers. In contrast, a community structured by **content area** may consist of all math teachers in the district. The district leader may determine which structure best meets the needs of the teachers and students. Professional learning communities are usually **goal-driven**, which encourages participants to collaborate in order to achieve the established goals. Professional learning communities are often guided by the following questions: What do we want students to learn? How do we know if they learned it? What do we do if they did not learn it? What do we do if they did learn it? While participation in professional learning communities may be voluntary in some districts, for many schools it is mandatory for teachers to participate.

Purpose of Professional Learning Communities

The purpose of professional learning communities, also referred to as **PLCs**, is to improve the educational performance and achievement of students through **educator collaboration**. PLCs are structured ways to facilitate **sharing knowledge** and **improving skills** among educators through data analysis, action research, exchange of expertise, and professional dialogue. In PLCs, teachers may discuss their practice and seek ways to improve. For example, teachers participating in a PLC may share lesson plans with committee members for feedback. Teachers may also share student work with committee members to calibrate grading practices or solicit ways to improve the quality of students' work. For example, a teacher may present a sample of student writing to committee members to get feedback on suggested focus areas for subsequent instruction. Teachers may also discuss student performance data in PLCs. This data may include summative assessment within the classroom or formative assessment, such as benchmark data or standardized testing data. Teachers may also use PLCs to discuss professional literature.

Collaborative Teaching and Learning

There are many benefits of collaborative teaching and learning. When teachers collaborate, they are able to **share ideas**. This fosters innovation and growth on the campuses. Collaboration also helps to **solve problems** more quickly. When a teacher has an issue, other teachers can provide resources, suggestions, or advice to help address the issue so the teacher does not have to research solutions independently and attempt to solve the problem through trial and error. For example, if a teacher has difficulty reaching a particular student, collaborating with other teachers who have that student in class and have been successful can help to identify ways that the teacher can reach the student. Also, collaboration among teachers builds **community** and fortifies the **school culture**. When teachers work and plan together, they build relationships with one another that can foster feelings of belonging and support. Teachers who are collaborative know that they can celebrate successes with their team members and that if they have a problem or challenge, they have a team of supporters. When teachers have these types of relationships and feel **supported**, it is easier to retain them in the classroom and encourage them to grow professionally.

Supporting Collaborative Teaching

A district leader is instrumental in ensuring that teachers are able to collaborate on the campuses. First, the district leader must plan a **school schedule** that allows for collaboration. This could mean that there are designated times for professional learning communities or that teachers who need to plan together have planning periods scheduled at the same time. For example, if the district leader expects all teachers in a certain grade level to collaborate, then the instructional schedule must accommodate a shared planning time for those teachers. The district leader also needs to **train staff** how to participate in a collaborative learning environment in line with the district vision and goals. This requires the leader to set clear expectations for the operation and outcomes of collaborative planning, such as those outlined in professional learning communities. Also, the leader must designate teachers or leadership team members to **lead collaborative planning** so that there is organization and accountability. Finally, the leader can support collaborative teaching and learning by **participating** in collaborative meetings when possible and **modeling** collaboration in other areas.

Collaborative Learning

Collaborative learning is an instructional strategy in which students are organized into **groups** for learning. These learning groups allow students to support each other and dialogue about the instruction and content. Collaborative learning reinforces **listening and speaking skills** in addition to the presented content. Teachers may employ several different strategies to organize students into collaborative groups. These include ability grouping (or homogenous grouping), heterogeneous grouping, and flexible grouping. In **homogenous grouping**, a teacher may organize students into groups based on proficiency with a certain skill so that targeted support and activities can be provided to groups based on their collective need. In **heterogeneous grouping**, students with different strengths or skills may be grouped together to balance out the group's deficits. Students may remain in these designated groups for a certain period of time, such as a grading period. **Flexible groups** are dynamic and take on different forms based on the instructional goals set by the teacher. These groups may have different sizes and composition based on needs.

Achieving and Maintaining Effective Instruction

Resources for Effective Instruction

Appropriate Physical Resources

Effective instruction requires appropriate physical resources. The leader can support instruction on the campuses by providing adequate physical resources for instructional staff. **Physical resources** include all of the tangible items needed to deliver instruction, such as furniture, books, and supplies. For example, **classroom spaces** must be able to accommodate teachers and learners, so there must be an adequate number of desks or tables and chairs, as well as enough physical square footage of the instructional space. Also, teachers need access to **instructional supplies** and appropriate **technology** for instruction. Other physical resources include curriculum, textbooks, computer labs, and other instructional resources. Leaders can identify necessary physical resources based on the school's **vision and goals**. For example, if the campus is striving to excel in STEM instruction, the leader needs to equip the school with science materials, computers, and other physical resources required for effective STEM instruction. Also, the leader may seek feedback from instructional staff regarding the necessary resources to be effective in the classroom. For example, a teacher may need additional bookshelves to accommodate leveled books within the classroom.

Appropriate Human Resources

Effective instruction requires the appropriate staff in place to deliver and support the instructional program. **Human resources** that are part of the instructional program include teachers, librarians, aides, and many others. A leader must ensure that the right number of people with the appropriate skills and qualifications are placed in the appropriate **instructional positions**. For example, it is the leader's responsibility to ensure that all classes are assigned a highly qualified teacher for the start of the school year. This may mean that the leader actively recruits and screens teaching candidates to have fully staffed campuses throughout the school year. Additionally, a leader must respond to needs for **additional staffing** or **changes in staffing** throughout the school year. For example, if students demonstrate deficits in math, the leader may identify math tutors to provide additional instruction. Also, a leader may notice that students with special needs require more support within the classroom and can implement a co-teaching model to support instruction. The leader can also seek **feedback** from staff to determine where additional instructional staff may be needed or where staff changes need to be made.

Importance of Resources for Effective Instruction

A leader must ensure that the appropriate resources are provided to instructional staff in order to support **effective instruction** on the campuses. A **lack of resources** on the campuses can make it difficult for teachers to teach and for students to learn. For example, if a teacher is assigned 22 students in her classroom, but there are only 20 desks, the teacher will have difficulty arranging her classroom in a way that is conducive to learning. Also, if a classroom does not have a highly-qualified teacher assigned to it, students will lose out on quality instructional time. In contrast, when teachers and other instructional staff are provided with the **physical and human resources** needed for effective instruction, both they and the students benefit. For example, if the school's vision is to cultivate reading skills in students, teachers would benefit from books, bookshelves, online reading programs, a library, and a librarian in order to achieve that vision. As a leader may not be able to provide all of the desired resources for instructional staff, he or she must decide which resources can be provided based on the district budget.

Overcoming Budgetary Challenges

At times, the district budget will not be sufficient to provide the desired instructional resources for teachers. In these instances, a district leader may need to seek additional ways to provide these resources. One way to overcome this challenge is to seek **funding from outside the school**. This may mean applying for **grants** or seeking **donations** from various businesses and organizations. The funds acquired can be used to purchase the desired resources. An additional strategy is to ask the **manufacturers** to donate the resources to the district. The school district may volunteer to be a pilot school district for the implementation of the resources. Also, parent organizations can conduct **fundraisers** to supplement the district budget and secure the needed resources. For example, the PTO may conduct a fundraiser to purchase supplies for the art program. The district leader should also determine whether the next school year's budget should accommodate the resources for the subsequent school year.

Time Management

Using Planning Time to Support Effective Instruction

Teachers have planning time scheduled into their instructional day. This **planning time** is determined when the master class schedule is designed for the campus, so leaders must consider in advance how much time is allotted to teachers for planning. A leader should encourage teachers to use this time to **support effective instruction**. For example, teachers can assess the quality of student work, prepare feedback for students, and determine which skills or content may need to be retaught. Planning time can be used to examine **resources** and determine how they can be incorporated into instruction or to identify differentiated instructional strategies for reaching diverse learners. Teachers may also choose to **collaborate** with other teachers in the planning and delivery of lessons. Leaders should ensure that teachers have adequate planning time and access to resources to support their efforts during planning time. Additionally, leaders should be considerate of teachers' planning time by avoiding scheduling meetings, conferences, duty, or other assignments during this time whenever possible.

Impact of Time Management on Instruction

Instruction on school campuses is delivered according to a strict **schedule**. Specific times are allotted for various aspects of the instructional program. A district leader's ability to **manage** his or her own time as well as to occupy the time of other **district staff** can affect instruction. For example, the leader's timeliness in approving decisions relating to instruction can impact the timeline of projects. The timeframe in which the district leader obtains **resources** for the instructional program can also impact instruction. For example, if the district would like to integrate technology into the curriculum, the leader's ability to secure computers for the students and teachers affects when instruction could begin. Additionally, the leader's daily decision-making regarding use of time can impact **instruction**, such as scheduling of meetings, school assemblies and activities, and conferences with staff. The leader must manage his or her time in planning, decision-making, and other duties throughout the school day to support the instructional program.

Preserving Instructional Time

Preserving instructional time means reducing the number of distractions and interruptions to the instructional program, specifically the time students spend in the classroom. **Interruptions** to instructional time may include announcements, school assemblies, meetings, or any other activities or events that distract from the instructional routine. For example, a district leader may desire to host a school-wide event such as a pep rally during the school day. The leader would need to consider the impact on the instructional day from hosting such an event. He or she may decide to adjust the day's schedule by taking a few minutes from each class, rather than having students miss a large portion of instructional time from one class, to accommodate the event at the end of the day. A leader may also decide that a pep rally does not warrant the interruption of instructional time and instead may postpone the event. Leaders who **preserve instructional time** use school-wide public announcements sparingly, adjust schedules for school assemblies to reduce the impact on instructional time, and try to schedule other meetings and events outside of the instructional day when possible.

Curriculum and Instruction

Rigor

Rigor in academic instruction refers to **challenging curriculum and instruction**. Rigorous instruction challenges students not only academically, but also intellectually, and even personally. Rigorous instruction is often complex and challenges students to think deeply and critically. Through rigorous instruction, students are able to develop the **soft skills** necessary for success in college, career, and adulthood, such as problem-solving, critical thinking, inferring, studying, time management, self-discipline, working in teams, and many others. Rigor does not mean something is excessively hard or difficult. However, rigor does involve stimulating and engaging instruction. Rigorous instruction often requires students to make connections **across academic content areas** and apply concepts to the **real world**. For example, if a high school English teacher wanted to assign a rigorous assignment based on a reading of *To Kill a Mockingbird*, he or she could assign a project in which students discuss the impact of the political setting in the United States at the time of the story on the plot. In contrast, a non-rigorous assignment could be a worksheet of multiple-choice questions.

Ensuring Rigor

A district leader must ensure that all students have access to a rigorous instructional program. First, a leader must evaluate the curriculum for **alignment to state standards**. This ensures that all curriculum is designed to instruct students based on the expectations set by the state. This prevents the lowering of standards in the classroom, which could lead to students falling behind. Next, a leader must determine that curriculum is taught in a **rigorous manner**. This includes creating lessons that require students to think critically. A leader may encourage instructional strategies such as differentiated instruction, project-based learning, and collaborative learning to help foster rigorous instruction in the classroom. Finally, the district leader must ensure that **assessment** of instruction is rigorous. This may mean encouraging the use of projects and other creative means that allow students to demonstrate mastery of standards and objectives. A rigorous instructional program avoids reliance on worksheets and other assessment activities that do not align with a rigorous instructional program.

Supporting Rigorous Instruction

Rigorous instruction must be challenging yet feasible for students. District goals can support rigorous instruction by motivating instructional staff to have **high expectations** for teaching and learning. When a goal is set high, it challenges instructional staff to work harder and with greater urgency, which requires utilizing **rigorous instruction**. For example, if a district has had prior reading performance of 65%, a district goal of 70% would not require significant change from the prior year's strategies and practice. However, setting a reading performance goal of 80% for the school year would encourage teachers to provide rigorous instruction to students to meet the higher performance expectation. Low expectations in goal setting will result in low expectations in instruction while high expectations in goal setting will result in high expectations in instruction. Similarly, when district goals include all populations and sub-populations of students, rigorous instruction is supported. This ensures that low-performing students and high-performing students receive instruction at their appropriate level of rigor.

Cross-Curricular Instruction

Cross-curricular instruction is the deliberate making of connections between **various content areas** so that students may apply their knowledge in more than one content area at a time. For example, students may examine the historical setting of a story in a reading class, utilize math strategies in a science class, or discuss geometric principles in an art class. Cross-curricular instruction is beneficial for students because it demonstrates the **relevance** of their content knowledge. When students understand that the instruction is not isolated to one particular area, but has applicability in other areas, students find the knowledge to be more **meaningful**. Additionally, utilizing concepts and skills in different contexts helps students to **master and retain** those skills. Cross-curricular instruction also aids students in their critical thinking skills such as inferring, drawing conclusions, predicting, and so forth. Cross-curricular instruction benefits teachers as well as students because it facilitates **collaboration** among colleagues. Teachers can plan together when lessons align across content areas, and they can even team-teach lessons.

Supporting Cross-Curricular Instruction

Leaders can support cross-curricular instruction by facilitating collaboration and providing resources for teachers. Cross-curricular instruction can be done independently but is more effective when teachers can **collaborate in lesson planning**. Leaders can provide **time** during the school day or at other times for teachers of different content areas to collaborate and examine the curriculum for opportunities for cross-curricular instruction. Also, leaders can support cross-curricular instruction by providing the appropriate **resources**. Teachers may have ideas that require books, supplies, or other materials to facilitate these lessons. Additionally, teachers may need **training or professional development resources** to help them present cross-curricular lessons effectively. Leaders can cultivate an environment where cross-curricular instruction is supported, encouraged, and praised.

Review Video: Creating Effective Lesson Plans
Visit mometrix.com/academy and enter code: 100377

Alignment of Curriculum and Instruction to Assessment

Curriculum and instruction must be aligned to assessment because what is taught must be measured and what is measured must be taught. If instruction is not aligned to the assessment, there will likely be no **measurement** of how well students mastered what was taught. Additionally, if instruction is not aligned to the assessment, students will likely be assessed on concepts and material they have **not been taught**. Neither scenario is fair or beneficial to students. In the case of district- or campus-created assessments, the **assessment** is often created first because this defines what students should know at the conclusion of the given time period. Then, based on the assessment's expectations, teachers can plan the order and pacing of the concepts and skills to teach. On state-mandated tests, students are expected to have mastered all skills and objectives provided by the state, but no one is aware of the test content until its administration.

Rigor and Differentiated Instruction

Rigorous instruction is challenging to students, but not impossible. However, classrooms are diverse and not all students perform at the same academic levels. As a result, teachers must provide an appropriate level of rigorous instruction to students based on their **current performance**. When teachers **differentiate instruction** for students, they cater to the individual needs of students, such as identifying the appropriate level of rigor for particular students or groups. For example, an eighth-grade math teacher would not give the same assignment to a struggling student as he or she would to a student who is performing above grade level. Each student needs a **unique level of rigorous instruction**. The teacher may identify that adding and subtracting fractions is a rigorous activity for the struggling student whereas the high-performing student may be able to solve algebraic equations that include fractions.

Relevance in Instruction

Relevance in instruction refers to how content is related to other content and to the real world, as experienced by the students in the classroom. When instruction is **not relevant**, students may have difficulty making connections to the instruction, identifying or connecting any background knowledge they may have, or retaining the information. In contrast, when instruction is **relevant**, students understand how the content connects to what they already know, what they are learning in other areas, and to the world around them. For example, a math teacher may explain to students how using an algebraic function can help them calculate their weekly paycheck on a job. An English teacher may compare a plot from classic literature to a modern-day movie or story to help students make connections. Teachers make instruction relevant by demonstrating how the new content **connects** with old content, with the content they are learning in other courses, and with the real world as they experience it.

Supporting Student Engagement and Performance

When instruction is relevant to students, they are more likely to engage in it and demonstrate better academic performance. Students are better able to **engage in relevant instruction** because they understand how the new content **relates** to what they already know, which can build their interest and provide them with a way to contribute to the lesson. For example, if the students are reading a story in which a character spends a day at the beach, a student who has never been to the beach may have difficulty engaging in the lesson, whereas a student who has visited the beach is more eager to share experiences and connections to the lesson. Similarly, when students are taught **abstract concepts**, they may have difficulty grasping and retaining them if they are not relevant. In contrast, when students understand how concepts are applied in the **real world**, they are more likely to retain them. For example, students may learn about chemical reactions in a science course, but if they are shown how these chemical reactions occur in everyday life, such as cooking, they will have a deeper understanding of the concept and be more likely to retain it.

School-Wide Practices and Focus on Standards-Based Instruction

Differentiated Instruction

Differentiated instruction refers to providing **customized or tailored instruction** to students to meet their diverse learning needs. These learning needs can be determined by previous academic performance, learning style, special needs such as a physical or learning disability, or other means. Based on the identified needs, teachers can **differentiate** the content, process, or product of the instruction. When teachers differentiate **content**, they provide different content to different students, such as a math teacher instructing one group of students on fractions and another group on algebraic equations. When teachers differentiate by **process**, a teacher provides different modes of instruction, such as video or media, field experiences, exploratory discovery, or other means. When a teacher differentiates by **product**, he or she provides different ways for students to demonstrate mastery of the content such as through writing, performance, or projects, among others. Teachers may differentiate instruction in all of these areas or in selected areas, based on the needs of the students.

Using Data to Support Differentiated Instruction

Instruction is differentiated based on **students' needs**. Data can be used to identify these needs, especially in the area of academic performance. **Historical student performance data** as well as current **formative and summative assessments** can help to determine the type of instruction a student may need. For example, the data may show that a certain group of students has deficits in reading. These students may benefit from not only reading a text, but additional methods of instructional delivery, as well as specific instruction that helps to build their reading skills. Data may inform campus leaders on what **courses** to offer. For example, if historical data demonstrates that many students have achieved advanced performance on state assessments, the leader may consider offering advanced classes in certain academic areas such as Advanced Placement, Gifted and Talented, Honors, and others. Other data that can be used to identify ways of differentiating instruction for students includes learning styles inventories, personality assessments, and observational data. These types of data can help teachers determine how to tailor instruction in a way that will support student learning and increase their academic performance.

Monitoring Curricular Programs

Ensuring Student Needs Are Met

The district leader must monitor curricular programs to ensure that student needs are being met. If curricular programs do not meet student needs, students will not be successful and campus goals will not be met. The curricular program must meet the **academic and social needs** of students. For example, if a population of students in a district is consistently exceeding the performance standards on assessments, they need a curricular program that extends their learning and supports their academic growth. If the entire curricular program is centered on remediation, that group of students will not have their needs met. District leaders examine student needs and design the curricular program based on those needs. Such decisions may include which classes to offer, the uses of self-contained instruction or content-specific instruction, the offering of the arts and other ancillary instruction, the integration of tutorials and remediation into the school day, and many others.

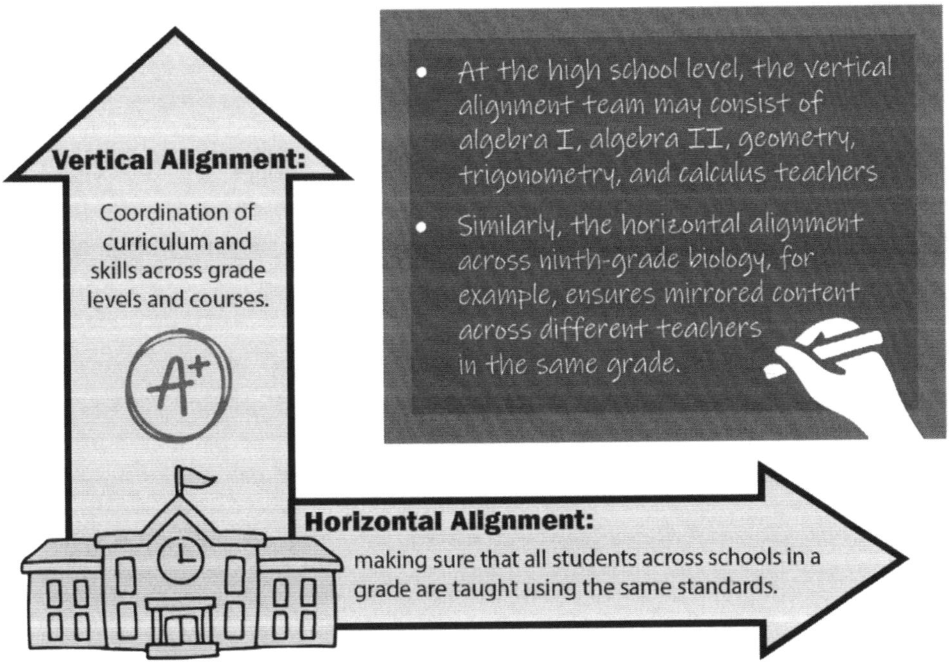

ENSURING CONTENT STANDARDS NEEDS ARE MET

The district leader must monitor curricular programs to ensure that they meet content standards. **Content standards** are determined by the state and are the basis for the design of **state testing**. Therefore, when curricular programs are not aligned to the content standards, students will not be prepared for state testing. If students are not prepared for state testing, they will not perform well and district goals will not be met. District leaders must be mindful of how students will be assessed so that the curricular programs support instruction to adequately prepare students for those assessments. Additionally, ensuring that the district curricular program meets content standards aids in **vertical and horizontal alignment** of instruction and curriculum. Vertical and horizontal alignment helps with collaborative planning among colleagues and ensures continuity of instruction for students, especially those with high mobility rates within the school district.

EFFECTIVELY MONITORING CURRICULAR PROGRAMS

Leaders can effectively monitor the curricular program by analyzing data, conducting observations, and soliciting feedback from stakeholders. If a curricular program is **appropriate**, student performance data relating to content standards will be reflective of that. If students are not performing well, the district leader may need to identify whether the curricular program has **deficits** or if the programming is **mismatched** with student needs. Also, the leader can identify if the curricular program is working based on **observations of instruction** on the campuses. For example, if the leader observes that students are demonstrating high levels of engagement in science courses, there may be an opportunity to expand the curricular program in science. Also, the leader can solicit **feedback** from stakeholders, such as teachers, students, and parents. These persons may identify needs or strengths of the curricular program for the leader to address. For example, Language Arts teachers may identify a need to separate reading and writing instruction in the curricular program to provide students with more time for instruction in these areas.

Assessment and Accountability

Evaluating the Quality of Teaching on Campus

A district leader can evaluate the quality of teaching on the campuses through observations and data. A district leader should spend time in the classrooms to **observe** teaching in action so that the leader will recognize effective and ineffective teaching practices. It is important to observe teaching to evaluate quality so that if corrections are necessary, these can be made in time to affect student performance. After teaching has been completed, the district leader can analyze **student performance data** to evaluate the quality of the teaching. If teaching is of good quality, the majority of students should be able to grasp the concepts and demonstrate mastery on assessments. If many students are unable to master these concepts and objectives, teaching efficacy needs to be evaluated. District leaders can use both formative and summative assessments as indicators of teaching quality.

Evaluating the Quality of Learning on Campus

Student learning can be evaluated in a number of ways. A district leader can determine the quality of learning on campus through observations, feedback from students, and student performance data. When the district leader **observes classroom instruction**, he or she has the opportunity to observe students in the learning process. If students are excited about the content, are engaging significantly in the process, and are successful when checked for understanding, there is likely a high quality of learning. Also, a district leader may solicit **feedback from students** regarding their learning. This can be in the form of surveys, focus groups, or individual interviews. The students can be asked about the learning environment, the relevance of content, and the rigor of the instruction, among other quality indicators. Finally, a district leader needs to **analyze student performance data** to determine the quality of learning. If students are not meeting expectations on assessments, the quality of learning can likely be improved.

Improving Teaching Already Deemed Effective

Even if teaching is deemed effective, there are still benefits to improving. Some district leaders focus solely on improving ineffective instruction, but that narrow focus results in a missed opportunity to develop and reinforce a **culture of high expectations** in the district. Effective instruction can become highly effective with additional support and strategies. When a district leader is committed to **improving all instruction** in the district, even instruction that is already considered effective, all staff are encouraged to grow professionally for the benefit of students. This fosters an environment of **continuous improvement** and also helps teachers to seek changes in the instructional program and to help address student diversity. This environment also encourages innovation in the classroom to find new and creative ways for instructing learners. Increasing the effectiveness of teaching can help high-performing students to grow and perform at even higher academic levels.

Address Ineffective Teaching

It is a district leader's responsibility to address ineffective teaching. First, the leader must **identify** the ineffective teaching. This is done through observations of classroom instruction and review of student performance. Next, a leader must **communicate** to the teacher which aspects of the instruction are ineffective. A leader should be strategic in communicating areas of improvement to avoid discouraging the teacher, and the leader should focus the teacher's growth in the areas that will have the most impact on students. Then, the leader must provide the **resources and support** to improve the ineffective teaching. This can include professional development and instructional coaching. The leader should also continue to **monitor instruction** to determine if improvements are being made. In some instances, depending on the severity of the deficits in instruction, the district leader may decide to change staff's instructional assignments or even remove staff from their current assignments. If staff is changed or removed, the district leader must adhere to district policies regarding staff changes.

Formative Assessments

Formative assessment is designed to **monitor student learning**. Formative assessment is useful in providing **feedback** to students so they will know which areas they need to improve and so teachers will also know areas in which to improve their teaching. The results of formative assessment may help teachers identify **instructional areas for re-teaching** or identify students for **interventions and tutorials**. Formative assessment may include checks for understanding within the classroom, classroom activities, and other guided and independent work. Formative assessments are usually activities that are low stakes, meaning that often no grade or point value is attached. For example, a teacher may ask students to represent their understanding of a concept using a graphic organizer. A teacher may also provide feedback on a pre-writing activity before a student writes an essay. Formative assessment may occur frequently and feedback should be timely in order to be relevant.

Review Video: Assessment Reliability and Validity
Visit mometrix.com/academy and enter code: 424680

Summative Assessments

Summative assessment is used to evaluate student learning for **mastery**. Summative assessment usually occurs at the end of an instructional unit or a designated period of time such as a grading period or school year. These assessments are aligned to objectives or standards and are usually **high stakes**, which means they may count for a significant portion of the grade or may determine students' progress in their educational careers. A summative assessment may be a midterm or final exam, a research project, a unit test, or a standardized exam. The results of summative assessments may determine a student's grade promotion or earning of course credit. Results from summative assessment may also determine a school's performance according to accountability standards. Summative assessment results are often used by district leaders for **instructional planning** and **goal-setting** for the subsequent school year.

Review Video: Formative and Summative Assessments
Visit mometrix.com/academy and enter code: 804991

Indicators of Effective Teaching

A leader can use several indicators to identify effective teaching on the campuses. With effective teaching, there is a clear **goal or objective** to be accomplished with the instruction. This objective is communicated to students and is evident throughout the lesson. Additionally, there is a clear **lesson cycle** throughout the instructional delivery, such as a gradual release teaching model in which students are supported throughout the learning process. When there is effective teaching, students are **engaged** in the learning and demonstrate **retention** of the concepts through formative assessment. Effective instruction includes **diverse instructional strategies** to meet the needs of learners and is responsive to the results of the formative assessment conducted in the classroom. Also, effective teaching is evident in **student performance data**. Students who receive effective instruction are able to perform to the selected standards on assessments.

Assessing Program Quality

A leader can assess program quality using data and feedback from stakeholders. **Data** that can inform a leader regarding program quality includes participation or attendance data, student performance data, and any other metrics that are collected, such as those specified by grants or state and national associations. If a program is good quality, parents and community members will **participate** in it, which is reflected in the participation and attendance data. Also, **student performance** will reflect whether a program is high quality. If student performance is below standard, this may be an indicator that the district's programming may be misaligned or below standard. Other metrics dictated by **outside agencies** may include the data relating to parent and community events, awards received, college acceptance, and others. A leader can also obtain feedback from **stakeholders**. Teachers, staff, students, and community members will generally be pleased with the implementation of a high quality program. Low approval of the school's program may suggest that the leader needs to examine its implementation or its appropriateness for the district.

ALTERNATIVE ASSESSMENT METHODS

Traditional methods of assessment usually involve a standardized test with closed questions, which require students to select an answer from several choices. Educators are now trying to incorporate a greater variety of assessment methods so that students can demonstrate mastery of content and objectives in different ways. These **alternative methods** may include writing assessments, project assessments, and performance assessments. **Writing assessments** may include responding to open-ended questions or writing an essay or work of fiction. **Project assessments** typically require students to conduct extensive research and compile a final product with multiple parts or aspects. Project assessments have typically been used in science and social studies courses but are now being incorporated across the curriculum. **Performance assessments** require the student to perform in front of peers or the teacher. These may include a speech, skit, dance, or some other physical demonstration of their learning. Many of these alternative assessments are also facilitated using technology applications.

Communicating Progress Toward Goals

COMMUNICATION WITH STAFF

It is important for a district leader to communicate with staff about progress toward goals to maintain or increase **momentum**, as well as to celebrate **successes**. A leader can communicate with staff about progress toward goals through **normal channels**: emails, employee newsletters, or staff meetings. Incorporating goal progress within these forms of communication helps the staff to view goal progress as something that is as important as the other topics that are being communicated. Also, it does not require staff to utilize a new or foreign form of communication to determine progress toward goals. However, a leader may want to publicize progress in more **public or visible ways.** These may include public announcements, posters or charts in hallways and meeting rooms, or special charts and graphs that can be shared with staff. Reaching goals or goal milestones can also be celebrated with awards, certificates, or other means.

COMMUNICATION WITH PARENTS AND COMMUNITY

A leader should communicate with parents and community about goal progress often and in a variety of ways. This can include **community meetings** in which stakeholders are invited to hear about district performance in a variety of areas, with a focus on goals. Additionally, the leader can provide a **newsletter or bulletin** to update the community on district performance, upcoming events, and ways to get involved with the district to help achieve its goals. Many districts feature phone systems that can **mass call** the homes of students, which can be used to communicate announcements regarding district goals and progress toward them. Similarly, district leaders can mail **letters** to parents with updates regarding the district goals. Progress toward district goals can also be communicated in other **meetings** that involve parents and community members, such as committee meetings, parent teacher organization meetings, and advisory board meetings.

COMMUNICATION WITH STUDENTS

Teachers can communicate with students about the district's goals and how their individual efforts and performance contribute toward achieving them. For goals that are related to student academic performance, teachers can help students take ownership of their own performance by setting **individual goals** and tracking their progress toward them. Students can be provided with **data trackers** to track their own progress toward their individual goals. Teachers can speak with students individually about the support they need to accomplish their goals. Teachers can also set **class goals** that align with district goals and encourage students to reach them. For example, if the district has a goal of 90% proficiency in math performance, a math teacher can help students set individual goals in math. This ensures that students understand how their behaviors affect their class and school district, and it demonstrates how they can contribute to the district's success while achieving their own success.

Two-Way Communication

Two-way communication on progress toward goals is important because it provides stakeholders with the opportunity to convey to the leader why **goals** may or may not be achieved. When a leader facilitates two-way communication, he or she can receive **feedback** on the efficacy of existing strategies, ideas for additional strategies, or requests for additional resources or support. For example, if the district has a goal to increase student proficiency in technology and the leader has purchased certain technology hardware to accomplish this goal, teachers may provide feedback that the chosen hardware has not been effective in exposing students to technology and that another type of hardware may be necessary. Additionally, two-way communication may reveal unexpected **barriers** to achieving goals. For example, a teacher may inform the leader that the technology goal may be difficult to achieve because the district technology infrastructure cannot support the increased Internet usage on the campuses. A leader can benefit from two-way communication about progress toward goals by receiving additional information that can lead to **refining or revising goals**, or that assures the leader that the right actions have been **implemented**.

Safe Environments

Physically Safe Environments

A physically safe environment is free from seen and unseen dangers that would pose a threat to the physical safety of anyone exposed to that environment. A **physically safe environment** is in good repair, accessible to all, and accommodating to its designated purpose. For example, a physically safe classroom would be free from damaged walls, ceilings, or floors; broken or damaged furniture; leaky pipes or plumbing; and electrical hazards. Additionally, a physically safe environment includes **well-controlled people** so that no one is physically harmed by the presence of others. This includes adhering to **capacity limitations** and monitoring the **conduct** of those present in the environment. For example, a school cafeteria should not exceed the posted maximum capacity of persons, even for special events, and persons should be able to move safely and freely in the cafeteria in accordance with its purpose.

Emotionally Safe Environments

An emotionally safe environment is an environment in which all persons are able to **learn**. This type of environment is free from all obstacles, emotions, and conflicts due to **preventative strategies** and **quick resolutions**. When an environment is not emotionally safe, children can feel fear, anxiety, and a host of other emotions. In an **emotionally safe environment**, both adults and children feel comfortable participating in the learning environment and interacting with one another. There is an absence of peer-to-peer and peer-to-adult conflict as well as bullying. **Procedures and systems**, such as counseling, mentoring, and other interventions, are in place to ensure the emotional safety of students on campus. There is an emphasis on **communicating** one's needs to foster active participation and engagement in the learning process. Additionally, the **physical arrangement** of the environment is designed to contribute to emotional safety, such as including windows and natural lighting, inspirational and positive posters and bulletin boards, and aesthetically pleasing furniture and decoration.

Operation of Physical Plants, Equipment, and Support Systems

A leader must ensure that the physical plant, equipment, and support systems on each campus operate safely, efficiently, and effectively. The first step is to identify the appropriate staff to **manage** the physical plants. These people have the primary responsibility to ensure the safe functioning of everything on the campuses, so the leader must have the right persons in place and must monitor their performance. Also, the leader must provide the plant managers with **competent staff** to support plant maintenance. In partnership with the managers, the leader can develop systems of **monitoring and inspection** to ensure that all aspects of the plants are running efficiently and safely. The district leader should also solicit **feedback** from other staff members who use certain aspects of the school plants. For example, if a school has a swimming pool, the leader should get feedback from the swimming coach or athletic director regarding the pool facilities. This feedback can help to identify areas of improvement, repair, or replacement needs.

Laws and Policies Regarding Maintaining a Safe Environment

Local, state, and federal laws and policies help district leaders maintain a safe environment for students and staff. These regulations and policies, when adhered to, create a minimum level of safety. For example, **federal laws** regarding aspects of school safety such as asbestos management, ADA compliance, Internet safety, and others are interpreted into district policies. **School districts** may have additional safety requirements, such as the presence of police officers on campus, campus visitor policies, volunteer policies, and others. **Local laws and policies** may include fire codes and occupation limits, as well as other mandates for building safety that are not particular to schools but are implemented in all public places in the area. Each of these regulations and policies is meant to **enhance the safety** of the schools, so the district leader should prioritize adherence to these regulations and policies. Failure to comply with local, state, and federal laws and policies can result in sanctions, fines, or other repercussions.

Maintaining a Physically Safe Environment for Students

A leader should take proactive steps to maintain a physically safe environment for students. First, the district leader should conduct regular **inspection and maintenance** of all parts of the buildings to ensure that no aspects of the physical buildings pose hazards to students. Next, the district leader should **monitor flows of traffic** within the school buildings to maintain safety. For example, a leader may notice that a school banner obstructs visibility in a hallway, causing students to bump into one another during transitions between classes. To promote safety, the leader should relocate the banner to a different area of that school. The leader should also ensure that common assembly areas such as hallways, courtyards, and auditoriums are monitored by school staff to prevent or identify **conflict between students** that could lead to physical harm.

Maintaining an Emotionally Safe Environment for Staff

Like the students, staff members need an emotionally safe environment. A leader can establish and maintain an **emotionally safe environment** through leadership style, communication, awareness, and support. When a leader has a **caring and empathetic demeanor**, employees will feel emotionally safe. In contrast, **high-strung, micromanaging leaders** can create fear and anxiety in staff. Also, leaders need to maintain **open lines of communication** with staff members. This allows them to communicate their needs so the leader can address them when possible. A leader should be able to recognize or be aware of aspects of the environment that **endanger emotional safety** for staff and should be able to address those concerns. For example, a lax discipline policy can create a challenging environment for teachers and staff. A leader can take steps to remedy this and create a safer environment. Finally, a leader should provide **avenues of emotional support** for staff. This may include staff counseling, referrals, or other accommodations and support that can help staff members feel emotionally safe.

Disciplinary Expectations and Behavior Management

Behavioral Expectations for Staff and Students

Safe Student Behavior

Student behavior must be regulated and controlled for a safe school environment. Students who are unsupervised or do not adhere to established rules and procedures pose a **threat** to the safety of the school and to themselves. As a result, **student behavior management** is necessary to maintain a safe environment. School staff and ultimately the district leader are responsible for the safety of students the entire time they are at school. Unsupervised students may lead to an unsafe environment since they are less prone to follow rules when supervision is absent. All students should be accounted for at all times and actively monitored. Additionally, students who misbehave can cause disruption, conflict, destruction of property, and a host of other actions that threaten the safety of the school environment. As a result, negative student behavior must be addressed quickly and effectively to maintain a safe environment.

Review Video: Promoting Appropriate Behavior
Visit mometrix.com/academy and enter code: 321015

Behavior Management and Discipline Strategies

A leader may use a variety of behavior management and discipline strategies, as well as instructing staff to use them, to properly manage student behavior. These different techniques and strategies almost all have certain characteristics in common. Effective **behavior management** requires active **supervision.** It is not enough for adults to be present wherever students are. They must survey students, anticipate student behaviors, and be prepared to intervene when necessary. Also, most strategies require that adults set clear **expectations** for student behavior. This can be done through establishing rules, behavior contracts, or other ways to articulate expectations. Finally, there must be clear **consequences,** applied fairly and equitably, for behavioral infractions. Many behavior management strategies encourage building relationships and rapport with students, incorporating positive consequences for appropriate student behavior, and addressing student behaviors without overly emotional responses such as yelling, sarcasm, or unprofessional language.

Student Behavior Management and Student Success

Student behavior management and student success are related because poor student behavior detracts from the learning environment. If a student is behaving in a disruptive or disengaged way in the classroom, he or she cannot **learn effectively**. If the poorly-behaved student misses the instructional content, he or she will be less likely to succeed academically in that class. Poor student behavior can also negatively impact the **academic success of other students** in the room. For example, speaking out of turn, interrupting, and bothering others detracts from the learning environment. Finally, some behavioral consequences require the misbehaving student to be **removed** from the classroom. In these instances, the student often loses out on instructional opportunities, which can negatively impact academic success. Consequently, when student behavior is appropriately managed, the learning environment is preserved and all students have an opportunity to learn in a safe environment.

Review Video: Student Behavior Management Approaches
Visit mometrix.com/academy and enter code: 843846

Fairness and Equity

Student behavior management strategies and discipline must be applied in a fair and equitable manner to be effective and maintain a positive school environment. **Fairness** involves **communicating expectations** prior to applying discipline. If expectations are unknown or unclear, students can be frustrated and deem it unfair to be held responsible. Fairness also means that the adults **adhere** to the expectations and consequences that have been communicated to students and parents. For example, a behavior strategy may be to give a student a warning before applying consequences. A teacher may give students multiple warnings on one day and never give consequences for a particular behavior, but on another day, the teacher may immediately give a consequence for the same behavior without a warning. This type of inconsistent behavior from the teacher would be deemed unfair. Also, staff must practice **equity** in discipline. Adherence to written policies and procedures can ensure that all students are disciplined in an equitable manner, regardless of race, gender, or academic and behavioral history.

Emergency Preparedness and Response

Planning for Crises

Even though crises are unpredictable, a leader can plan in advance to ensure that the school district is as prepared as possible. First, the leader should have **emergency plans** in place for events such as natural disasters, fire, medical emergencies, intruders on campus, etc. These plans should be clearly written, and key emergency staff should be trained on how to implement the plans in time of crisis. Additionally, the leader can implement **drills** to practice the crisis plans. The leader can evaluate staff and student performance during these drills and provide feedback to participants or revise the emergency plans based on the performance. The leader should also be familiar with **district policies** regarding emergency plans, drills, and reporting. A leader should make contact with **local emergency services** in the community to establish a relationship and ascertain important information and contacts to help in the event of an emergency or crisis.

Procedures in Emergency Situations

Procedures are necessary in emergency situations to ensure the safety of everyone affected. In emergency situations, emotions can cloud thinking and judgment. Additionally, persons who are not familiar with a particular emergency situation may not know what to do in these instances. Having a **procedure** in place ensures that the right actions are taken in the event of an emergency, regardless of the emotional state or expertise of those involved. For example, if a person has a health emergency on campus, procedures should be in place for addressing the situation, including calling an ambulance, providing emergency aid, and maintaining the safety and order of the staff and students not immediately involved in the situation. These procedures should be taught to all **staff** in the district and be available in **written form** so they are accessible in the event of emergency. Having written procedures in place and abiding by them in the event of an emergency can also serve as legal protection for the district leader and staff.

Key Emergency Support Personnel

The district leader should identify key emergency support personnel **on the campuses** to prepare them for emergencies. These key staff members should know their **roles** in each emergency instance and be trained on how to fulfill those roles in the event of an emergency. These staff members may include the school nurses, counselors, police officers or security personnel, administrators or other district leaders, clerks, and others, depending on the nature of the emergency. For example, a different team of personnel may be needed to respond to a health emergency than a natural disaster emergency. Emergency support personnel **outside of the schools** may include key district staff members and personnel at various emergency response organizations, such as the fire department.

Emergency Preparedness

Emergency preparedness means that the district leader and staff have identified **potential types of emergencies** and planned the **procedures, staff, and resources** needed to address each type. Emergencies may include health emergencies, fire, natural disaster, intruders on campus, and many others. For each of these potential emergencies, a **written plan of procedures** should be created, detailing how everyone on the campuses should behave in the event of such an emergency. **Key personnel** with specific roles and responsibilities should be identified in the written plan. Everyone should be trained prior to the emergency to follow the written procedures. For many emergencies, **practice drills** can be conducted, such as fire drills or school lockdowns. Also, **resources** should be acquired, stored in designated locations, and inspected periodically. These resources may include printed copies of emergency procedures, fire extinguishers, automatic defibrillators, first aid kits, and other resources.

INCIDENT COMMAND SYSTEM (ICS)

The **Incident Command System (ICS)** is a framework designed to enhance the coordination and management of emergency responses. In the context of school emergency response teams, ICS serves as a comprehensive structure that delineates clear roles, responsibilities, and communication channels during crises. One of the primary functions of ICS is to establish a unified command structure, ensuring that all involved parties—from school administrators to first responders—operate under a centralized leadership. This organizational clarity promotes efficient resource utilization and aids in effective decision-making, contributing directly to maximizing a safe and effective learning environment. By implementing ICS, school emergency response teams can optimize their use of resources, both human and material, to respond swiftly and appropriately to emergencies. The system allows for a strategic and coordinated approach that reflects effective fiscal management while prioritizing the safety and well-being of students and staff. Through standardized procedures and clear lines of communication, ICS minimizes potential chaos, enabling schools to navigate emergencies with precision. This not only aligns with the objective of maintaining a safe learning environment but also underscores the significance of judicious resource allocation in achieving this goal.

Protecting and Advocating for Students

PROTECTING AND ADVOCATING FOR STUDENTS

A district leader should have systems in place for the protection and advocacy of students. These systems should be based on the needs of the student population and should be responsive to the changing needs and concerns of these students. A district leader will know if these systems are **appropriate and effective** in various ways. First, there should be a **student culture of safety** in the schools. This culture involves students feeling free to engage in the academic program, social activities, and extracurricular activities. Also, students should have an **adequate voice**. An appropriate and effective system for protection and advocacy will allow various avenues for students to contribute their ideas and voice their concerns. Additionally, there will be evidence that students are **supported** in times of need or crisis. This means that socio-emotional needs are identified and addressed quickly so that students can engage in the district program. These systems are effective and appropriate only if they benefit all students. If some groups of students are **marginalized or neglected** on campus, the district leader must revisit the appropriateness and efficacy of the district's systems.

Review Video: Crisis Management and Prevention
Visit mometrix.com/academy and enter code: 351872

OPPORTUNITIES TO SERVE AS AN ADVOCATE

Advocacy for students is necessary whenever any group of students is or has the potential to be **marginalized**. These groups are commonly students of low socioeconomic status, minority status, immigrant status, or a different sexual orientation. However, any student or group of students can need advocacy at any given time. There is an opportunity to advocate for these students when their **right to an equitable education in a safe environment** is threatened. For example, a district leader may observe that an academic program offered in the district consistently leaves out students who receive special education services. The district leader may advocate for that group of students by calling for a review of the application and acceptance criteria to drive change. Opportunities for student advocacy can occur on campus, within the school district, or within the local, state, and federal political arenas.

Maintaining Student Confidentiality

A district leader must maintain student confidentiality according to the Family Educational Rights and Privacy Act (FERPA). This involves keeping **student information and records** confidential. However, when advocating for students, the district leader may be informed of student information by other staff members, parents, or the students themselves that should also be kept confidential. Keeping the students' confidentiality means not sharing private information with outside parties unnecessarily. This fosters **trust** between the district leader and the student or other stakeholders. Establishing this trust helps to create a district culture in which students and their families are willing to share sensitive information with the district staff to help **advocate** for a student. For example, a parent may inform the district leader that the family has recently become homeless. Certain documents must be completed and certain staff need to be informed of this information to advocate for the homeless student, but the district leader must ensure that the sensitive information remains as private as possible. There are circumstances in which the student's confidentiality may need to be breached, but the district leader should make an effort to maintain that confidentiality wherever possible.

Situations in Which Student Confidentiality Must Be Breached

A district leader and other district staff must do their best to maintain the confidence of students, but under some circumstances a student's confidentiality must be **breached**. If students confide in a staff member that they are being **harmed**, pose **harm to themselves**, or pose **harm to others**, school staff members have the responsibility to act on that information for the protection of those students or others. For example, a student may confide in a teacher that he or she is contemplating suicide. The teacher would then break the student's confidentiality and inform the district leader of the student's intentions. The teacher and the district leader would then contact the student's parents and the proper authorities to obtain immediate help for the student. Other examples that warrant a breach in student confidentiality include information related to **child abuse or neglect** or **threats of violence to others**.

Motivating Students

Intrinsic Motivation

Intrinsic motivation is motivation that comes from **within**. It is a person's own drive to succeed or to accomplish a goal. For students, this **intrinsic motivation** may be the result of education and career goals, family expectations, social influences, and more. Intrinsic motivation may drive students to meet or exceed academic performance expectations, participate in and excel in extracurricular activities, or choose certain education and career pathways. Intrinsic motivation is affected little by **outside influences** because the drive comes from within. For example, a high school student may desire to become a writer and consequently excels in English Language Arts classes. This student may have an English Language Arts teacher that he or she does not get along with, but because the drive to become a writer is intrinsic, the student may still work hard and perform well in that class. Intrinsic motivation is considered more effective than extrinsic motivation. Students who excel in school, especially in the face of obstacles and challenges, are often highly intrinsically motivated.

Extrinsic Motivation

Extrinsic motivation is motivation that comes from an **outside source**, such as another person, and is in the form of a reward. The reward can be **tangible**, such as money, prizes, or gifts, or it can be **intangible**, such as an experience, recognition, or approval. Teachers and other staff often use extrinsic motivation to encourage students to perform at a certain level or behave in a certain way. For example, a teacher may tell her third-grade class that all students who complete their homework will receive stickers. The students will be motivated to complete their homework and earn stickers. **Extrinsic motivation** can be effective with students, especially when they are lacking intrinsic motivation. However, extrinsic motivation is considered less effective than intrinsic motivation because in the absence of the reward, motivation significantly decreases. Additionally, if the reward loses its appeal, motivation will decrease. For example, if the third-grade teacher were to stop offering stickers for homework, the number of completed homework assignments might decline. Similarly, students may be less excited about receiving stickers for homework near the end of the school year, resulting in fewer completed homework assignments.

Motivating Students

District staff can create **systems of rewards** to motivate students to engage in the academic program, perform at higher levels, and behave in an acceptable manner. Rewards can be given for individual and collective behaviors. Some districts have used **point systems** or **merit systems** to reward and motivate students. Students can redeem points for prizes, participation in field trips, or participation in other school activities. Some districts use stickers, tickets, or other means of reinforcing positive student behaviors, which can be redeemed as well. For example, a student may earn a ticket for participating in class discussion, which can be redeemed for a prize. This reward would encourage the student to increase participation in class discussion. Students may also be motivated by public recognition, such as receiving an award at an awards ceremony, being identified on the school website or a classroom bulletin board, or having their names announced during school announcements. Students are **motivated** when rewards systems are clear, fair, and consistent and when expectations are clearly outlined.

Aspects That Demotivate Students

Perceived negative aspects of the district can decrease student motivation, causing them to disengage in the district program. If a student perceives school as **unsafe**, he or she may have poor school attendance or arrive late to school. If a student perceives the teacher to be **unfair or ineffective**, the student may not desire to perform well in that class, resulting in poor grades and possibly behavioral problems. When students perceive **school rules or policies** as unfair or inequitable, they may be discouraged from abiding by those policies or engaging in the programs that the policies or procedures apply to. For example, a student may desire to audition for a role in the school play. However, the student may view the audition process as unfair, believing that certain students will be chosen for the roles regardless of who auditions. Consequently, that student will choose not to audition for the play or engage in the theater program. District leaders must identify aspects of the district and district program that may **demotivate** students and remedy these where possible.

Professional Influence for Systemic Change

Professional Education Organizations and Associations

It is important for district leaders to participate in professional education organizations and associations. Many organizations have been created to **support educators** in various stages of their career. There are organizations primarily created for teachers in the classroom, with some organizations specific to particular content areas. There are also organizations created specifically for **school administrators**. District leaders may consider joining organizations related to the **field** in which they obtained their degree. These organizations provide training, information, and networking opportunities. Some offer legal help and protection as well. Most organizations charge a fee for membership, and members have access to a website, newsletters, training opportunities, job postings and leads, networking events and much more. The information provided through these organizations can also help district leaders stay **current** on trends in education, changing laws and policies, and politics that affect the field of education. Additionally, **networking** within these professional organizations can provide opportunities for growth, advancement, and partnerships.

Impact of Professional Influence on the School

The district leader often has influence in the community due to the position of leadership. This **influence** comes from the connection to others who are in a position to support the district's vision and goals. Additionally, the size and diversity of a district leader's **network and contacts** can increase the power of that influence. The district leader's professional influence can be used to bring **positive attention and resources** to the school district. For example, a district leader may know professional athletes, musicians, or actors within the community and can invite them to speak to or mentor the students on the campuses. Having such persons on campus can inspire the youth and encourage them to succeed academically. The district leader can also use his or her influence to secure **opportunities for students** from businesses and organizations in the community, such as field trips, internships, or other educational opportunities. Finally, the district leader's professional influence can be used to **promote social justice** within the district and the community. For example, the district leader may advocate for a public library within the community.

Sphere of Influence

A sphere of influence refers to a leader's power to affect others, even without formal authority. School leaders have **authority** over staff and students. Staff can be reprimanded or terminated and students can be disciplined. Staff and students conform their behavior to the expectations of the leader because of the leader's authority over them. In contrast, the leader does not have authority over **parents, community members, district personnel, and other stakeholders**. However, the leader has the ability to **influence** these persons through speech and other communication, as well as behavior. For example, a district leader cannot mandate that a neighborhood organization offer childcare services on campus after school because the district leader has no authority over that neighborhood organization. Instead, the district leader could use his or her influence to **encourage or persuade** the neighborhood organization to provide childcare services in partnership with the school. A district leader must recognize that when operating within this larger sphere of influence, skills such as understanding, compromise, persuasion, and clear communication are necessary to reach desired outcomes. This skillset differs from the skills used with those under the district leader's authority.

Educating Community Stakeholders

Local Education Processes

The purpose of educating community stakeholders about local education processes is to help them understand the reason for **local policies and procedures** and to help them engage in the **local education processes**. Community stakeholders who are uninformed or misinformed on local education processes and issues may mistakenly assign responsibility or culpability to the school and district leader. Stakeholders should be aware of the **decision-makers** within the school district, the **processes** for decision-making, and how they can **participate** in those processes. This can help stakeholders to be effective in **enacting change** for decisions and processes that they do not agree with. For example, if a school dance program is eliminated, stakeholders may mistakenly believe that this was the district leader's decision when, in reality, funding for these types of programs was eliminated for the whole area. Stakeholders should be educated regarding the **budgeting process** and how they can participate in the decision-making process behind district and school budgets.

State and Federal Education Processes

The purpose of educating community stakeholders about state and federal education processes is to help them understand the reason for the **laws and policies** that govern the education system and to help them engage in the **state and federal processes**. Many district policies and procedures are developed in response to state and federal laws. When community stakeholders are aware of the laws that impact their children, they are more likely to engage in the processes to **effect change**. For example, a community may believe that their students should not be subject to standardized testing. Those community members would need to be informed of the accountability laws that require assessment of students. Then the community members would be able to participate in the processes that could affect those laws in the future, such as voting or communicating with lawmakers.

Identifying Areas in Need of Improvement

Facilitating Discussions with Students

Students can help the district leader identify areas of the district in need of improvement from the **student perspective**. This perspective is invaluable when evaluating **district programming** and **district culture**. For example, the district leader may have instituted an art program for students based on the perception that students wanted more arts on campus. Students can inform the district leader about how well that art program meets their needs. They may explain that the student body was interested in digital arts rather than classical arts, therefore making the district leader's art program ineffective. Students have to abide by the **rules and policies** that district leaders design and can often provide feedback on how effective those rules and policies are. Students can inform the district leader of aspects of the district that do not enhance school safety, are deemed unfair or inequitable, or are simply ineffective. Students are also helpful in providing solutions for areas of improvement on the campuses.

Facilitating Discussions with Teachers

Teachers can help the district leader identify areas of the school in need of **improvement** from their perspective. Teachers are responsible for **implementing** the district program that the leader designs. As a result, they are often aware of needed areas of improvement that the district leader cannot see. When a district leader facilitates discussions on school improvement with teachers, they are in a position to **gather information** that may not have discovered otherwise. For example, the teachers may point out a misalignment between the curriculum's scope and sequence and the assessment calendar, which causes the performance data to be skewed. This information can help the leader analyze data that has already been collected and devise a plan for revising the assessment calendar. Additionally, including teachers in this discussion increases buy-in. This process allows them to voice their concerns and to identify areas of the district program that need improvement for them to do their job more easily and effectively.

Facilitating Discussions with Community Stakeholders

Community stakeholders can provide the district leader with the **community perspective** of district areas in need of improvement. The school district is an integral part of the community and plays a significant role in **meeting the needs of community families**. Community stakeholders can inform the district leader of areas in which the district is not meeting needs. For example, community members may inform the district leader that school dismissal procedures are inadequate and that the schools are creating disruptive traffic congestion in the community at dismissal time. The district leader can work with community members to develop a plan that is appropriate for the district and respectful of the surrounding community. Engaging community stakeholders in discussions relating to the efficacy of the district program also creates **buy-in of the district vision and goals**, as well as building relationships between the district and the community.

Facilitating Discussions with District Personnel

Feedback from district personnel regarding areas of campus improvement is valuable. **District personnel** offer a unique perspective because they are able to view the district as it relates to the entire district's curricular program, mission, and goals. As a result, their perspective can help the district leader remain in alignment with **district expectations**. District personnel can also provide feedback based on how the various campuses in the district **compare** to each other. District leaders may not be able to spend sufficient time on each campus to gather ideas and best practices, but district personnel can provide this perspective. Additionally, district personnel are often the persons responsible for **evaluating** the district leader's performance. Addressing weak areas identified by district personnel can ensure that the leader is meeting the district's performance expectations.

Root Cause Analysis

Conducting a root cause analysis involves identifying the root cause or underlying source of a problem. A **root cause analysis** begins with identifying the problem, then systematically identifying the source of that problem with the understanding that a sequence of events (or chain of causes and effects) may have led to the problem's manifestation. Conducting a root cause analysis is valuable because the **main source of the problem** can be addressed rather than just the symptoms. For example, the district leader may notice that math scores are below expectation. A further analysis of the data may indicate that the majority of the low performing students have their math class in the morning. A further analysis may indicate that a significant number of students arrive late to school every day and are missing the math instruction needed to perform well on the assessments. The district leader may conclude that addressing the tardiness may help to improve math scores. Root cause analysis helps the district leader to address the right problem in order to improve outcomes.

SWOT Analysis

A SWOT analysis is a method of identifying the strengths and weaknesses of an organization in order to develop an **improvement plan**. SWOT stands for Strengths, Weaknesses, Opportunities, and Threats. The **strengths** of an organization are what provide the district with a competitive advantage over other districts. A district may be technology-rich, which is a strength. **Weaknesses** describe areas of disadvantage relative to other districts. A district may have a poor attendance rate in comparison to other districts. **Opportunities** are areas the district may be able to use by leveraging strengths to address weaknesses. The district may identify that the technology can be used to provide students with instruction at home when absent or to provide accelerated instruction when they return to school. **Threats** are aspects of the environment that the district has little or no control over but may negatively affect the district. The district may identify that the closure of a chemical plant has resulted in the layoff of many students' parents. Conducting a SWOT analysis is helpful in identifying areas of potential improvement, even for districts that are already high-performing.

Areas to be Evaluated for Weakness

All areas of district programming should be evaluated for weaknesses. **Academic performance** is most often evaluated because this is the basis for district accountability measures. A district leader should examine the alignment of curriculum to assessments, the quality of the instruction that is delivered, and the rigor at which it is delivered. However, other aspects should also be evaluated. These include school safety, district culture, parental and family engagement, and more. For example, a district leader should determine if school **safety procedures** are up-to-date and should also assess the performance of students and staff during safety drills. **District culture** can be evaluated based on student and staff perceptions as well as by the experiences and feedback of visitors on campus. Also, the district leader can identify whether the district is achieving **family engagement** on campus, if it is in the desired areas, and if it is producing the desired outcomes. There are always aspects of the district program that can be improved, so the district leader should have a mindset of continuous improvement.

Data Used to Identify Areas of Weakness

Data is essential in the identification of weaknesses in the district program. Differences and changes in the data, identifying potential **areas of improvement**, may be observed. The district leader may identify **disparities** in the data between the district and others nearby. For example, the district leader may note that on a regional benchmark assessment, his or her district had the lowest overall performance. Based on that data, the leader could develop a plan for improvement. Data may also reveal a disparity in performance of a school from one school year to the next, or between various groups of students. Other data that can be used to identify areas of needed improvement include student attendance data, discipline data, compliance in data reporting, staff performance or evaluation data, and more. All data collected on the campuses has the potential to indicate **needed improvements** in the district program. The district leader should analyze the data in comparison to other data as well as changes, trends, and gaps in the data over time.

Advocating for Change

Promoting Awareness and Activism

The district leader has the influence to encourage stakeholders to lobby and use political activism to bring about change, especially in regard to social justice. The primary way that the leader can encourage engagement is by **educating** the community on present issues. The leader often has several opportunities to speak to community families en masse. These opportunities can be used to educate families about education trends and politics that will ultimately affect their community, school, and families. By **promoting awareness**, the leader can empower parents and community members to become active. The second way the district leader can encourage engagement is by showing community stakeholders how they can become directly **involved**. The district leader can invite community stakeholders to be active in bringing about change by writing letters, sending emails, making phone calls, or engaging with political leaders.

Caution for Political Activism

In the district leader's efforts to advocate for students and for social justice, he or she must engage carefully. Most school districts have **guidelines** for how a district leader can represent him or herself in the community while representing the school district. These guidelines usually apply in regard to supporting specific political parties or candidates, persuading others how to vote in elections, and various other activities. A district leader must identify what actions they are allowed or not allowed to take while in the position of leader. Outside of school hours, the leader may have additional freedom to engage in such activities, but must still be aware of how his or her **influence and authority** are used in such activities. The district leader should consult with the school district or the leadership of appropriate professional organizations regarding the implications of **political engagement** prior to doing so.

Chapter Quiz

Ready to see how well you retained what you just read? Scan the QR code to go directly to the chapter quiz interface for this study guide. If you're using a computer, simply visit the online resources page at **mometrix.com/resources719/osatsuper248** and click the Chapter Quizzes link.

Organizational, Resource, and Operational Management

Employment and Fiscal Responsibilities

Recruiting Teachers and Staff Members

A leader should be strategic in recruiting new teachers and staff members. To determine whether candidates will be a good fit in the district, the leader should examine them in relation to the district culture, vision, and goals. A leader should first use the **district culture** as criteria for recruitment. For example, if the district culture is one of innovation and creativity, the leader will want to recruit candidates who have demonstrated creativity in the past and are comfortable taking the risks necessary to try new things. Also, the leader will want to recruit candidates with the necessary skills to aid in implementing the **district vision and goals**. For example, if the district vision is to become exemplary in the integration of technology into the learning process, the leader should recruit candidates who are skilled with technology and are comfortable utilizing it. Using such criteria when recruiting teachers and other filling other roles will ensure that they will be a good fit in the district and contribute to the district's success.

Including Other Team Members in the Recruitment Process

Including other team members in the recruitment process is beneficial for several reasons. First, having more than one person participating in this process reduces the potential for demonstrating **bias** during the recruitment and hiring process. Other team members may notice aspects of potential candidates that the leader missed, which can help to provide a **well-rounded view** of each candidate. Also, other team members may have different perspectives regarding the **needs and dynamics of the district**, which can help to determine whether potential candidates are a good fit for open positions. Lastly, **staff morale and district culture** can benefit from allowing team members to participate in the process of selecting their future coworkers. Some districts allow students to participate in the recruitment and selection process of teaching candidates because they are the ones who will ultimately be affected.

Teacher Tenure

Teacher tenure refers to the ability of teachers to attain **tenure**, a particular contract status, as the result of long-time service to a school district. Obtaining tenure does not guarantee that a teacher cannot lose their job, but it does mandate that **due process** is granted before a tenured teacher is terminated. The purpose of granting tenure is to prevent teachers who are educated and qualified from being **removed** from the classroom as the result of fluctuations in the academic program, changes in leadership, or other temporary circumstances. However, the issue of concern is that granting tenure makes it difficult for school and district leadership to remove **underperforming teachers**. Tenured teachers, especially those who belong to a teachers' union, must be granted due process if being considered for dismissal, which is often determined based upon collective bargaining provisions. Following due process is time-consuming and may result in an ineffective teacher remaining in a classroom or being moved to another campus rather than being terminated. School districts may have policies in place that make teacher tenure difficult to earn in order to avoid the difficulty of dismissing a tenured teacher.

Performance-Based Pay

Performance-based pay or merit-based pay is compensation for teachers or staff above their normal salary as a reward for **performance**. Performance is defined by school districts and school boards and often involves student performance on standardized assessments, teacher evaluations, or other performance indicators. The intent of performance pay is to compensate for inadequate teacher salaries and to reward teachers for performance related to **district goals**, such as student academic achievement. Performance expectations for compensation may involve achieving certain standards, demonstrating growth by certain standards, or a combination of the two. A criticism of performance pay is that it is not always sustainable, the formulas for compensation are often confusing, methods for calculation are often not transparent, evaluations or performance measures are subjective, and incentives are not large enough to influence teacher or staff behavior. Proponents of incentive pay believe that it is an effective strategy for retaining effective teachers and attracting teachers in hard-to-staff districts and subject areas that are in high demand.

Contractual Agreements

The superintendent is responsible for the hiring, evaluation, promotion, and training of personnel. To effectively carry out this responsibility, the superintendent must understand the implications of **contractual agreements**. Contract terms for employment determine how long the school is contractually obligated to employ personnel and contract types can determine the process that must be completed in order to terminate an employee. These contractual agreements have implications for **budgeting**, compliance with **federal and state laws**, and other aspects of **district operations**. For example, if a teacher is employed under a three-year contract, but must be laid off due to low enrollment during the second year of employment, the district is responsible for compensating that employee for the remaining terms of their contract or continuing their employment at the district in some capacity per the terms of the contract. A superintendent must also be aware of the implications of offering **tenure contracts** to teachers, as these contracts can impact the district's ability to terminate the employment of these teachers.

Local, State, and Federal Requirements for Financial Management

The superintendent must be aware that there are differences between local, state, and federal requirements for **financial management**. Revenue from the local, state, and federal levels often have different requirements for how funds are allocated and how expenditures related to these funds are reported and monitored. **Local financial management** may include requirements specific to local taxes, bonds, or other aspects of finances that are particular to the city or county in which a school district operates. At the **state level**, there may be finances related to state funds and programs that require specific financial management processes. Finally, **federal funds**, including grants, may require financial management processes that are unique to those funding sources. As a result, the superintendent must be aware of the various procedures such as record keeping, reporting, and accountability related to these various levels of funding.

Monitoring Financial Accounts

There are several aspects of school finance that a superintendent must consider when **monitoring financial accounts**. The superintendent must determine whether finances have been allocated in alignment with the **goals and priorities** established by the school board. For example, if the school board has determined that there will be a focus on reading achievement in the district, the budget should mirror that focus through allotments to reading curriculum, personnel for instruction, resources, or other initiatives related to reading. The superintendent must determine if resources are allocated **equitably** across schools to address student needs. Needs may vary across the district and equity does not imply equality. For example, an impoverished area of the school district may require more funding and resources to provide an equitable education when compared with other schools in the district. The superintendent must also gauge the cost-effectiveness of district policies and programs and ensure that grant money is spent wisely.

Standard Accounting Practices

The primary reason that school districts should use standard accounting practices is to ensure that comparable financial data is **reported** to the state by the various public school entities. This results in accurate reporting and monitoring at the state level, including annual audit reports. **Parity** in financial reporting makes it easier to track financial data and compare the data with other educational institutions as well as other government institutions. The Governmental Accounting Standards Board establishes the **generally accepted accounting principles (GAAP)** that government organizations utilize, which includes public schools. For example, GAAP dictates what is considered revenue, assets, and liabilities in accounting. Adhering to these guidelines streamlines the auditing process and helps to maintain the transparency of the budgeting process. Additionally, following standard accounting practices allows for the use of financial data to support financial decisions such as cost increases in payroll or other aspects of the operational budget, the need for school bonds, or other costs associated with school programming.

Enrollment and Staffing Projections

The size of student enrollment impacts the number of staff persons employed at the campus and district levels. **Student enrollment** determines much of the funding that schools receive. If student enrollment is greater than expected, more **revenue** is generated for the school, which allows for budgeting of more staff positions. In contrast, if student enrollment is less than expected, the **decrease in funding** can cause the school district to cut positions or reorganize staff assignments. Additionally, there are regulations and policies that help to determine **class sizes** in schools. For example, elementary classrooms are limited to 22 students without a class size waiver. If enrollment increases would result in exceeding this limit, **more teachers** will be needed. If enrollment decreases, **fewer teachers** will be needed. Increases in enrollment in the district overall, in particular areas of the district, or in certain grade levels can affect staffing projections. For example, if a new apartment complex is built in an area of the district and causes a surge in student enrollment at the nearby elementary school, the influx of students may be large enough to require that additional teachers be hired to keep class sizes at an acceptable level.

Revenue Forecasts and Enrollment

Student enrollment is a key component of how school funding is determined. **Enrollment projections** are used to estimate the number of students that the district will serve for the upcoming school year. Determinants of enrollment projections may include historical enrollment, population trends in the area, and migration trends, among others. This projection can be used to **forecast the revenue** that the school district will receive, and it is then used to develop a district budget. If a superintendent overestimates student enrollment, this can result in a **shortfall** in the budget. A budget shortfall can result in layoffs or elimination of various school programs. For example, an elementary school may expect to serve 750 students, but only 700 students enroll. The difference of 50 students creates a financial deficit that could require the loss of two teachers. On the other hand, if a superintendent underestimates student enrollment, there may be a **surplus** of funds. This surplus of funds may be recaptured by the state or federal government if it is not allotted and utilized. Neither situation is ideal because the school district budget should be as accurate as possible to ensure that academic programming, staffing, and resources are stable and effectively utilized.

Managing Operational Systems

Organizational Systems

A district organizational system refers to how a district is organized in relation to resources, personnel, time, and space to achieve student learning and success. Examples of **district organizational models** include departmental models, project-based learning models, academy models, integrative models, small community models, and the school-within-a school model, among others. The organizational system dictates the **structure** of the district and its systems, what personnel are needed and how personnel are allocated, what resources are needed, and how the physical space of the school is designed and utilized. Consequently, the organizational system in a school district dictates how **instruction** is delivered and how **student learning** is achieved.

Types of District Organizational Systems

The different types of district organizational systems affect how instruction is delivered on campus. In the **departmental model**, the different subject or content areas are separated and distinct. Each of the subject-area departments have leaders or chairs who report to administration. In an **integrative model**, disciplines are combined or grouped together, such as in the pairing of math and science classes or English and history classes. **Project-based learning models** facilitate interdisciplinary learning through student completion of large, extended projects. In **academy models**, a district may group students and classes based on college or career pathways. **Small community models** and **school-within-a-school models** are similar in that students are grouped into cohorts and remain within a small community for their instruction; each community operates like a small school. In the school-within-a-school model, the small communities often have their own administrators. Other types of district organizational systems have developed as **technology** has become more accessible in districts, such as virtual schools and flipped classrooms.

Determining the Best Organizational System

To determine the best organizational system for a school district, a leader should first examine the district vision and goals. The organizational system should directly support the **district vision** and facilitate achievement of the **district goals**. For example, if the district is focused on reading performance and instruction, the leader may select a block scheduling structure to provide students with more instructional time in reading. A leader may also determine that, in order to provide socio-emotional support to students, dividing a large school into teams or houses would best facilitate relationship building and cultivate a small-school feel. A leader can also analyze the **district's culture** and identify the appropriate organizational system to support the ideal culture. For example, if the district vision is to create independent, life-long learners, the district organization system may involve giving students autonomy in their learning when possible. For example, the district could offer self-paced instructional programming, student course selection, and other exploratory opportunities for students.

Areas of the Organizational System Unrelated to Classroom Instruction

Many organizational systems are part of the district system but are not directly related to **instruction**. For example, the **cafeteria** represents a large system within a school. The process of feeding breakfast, lunch, and even dinner to students can be a complex organizational system. It involves providing the food, serving it, and maintaining the facilities in which it is served. This particular system may be regulated by state and federal regulations which add additional complexities. Another organizational system is **behavior management and discipline**. There are processes in place to promote positive student behavior and deter negative behavior. This system may include the development and distribution of handbooks, training and communication regarding behavioral expectations, and imposing consequences for infractions. Other systems include student arrival and dismissal, extracurricular programming, and counseling. Even though these systems are not directly related to classroom instruction, they often **support** effective classroom instruction.

Systems Thinking

Systems thinking involves understanding how a system or an organization is constructed. It is an understanding of the many **parts** that make a system work, how those parts **interact** with one another, and how those parts **relate to the larger context** of the system. For example, the system of providing food to students in the cafeteria is one part of the larger district system. A leader who understands systems thinking understands that how the cafeteria functions can directly or indirectly affect the way other systems function, such as the classroom. If the cafeteria is unable to serve breakfast efficiently in the morning, students may be delayed in getting to class, which in turn impacts instruction. Therefore, systems thinking helps in understanding how the organization or system as a whole can best function by improving the function of the **smaller systems** that make up the whole.

Effective Data Systems

Effective data systems are important for managing the **organizational systems** across campuses. Data systems relating to student and staff population data are essential to the effective planning and management of the organizational system. For example, **staffing** is often determined by the number of students enrolled in the district and the allocation of those enrollment numbers to various aspects of the instructional program, such as grade levels, special populations, magnet programming, and more. Leaders must have **accurate data** for student enrollment in order to allocate staff to the various programs on the campuses. This type of data also impacts class sizes and student to teacher ratios. Additionally, areas of each campus have **capacity maximums** as dictated by fire code, and these limitations must be taken into consideration when planning lunch schedules, school assemblies, and other uses of school facilities. Effective data systems are also necessary to make decisions related to **funding** and **resource acquisition and allocation**, in addition to **instructional decision-making**.

Improving Organizational Systems

Short-Term Improvement

A leader should evaluate the district's organizational system for continuous, short-term improvements. Factors to consider include functionality, training, and resources. The organizational system should function smoothly and efficiently. This is indicated by **student and staff transitions** throughout the day as well as **flow of information and resources**. For example, if the district's organizational system is made up of small learning communities, it would be effective to place resources such as supplies and copiers near the learning communities. Also, the leader should ensure that staff has the appropriate **training** to support the organizational system. For example, if the organizational system is based on a project-based learning environment, staff will need appropriate, ongoing training to support this type of system. Finally, the leader should ensure that the district has the appropriate **resources**, both physical and human, to support the organizational system. This may include reassigning certain resources from one area of the district to another.

Long-Term Improvement

For long-term improvement of a district's organizational system, the leader should consider **alignment** to vision and goals, availability and allocation of resources, and spatial designs. First, the organizational system should support the **district's vision**. For example, a virtual school environment may not be appropriately aligned to a district vision that prioritizes building social and collaborative skills in students, due to its focus on individual, computerized work. Consequently, the leader needs to determine if the district's **organizational system** needs to be changed to reflect the changing needs of the students and community that the school serves. Next, the leader needs to determine the availability of both **physical and human resources** and how those are allocated to support the district's organizational system. This may require hiring additional staff, replacing or redesigning staff positions, or acquiring new resources such as technology devices. Finally, the leader needs to consider whether the layout and organization of the **physical space** in the schools is conducive to the district's organizational system. To implement a school-within-a-school model, for example, the leader may need to redesign or relocate certain classrooms and offices.

Physical Plant Safety and Compliance

Failure to ensure the physical safety of the **school plants** and comply with building regulations can negatively affect the instructional program. If students and staff are in danger of being injured or hurt due to aspects of a plant that are in disrepair or do not meet codes and standards, this can **interrupt** the school day and cause the school and school district to be **liable**. For example, if a school has an elevator in use that is not up to code, there is danger of a student or staff person becoming trapped in the elevator due to malfunction. This is dangerous to the person in the elevator and would necessitate emergency personnel, causing a disruption to the instructional program. Additionally, malfunctioning equipment such as leaks, loud machinery or A/C equipment, or pest infestations are distracting to the instructional environment and may cause damage to instructional resources such as books and technology equipment. **Compliance** with regulations, such as ADA codes, is important to ensure access of all students and staff, especially those with disabilities, to all areas of the campuses.

MONITORING SAFETY AND COMPLIANCE

A leader can monitor the physical plants for safety and compliance in several ways. First, a leader should have **plant operators** who are responsible for ensuring the plants' safety and compliance. The leader should meet with the plant operators regularly to address any concerns that may arise. Second, the leader should conduct **regular walks** of the plants to inspect them for safety and compliance. During these walks, the leader should take note of plant aspects that may need repair or maintenance. Also, the leader may receive formal or informal **feedback** regarding needed repairs and maintenance from instructional staff. Finally, city or county officials will conduct regular **inspections** and provide **reports**. These reports will detail aspects of the campuses that are in compliance, out of compliance, or in danger of being out of compliance with regulations. The district leader can use these reports to ensure the plants' safety and compliance.

BOND REFERENDUM

A bond referendum is a proposal to borrow funds long-term to fund **major capital improvements**. Since these capital improvements are costly, the bond allows the expenses to be spread over time so that the costs are covered by current and future taxpayers. The bond must be approved by **voters** because of the obligation that taxpayers will have in paying for the expenses incurred by the capital improvements. Funds secured through a bond referendum can be used for construction of new schools or district facilities, **renovation** of existing schools or district facilities, and other **updates** related to the physical aspects of the plant. Bond funds can be used to help schools update their buildings to new city or county building codes, ADA requirements, and technology requirements. Construction due to capital improvements may cause the **displacement** of students and staff from certain areas of the school plant where construction occurs or, in more substantial projects, **relocation** to another setting until construction is completed.

Acquisition and Maintenance of Equipment and Technology

DETERMINING EQUIPMENT TO ACQUIRE

A leader must decide if new equipment is necessary for the effective operation of the physical locations as well as the implementation of the instructional program. A leader should be aware of the **life expectancy** of the various equipment that is already on the campuses so that he or she can determine when new equipment may be needed. This helps in the planning of maintenance, repair, and replacement cycles. Also, the leader must determine if equipment is **mandatory** or **optional**. Equipment that must be present on campus for its operation is prioritized over equipment that can be acquired or repaired at a later date. For example, a leader may need to postpone the acquisition of new science lab equipment in order to repair air conditioning units. **District finances** must also be considered when contemplating the acquisition of new equipment. A leader may need to postpone the purchase of major equipment until a new fiscal year due to budget constraints. The district leader should also consider the **impact** of the new equipment. If the purchase of new equipment will impact the majority of the students or staff, it can be placed higher on the priority list than equipment that may impact a small group of students, such as a student organization or specialized instructional program.

ROLE OF TECHNOLOGY

Technology on the campuses impacts campus safety, communication, and instruction. Technology hardware and software are vital to the school district. Technology can be used to assist with **campus safety**. For example, cameras are placed on the campuses to monitor activity. These cameras and the associated software necessary for monitoring and recording the camera feeds are important to school safety. Other technology used for safety includes intercom systems for screening of visitors, software to conduct background checks of visitors and volunteers, and automated door locking systems. Technology also aids in **effective communication** on campus. Emails, intercoms and radios, PA systems, marquees, and other forms of technology are used to communicate to staff and students. Also, technology is very useful for **instruction**. Computers, projectors, printers, and many other technology devices enhance the quality of instruction that is provided to students. Both staff and students may use these technology devices as part of the instructional routine.

Allocating Funds and Budgeting

Calculating District Funding

District funding comes from a variety of sources. The **federal government** provides some funding. This is not usually substantial and may fluctuate due to changing budget decisions at the federal level. The **state government** also provide funding to school districts based on income and/or sales taxes. The majority of school funding in most states comes from property taxes within the school district. Both residences and commercial properties are taxed and a portion of those taxes are allocated to school districts. Some states, such as California, allocate school funding differently and may use income taxes instead of property taxes as the primary funding source. Schools generally receive an allotment of funds on a **per-pupil basis**. The per-pupil allotment differs by school district but may average about $10,000 per pupil. However, certain programs warrant extra funds on top of this allotment, such as special education programs and technology programs. School districts often seek grants and donations from **foundations** to supplement their budget.

Centralized Budgeting and Decentralized Budgeting

Centralized and decentralized budgeting refers to the point of control for budgeting decisions within a school district. In a **centralized school district**, all budgetary decision-making is conducted by **district leaders** within the district office. The benefit of a centralized budgeting process is that budgeting decisions are controlled and quality and efficiency can be easily monitored. However, this type of system can prevent staff buy-in and cause school leaders to feel they do not have the authority to make the changes necessary for their school to be successful. In contrast, in a **decentralized district**, **principals** of individual campuses have authority to make budgetary and purchasing decisions. This allows them to determine which resources meet the needs of each individual campus and gives them the latitude and flexibility to address campus needs. The benefit of a decentralized budgeting process is the flexibility and increased buy-in of leaders on the campus level. However, this type of system can be more difficult for the district leader to monitor and may cause more instances of mismanagement of funds.

Allocating Funds

A leader should consider multiple factors when allocating funds. First, the leader should refer to the district's **vision**. The allocation of funds should align with that vision. Similarly, the leader should align the allocation of funds to the district's **goals**. It is likely that the goals that are set for the district require funds and resources to accomplish them, so these funds should be allocated first. A leader should also consider whether funds are **recurring or one-time funds**. When a district receives funds that will not be renewed, a district leader must ensure that whatever is completed with those funds is sustainable for the future once those funds are gone. The district leader must also evaluate the **district program** and **organizational structure** to ensure that sufficient funds are allocated to the successful and efficient operation of the district program.

Factors Affecting a District's Budget

A district's budget is not fixed but can vary from year to year based on a variety of factors. Funding from the federal and state government can fluctuate and impact district budgeting. In some years, the government provides **one-time funding** that cannot be expected in subsequent years, which causes fluctuations. Additionally, the government can **change allocations** of funding for specific programs. For example, allocation of funding for Career and Technology Education may be altered, so even though the number of students participating in the program does not change, the received funds do change. **Local property taxes** may change in a school district, affecting the money allocated to schools. Additional factors include changes in student enrollment, changes in school programming, and other factors. Each year, a district leader must evaluate the proposed budget for the school year and make decisions based on each year's **budgetary allocations**.

Community-Based and Additional Resources Needed for Accomplishing Goals

Additional Resources

A district leader may seek additional resources for accomplishing goals because there may not be sufficient school funding to accomplish everything that needs to be accomplished. When planning school budgets, leaders have to determine how to **allocate funds**. Often budgets have **shortfalls**, especially for initiatives that are lower on the priority list. As a result, a leader may have to seek funding and resources from **outside of school** to accomplish these goals. These additional resources may be in the form of grants, donations, volunteers, and many more. For example, if a district leader wanted to establish a garden on one of the campuses, rather than using school funds for the gardening supplies and staff to tend the garden, the leader may solicit donations of gardening tools and volunteers to work in the garden. These types of resources can be very beneficial to the instructional program and alleviate some of the constraints of the district budget.

The Leader's Role in Advocating for Resources

The leader has the primary role in ensuring that **sufficient resources** are available to accomplish the set goals. First, the leader should properly allocate the funds and resources allotted by the **school district** to meet goals. If there is a shortfall in resources, the leader is responsible for advocating on behalf of the district to solicit **additional resources**. This may include petitioning for additional resources from the school district or seeking resources from community organizations and businesses. A leader may apply for grants to support the district program; seek donations of funds, resources, or equipment; or gather volunteers for staffing support. For example, if the district cannot afford to purchase new computers, a leader may ask a business organization to donate used computers to the schools. The leader should take initiative in securing the resources necessary to accomplish the goals that he or she set for the district.

Community-Based Resources

There are many community-based resources that are likely available to school districts. For many communities, **local churches** offer a variety of resources that can support the schools, such as volunteers, food and clothing for students and families in need, and much more. Also, many cities have **local community programs** to support the physical and mental health needs of the community and to provide nutritional support to families in need. There may be programs related to local transportation, arts, sciences, sports, clubs, and others that are available in the community. A district leader should be aware of all of the **organizations** in the surrounding community and communicate with these organizations to determine how they can partner to support students and their families. Often, these community-based resources can support students' **non-instructional needs** so that they can participate in the district program. These needs may include counseling, health-related issues, food and housing issues, and others.

Recruiting Highly Qualified Personnel

Highly Qualified Personnel

The term "highly qualified" is used to describe the **minimum qualifications** of a teacher according to the No Child Left Behind Act, enacted in 2001. To meet staffing expectations, a leader has the responsibility of ensuring that teachers are highly qualified. This means that the teacher must hold a **bachelor's degree** and either have full **state licensure/certification** or **demonstrate knowledge of the subject** that he or she will teach. Based on this definition, states have enacted various procedures that enable teachers to demonstrate their content area knowledge, such as testing. A teacher may be highly qualified in one subject area and not in another. For example, a teacher may be deemed highly qualified to teach chemistry due to holding a bachelor's degree in science and being state certified in chemistry, but that same teacher would not be highly qualified to teach biology. Having highly qualified staff on the district campuses ensures that teachers are knowledgeable in their assigned content areas and capable of teaching the content to students.

Recruitment Strategies

Leaders can employ several strategies to recruit highly qualified personnel. Leaders can participate in **recruitment fairs**. These are often hosted by the school district or by community organizations. Leaders can follow up with persons from the event for interviews or may even conduct screening interviews at these fairs. Also, leaders can contact **teacher preparation programs** for referrals of recently certified teachers. These entities have lists of recent graduates along with their areas of specialization. However, these lists include persons with limited or no teaching experience. It can also be helpful to post advertisements on **traditional recruitment sites**. Some sites specialize in recruiting for education. Finally, leaders can use **word of mouth advertising** to recruit highly qualified personnel. Teachers and district staff may have colleagues in other locations who would like to work at a new school. For example, a person may want to work at a school that is closer to home or teach a different grade level.

Importance of Being Fully Staffed

If a district has numerous teaching vacancies, it can be difficult to have all staff in place at the outset of the school year. However, the **beginning of the school year** is a critical time that can impact the success of the entire school year, so a leader should strive to have 100% of staff in place before school starts. First, important **training and professional development** occur prior to the start of school. A teacher who is hired later will miss these. Additionally, teaching staff begin to **bond and unite** as a team prior to the start of the year and a teacher would miss this opportunity if hired late. Also, students learn **procedures and expectations** for behavior and learning at the beginning of the school year. A teacher who is hired late may have to reset expectations for students, which could cause a difficult start for both teacher and students.

Temporary Staff

At times it is necessary to have temporary staff to support the instructional program. If there is a teaching vacancy or if a teacher is absent for an extended period of time, a leader may have to obtain **temporary personnel** until a permanent solution is found. Often, however, temporary staff persons are **not highly qualified** and do not have the same **training and experience** that permanent staff members do. As a result, the quality of instruction may be reduced when temporary staff persons are in the classroom. Additionally, with temporary staff persons, there may be a need for increased monitoring and support from other permanent staff persons, such as clerks and administrators, to ensure the effective and efficient progress of the instructional program. This can produce further strain on staff and the instructional program. To ensure that the instructional program is excelling and that students are receiving high quality instruction, the district leader should minimize the need for temporary staff.

Recruitment Considerations

Impact of School Culture

School culture is determined by the leader and the staff of the district. The school culture can create a welcoming environment for new teachers or it can inadvertently repel them. When the school culture is **positive**, focused on students, and driven by excellence, teachers will want to be part of that culture. They will be motivated by the positive culture and will recruit others to join the team. Additionally, when the culture is positive, students thrive, which can make the teacher's job easier and more enjoyable. On the other hand, if the school culture is **negative**, teachers and staff will likely have negative attitudes as well. Teachers will seek a way out of that school environment rather than encouraging others to join the team. This negative culture can negatively affect student academic performance and behavior. If a potential teacher candidate observes a negative school culture, he or she may be unwilling to work in that district.

Impact of Leadership Style

The leadership style of the district leader and other leaders in the district can positively or negatively impact **teacher recruitment**. A leadership style that is perceived as **negative** can deter teachers from wanting to work in that leader's district. During the recruitment process, a candidate may observe how the district leader speaks to him or her, the way the leader treats staff and students, and other indicators of leadership style. For example, if a leader is perceived as being overly demanding, negative, or micromanaging, a teaching candidate will not want to work for him or her. In contrast, if a leader is **fair, supportive, or warm**, a teaching candidate will be attracted to the position. Effective leaders attract effective teachers. Teachers will seek to work in districts where they will thrive and grow, and the district leader is an indication of whether the district will meet a teacher's professional needs.

Chapter Quiz

Ready to see how well you retained what you just read? Scan the QR code to go directly to the chapter quiz interface for this study guide. If you're using a computer, simply visit the online resources page at **mometrix.com/resources719/osatsuper248** and click the Chapter Quizzes link.

District Governance and School Law

Local, State, and Federal Laws and Policies

Federal, State, and Local Educational Laws, Policies, and Practices

Almost all aspects of the education process are governed by laws, policies, and practices. **Laws** governing the education process are established at the national and state level and supersede district and campus policies. **Federal laws** take precedence over state laws. **State laws** supplement and complement the federal laws. Local Education Agencies (LEAs) then interpret federal and state laws to create **policies** for their school districts that help schools to adhere to those laws or to clarify areas that the laws do not explicitly address. Individual campuses create **procedures** to address areas not explicitly outlined by district policy. For example, federal law states that students must be assessed by a standardized exam for grade promotion and graduation. State law dictates which tests the students take and when they are tested. School districts determine the policies for administering those tests, within the guidelines set by the state. Campuses implement district policy and may incorporate their own practices such as cell phone policies, dress code polices, or other school day aspects that are impacted by testing. Whenever there is a conflict between law and policy, law takes precedence.

Me on the Map

Sample

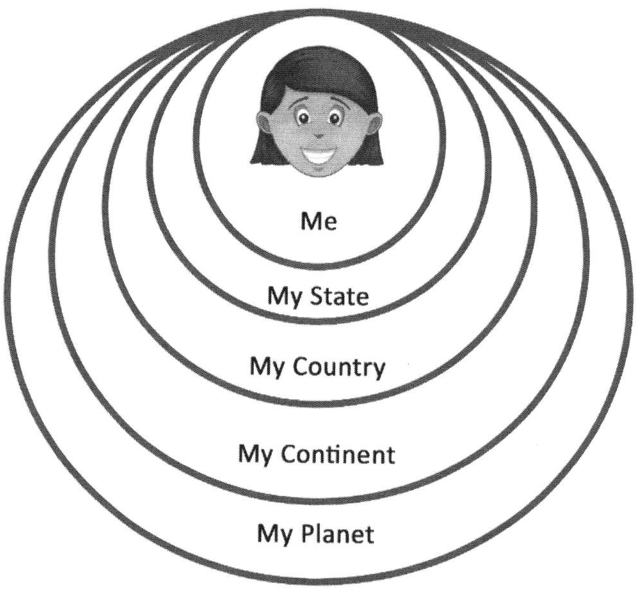

Areas of the Education Process Impacted by Laws

Federal and state laws impact almost every aspect of the education process. Often these laws require additional policies and procedures to ensure adherence to the laws. However, there are specific areas of the education process that are highly **impacted by federal and state law**. These include educating students with disabilities, educating English language learners, standardized testing, student confidentiality, school liability, school performance expectations, technology use, school finance, and many more. District leaders must understand the laws and how these laws can influence the development and implementation of their **vision and goals**. While many school districts develop policies and practices that aid district leaders in adhering to the law, it is the district leader's responsibility to remain current on school law at both the state and federal levels.

Impact of Laws and Policies on Professional Ethics

Federal and state laws dictate the requirements that educators must meet to be certified. As part of these requirements, educators must adhere to ethical codes and standards of behavior. The **ethical codes** address areas such as general conduct, conduct toward colleagues, and conduct toward students. Educators are expected to adhere to these standards of behavior; otherwise, sanctions may be placed on their educator licenses or their licenses and certifications may even be revoked. On any given school day, an education leader may make a number of decisions and must be fully aware of the legal and ethical ramifications of each one. Additionally, district leaders must understand that ethical decision-making is not only a result of personal morals and values but also of **codes and standards of behavior** that are set forth by federal and state government. The code of ethics requires that educators abide by all laws, but some decisions address "gray areas" in which there are no explicit laws, policies, or procedures. In these instances, district leaders must ensure that their decisions align with the educator code of ethics.

Development of Policies

School districts often develop policies as a **safeguard** for staff and students. Laws enacted at the federal and/or state level are often broad and subject to interpretation. As a result, policies are developed to **define** specific actions and behaviors that adhere to those laws, with the purpose of trying to ensure that persons abide by the law by adhering to policies. Policies are meant to be a **protection** to those who adhere to them. For example, a law may broadly state that schools must administer a confidential and secure assessment of student performance in Math and Reading. The school district may then develop policies to ensure that tests are administered to students in a confidential and secure manner. A person who violates a policy does not necessarily violate a law, but this is possible. District leaders and staff should abide by local policies as a protection, ensuring that they are adhering to state and federal laws.

Relationship Between Vision and Goals with Legal Responsibilities

Aligning Vision and Goals to School, Local, State, and Federal Policies

The district vision and goals must be **aligned** to local, state, and federal policies so that they can be legally and ethically accomplished. If the district vision and goals are not aligned to these laws and policies, it is possible that working toward these goals would constitute breaking the law or violating policy. Because laws and policies supersede district initiatives, it is important to align goals to these so that **resources** can be used efficiently. Even if the misalignment of the goal to the laws and policies does not constitute a violation of the law or policy, it could cause resources and efforts to be diverted, resulting in **loss of efficiency and impact**. For example, students with disabilities may require additional academic services, as dictated in special education law and policy. The district leader must provide the resources necessary to meet these students' needs, so it would be efficient to align the district's other goals and resources to this requirement.

Communicating District Laws and Policies

It is important to communicate district laws and policies to the community so that they can be **informed** of the requirements and constraints that govern the district leader's actions, decision-making, and goal-setting. The community should be aware of the laws and policies that helped to shape the leader's vision for the district. The community may be **unaware of laws and policies** that can influence the operations of the school district and how these laws and policies may affect the feasibility of their ideas and suggestions. For example, the community may wish to do away with a particular extracurricular sport because of low participation and lack of performance by the athletes, but they may be unaware that certain sports must be offered due to compliance with Title IX of education law. A superintendent could explain that the current education law requires that the particular sport be offered so that there is no perceived discrimination in sport offerings within the district.

Impact of Laws, Regulations, Policies, and Procedures on Vision and Goals

Laws, regulations, policies, and procedures should be reviewed and considered during the development and implementation of **district vision and goals**. Adherence to these laws and regulations supersedes district initiatives, so it is efficient and effective to align these with the vision and goals to prevent conflict or inefficiency in use of resources. A leader can evaluate these first, and then determine how the vision and goals can be designed in a way to help the district meet or exceed these regulations. For example, if accountability standards require that schools have a passing rate of 90% or above for the state exam in reading, then the district leader should set a goal to meet or exceed that requirement. If the district leader were to set the school goal at 85%, then meeting the district goal would still cause the district to fail according to state accountability standards. In order to be strategic, a district leader should determine what is **expected** of the district according to law and policy, and then determine how their vision and goals can **align** with those laws and policies.

Communication and Data Systems

Federal Laws and Regulations

Campus and district facilities must adhere to the **laws and regulations** dictated by various federal agencies. These agencies and regulations include OSHA, ADA, EPA, and IDEA 2004. **OSHA**, the Occupational Safety and Health Administration, oversees federal laws to ensure occupational health and safety in the workplace. **ADA**, the Americans with Disability Act, included laws and regulations to ensure that persons with disabilities are accommodated. **EPA**, the Environmental Protection Agency, oversees laws that regulate the impact that facilities have on the environment. **IDEA**, the Individuals with Disabilities Act, regulates the accommodations of persons with special needs. The superintendent must take into account these regulations when constructing facilities, repairing facilities, maintaining facilities, or inspecting facilities. The superintendent must also understand that staffing and funding may be necessary to ensure that all district facilities are in **compliance**. Additionally, facilities must be monitored for **continuous compliance** because these regulations may change from year-to-year. Failure to comply with federal laws and regulations in facilities management can result in costly repairs, fines for violations, or even closure of facilities.

Chapter Quiz

Ready to see how well you retained what you just read? Scan the QR code to go directly to the chapter quiz interface for this study guide. If you're using a computer, simply visit the online resources page at **mometrix.com/resources719/osatsuper248** and click the Chapter Quizzes link.

Stakeholder and Community Relationships, Professional Norms, and Ethics

Promoting the Welfare of Staff and Students

Key Staff That Can Promote the Welfare of Staff and Students

The key staff member responsible for promoting the welfare of staff and students is the **district leader**. The district leader creates a **district culture** in which students and staff feel safe, as well as **structures and systems** to provide support and intervention for students and staff in need. The district leader also sets the **example** for treatment of students and staff, such as displaying understanding, empathy, and compassion. The district leader should also identify other key staff who can promote the welfare of staff and students. Each member of the **leadership team**, such as assistant superintendents or deans, should take the lead in promoting the welfare of all and lead by example. The district leader should also enlist the support of counselors, nurses, and others who can be proactive in identifying and responding to the needs of students and staff. Additionally, teachers play a key role in identifying the needs of students and promoting their welfare within the classroom.

Promoting Counseling and Wellness

A leader should promote counseling and wellness to encourage staff and students to take advantage of these supports for their own welfare. A leader can do this by making **counseling and wellness programs** visible to all. This may mean having signs and displays around the school that promote these programs. Also, the leader can communicate the **availability of these resources** using common means of communication, such as emails, news bulletins, school public announcements, and announcements in staff meetings. The staff members who lead counseling and wellness programs can be included in other school projects and programs, such as in behavior intervention meetings or academic interventions, so that they are viewed as an **integral part of the district team**. A district leader can also consider hosting **mental health and wellness fairs** for school members and the community to raise awareness about potential health concerns and to promote available services.

Staff Health and Emotional Support

A leader can watch for several indicators to determine that staff members may need a recommendation to **counseling and health services**. Teachers and staff who need help may be **frequently absent** without a reasonable excuse. These absences may be referred to lightly as "mental health days," but they are often indicators that a staff person is stressed or overwhelmed. Another indicator of a need for counseling and health services are **overly emotional responses** to everyday stimuli. These responses may include yelling, crying, or bursts of anger. The district leader can also look for **changes in staff behavior**. For example, if a staff member who is usually outgoing, energetic, and talkative becomes withdrawn and disengaged, this may indicate a need for additional support. Staff who are unable to do their jobs satisfactorily, especially if they have a history of satisfactory performance, may need support from counseling and health services. The district leader should keep communication open so that staff are comfortable communicating that they need help.

Student Health and Emotional Support

A leader can watch for several indicators to determine that students may need a recommendation to **counseling and health services**. A student may begin to act out and display **negative behaviors** in the classroom with other students or with adults on a campus. This can be an indicator if the student does not usually display poor behavior at school. Additionally, a student who is usually engaged in classroom activities and with peers but becomes **withdrawn and disengaged** may also need help. These indicators can also lead to poor academic performance, indicated by falling grades. Students in need of support may also demonstrate **emotional responses** in school such as angry outbursts, crying, yelling, or even physical altercations with other students. In some instances, a **parent** may communicate with a staff member that the child is having difficulty at home as well. A district leader should ensure that **systems** are in place on the campuses to allow students to express their needs so that they can be referred for services. This may include having walk-in counseling hours or open-door policies with key staff members.

Available Types of Mental Health Services Within a Public-School Setting

School counselors are trained to work with students, teachers, and families to identify and address issues that may affect students' well-being and academic performance. Through **individual or group counseling** sessions, students can develop coping strategies, interpersonal skills, and emotional resilience, all of which helps foster an environment where they can thrive academically. Schools often implement Social and Emotional Learning (SEL) programs to promote the development of crucial life skills. These programs aim to enhance students' self-awareness, emotional regulation, and interpersonal skills, thus creating a positive and inclusive school culture. **Partnerships** with external mental health organizations allow schools to provide specialized services such as therapy and interventions for students with more complex mental health needs. Such partnerships allow students to receive the appropriate level of intervention based on their unique needs. Monitoring the impact of mental health services involves regular assessments of students' emotional well-being and the overall school climate. This can be achieved through surveys, behavioral observations, and academic performance data.

SEL Programs

Social and Emotional Learning (SEL) programs aim to equip students with essential life skills by promoting self-awareness, social awareness, responsible decision-making, and relationship-building. These programs typically involve structured curricula, classroom activities, and resources designed to enhance students' emotional intelligence and interpersonal skills, contributing to their overall well-being and academic success.

SPBS Programs

The **School-wide Positive Behavior Support (SPBS)** program focuses on establishing a positive school climate through proactive strategies. SPBS emphasizes clear expectations for behavior, consistent reinforcement of positive actions, and the use of data-driven approaches to address behavioral challenges. By creating a school-wide framework that reinforces positive behaviors and teaches appropriate alternatives, SPBS contributes to a culture where students feel supported and motivated to engage actively in their learning.

CASEL

The **Collaborative for Academic, Social, and Emotional Learning (CASEL)** is an organization dedicated to advancing the integration of social and emotional learning into education. CASEL provides resources, research, and frameworks to support educators in implementing evidence-based SEL practices. This collaborative approach ensures that schools have access to the latest research and effective strategies, facilitating the development of comprehensive programs that address the academic, social, and emotional needs of students.

Making Reports to Child Protective Services

Child Protective Services is a service provided by state agencies to protect the welfare of children. This agency investigates allegations of **child abuse or neglect** and provides services to children should such allegations be proven valid. There will be instances in which the district leader or a school staff member has reason to believe that a child is being neglected or abused. Whenever there is suspicion of abuse or neglect, it is each staff person's responsibility, including the district leader's, to submit a **formal report** to Child Protective Services for investigation. For example, if a teacher reports to the district leader that one of her students has confided that his or her mother is hitting him or her with various objects and shows the teacher bruises, both the teacher and the leader should file a report. There can be legal ramifications for staff members who fail to report suspected child abuse or neglect.

Promoting the Wellness of Staff and Students

Being proactive in promoting the wellness of staff and students means that the leader is actively looking for ways to **maintain the wellness** of all before problems arise. This is important because **prevention** is often more effective and less costly than trying to address a problem after it has already occurred. For example, taking steps to prevent teen suicide is a better course of action than addressing a grieving student body after a teen has committed suicide. Similarly, it is more effective to help an unwell teacher obtain needed help than to lose the teacher for the remainder of the school year due to a health crisis. The district leader should **proactively** promote wellness and identify potential wellness needs among students and staff so that mental health crises can be prevented or at least detected early in an effort to prevent tragedies that directly affect the student body and staff. Being proactive demonstrates to all that the leader is concerned about the wellness of staff and students and is willing to take the needed steps to address their health concerns.

Helping Staff and Students Deal with Grief on Campus

At times the student body and staff members will experience the loss of a peer or colleague. In these instances, the district leader will need to implement strategies to address the **grief** that students and staff experience. The first step that the leader must take is to **acknowledge** the loss. The leader should not operate with a "business-as-usual" attitude. Many schools have access to grief counselors who can be present on campus to assist students or staff who need assistance in dealing with their emotions. The district leader should also demonstrate **understanding and compassion** during this time and recognize that grief may cause students or staff to behave out of character, such as missing school, expressing outbursts of emotion like sadness or anger in school, or being disengaged from academic activities. It is important to **listen** to the needs of the students and staff during this time. The leader may provide opportunities for students and staff to express their feelings or to honor the one who has died.

Preventing Teen Suicide

The district leader can take steps to aid in the prevention of teen suicide or self-harm. Although many factors and influences outside of the school district can lead a young person to commit suicide, the district and its staff can serve as a resource and support to students who experience suicidal thoughts. First, the leader should create a **district culture** in which students feel comfortable turning to teachers and staff for support. When this type of culture is present, a student is more likely to share thoughts of self-harm with a staff member, which can aid in prevention. The district should also have **counseling staff and resources** available for students who are experiencing emotional issues. Many districts discuss this topic with the student body and provide telephone hotline numbers for support 24 hours a day. Also, if an adult becomes aware that a student is contemplating suicide or self-harm, he or she has a duty to report it to the proper authorities.

Role of Social Media in Student Wellness and Mental Health

Social media has a large influence on students' wellness and mental health. Students who engage in social media often experience **negative emotions** as a result. Some students develop feelings of **inadequacy or low self-esteem** when they compare themselves to others online. This is the result of unrealistic beauty expectations and exaggerated portrayals of others' lives. Additionally, students may be exposed to **cyberbullying** via social media. This type of bullying can involve name-calling, threats, shaming, spreading rumors, and other negative behaviors that can negatively impact a student's well-being. Cyberbullying can lead to bullying and other conflict on campus as well. Finally, engaging in social media can be addictive for some youth. They may spend excessive amounts of time on social media or engage in risky behaviors in an attempt to gain social media attention. For example, a student may post provocative pictures of him or herself in an effort to attract attention. This can have negative consequences for the student's mental health and overall wellness.

District Leader and Physical and Mental Wellness

In addition to ensuring the wellness of students and staff, the district leader should take steps to ensure his or her own **physical and mental wellness**. A leader cannot fulfill job responsibilities properly if he or she is not well. Also, the district leader should set an **example** for staff and students by prioritizing personal health needs. This is primarily accomplished by being proactive instead of waiting until a health problem arises to address it. First, the leader should **delegate responsibilities** and **accept assistance** whenever possible to keep stress levels low. The leader should also get regular **checkups** to quickly identify potential health problems. **Eating and sleeping** properly are also key components of maintaining physical and emotional health. Finally, the district leader should take advantage of the **resources and supports** that are offered on the campuses and elsewhere in the school district. These may include counseling, use of workout facilities, support groups, nurse hotlines, and many other resources designed to support the physical and mental health of staff.

Utilizing Community Services to Promote Wellness

It is important for a district leader to utilize community services for staff and student welfare because district funds and resources are often insufficient to provide abundant resources for staff and students. Even if a district has sufficient budgetary resources, there is no need to spend funds on resources that may be available as a **free community service**. Also, utilizing community services may expand the number and type of resources that are available, which means more support and help for members of the district community. Most district services only provide services directly to students, whereas community services often have programs, resources, and support for the **entire family**, which can be more impactful to students and their families in many instances. Finally, utilizing community services builds **partnerships and relationships** between the school and the community, which can have long-range benefits for both parties. For example, districts and community organizations can partner in community events, student recruitment, and applications for grant funding.

Identifying Community Resources for Promoting Wellness

A leader can identify community resources for promoting wellness in a variety of ways. Often, these organizations desire to partner with the school district and will visit or call to inform district leadership of their services and identify ways that they can serve the district community. Sometimes school district offices maintain **directories** of community organizations and programs that support students and their families within the school district. The district leader can also do a basic Internet search to identify nearby resources. **Local resources** include branches of city, county, or state organizations and are easily identified online. Finally, the district leader can make an effort to venture into the community and make **connections** with the leaders of area organizations to determine how the district and the organizations can collaborate.

Disciplinary Policy

Discipline Policy and Conflict Resolution

Discipline

Discipline is training students to abide by a specific **code of behavior**. When discipline is present, **rules** are typically stated and taught and **expectations for behavior** are defined in a variety of contexts and situations. In addition to the rules that are outlined as part of the discipline policy, there are **consequences** associated with failing to abide by the stated rules and expectations for behavior. Many associate discipline with administering consequences for failing to follow rules. However, the essence of discipline is the practice of **training or teaching behavior**. In schools, rules are often set by the school district and written in a student code of conduct for district-wide discipline. School districts may also have campus-wide expectations for behavior as part of their discipline, as well as sets of rules for individual classrooms. When discipline is effective, students are fully aware of behavior expectations and the consequences associated with not meeting those expectations.

Promoting Conflict Resolution

Conflict resolution is the practice of resolving conflicts or disagreements, such as verbal or physical altercations, between students to prevent further disruption. To promote conflict resolution, staff members must be vigilant in **identifying potential conflicts** among the student body. **Early intervention** is essential in resolving conflicts effectively. Staff members also want to **build relationships** with students and create an environment in which students feel comfortable reporting conflicts to adults. Both persons experiencing the conflict should feel that there is an adult on every campus who is willing and able to help them to resolve the conflict. There should be **structures or systems** in place to practice conflict resolution, which can include identifying mediators, locating neutral spaces for conversations between the conflicted parties, including parents and guardians, and support services to meet students' mental health needs. Additionally, the campus culture should utilize and promote **conflict resolution**, rather than simply administering consequences. This can be done by promoting conversations between students and adults and among peers regarding various aspects of their school experiences.

Applying Disciplinary Policy

The district discipline policy must be applied to students in a fair and equitable manner. Many studies have shown that male students, especially minority males, are disciplined more often and more severely than their peers. **Unfair discipline** can lead to increased misbehavior from students who receive the discipline at a higher rate than others, as well as by students who witness the inequitable discipline. The student who is disciplined more frequently may believe that he or she will receive consequences regardless of behavior, so he or she may choose to misbehave and earn the consequences. Students who witness this may believe they will not be punished for their behavior, so they can behave however they like. Rules should be enforced **consistently**. For example, if a district rule states that students should not chew gum, this rule should be enforced at all times and with all students, not just when it is convenient for the teacher or other staff member. Additionally, applying discipline in an unfair or inequitable manner can **damage relationships** with students and parents and can negatively influence the district culture.

Communicating the District's Discipline Policy

The district's discipline policy should be communicated to students, staff, and parents. Students must understand **behavioral expectations** if they are to meet them. It cannot be assumed that all students and their families hold the same expectations for behavior. As a result, the district's discipline policy must be **clearly communicated**. This can be done with a printed **handbook** for student behavior, as well as through **verbal communication**. When the discipline policy is not communicated clearly, this can lead to confusion and anger when consequences are administered. Emotional reactions from students and their parents or guardians can be expected when consequences are administered, especially for severe consequences. Ambiguity around rules and consequences makes it difficult to administer discipline and can lead to the nullification of warranted consequences due to ineffective communication of the discipline policy.

Bullying

Bullying occurs when one uses strength or other means of influence to **intimidate** another person. Bullying can be verbal, social, or physical and involves an imbalance of power. To prevent bullying, a district leader must employ several strategies. First, students and staff must be aware of what bullying is and is not. This will help to **identify** bullying quickly if it occurs. Also, the leader should create an environment in which bullying is **not acceptable or tolerated**. This will encourage those who are being bullied and those who observe bullying to report it so that it can be stopped. The district leader and the staff should also **model healthy, respectful relationships** with one another. The leader should not be a bully to staff, nor should staff bully students, as this would set an inappropriate model for students on the campuses. Additionally, acts of bullying should be addressed **swiftly and effectively**. This may include disciplinary consequences or other interventions such as peer mediation, counseling, or other strategies.

Common Disciplinary Problems

Many disciplinary issues among students are common and can be prepared for with effective **classroom management strategies**. One category of common discipline problems is **disengagement**. Students who disengage are not usually disruptive of others in the instructional setting but are not receiving instruction. These students may put their heads down and sleep or participate in off-task activities such as drawing, reading, writing, or daydreaming. Another category of discipline problems is **disruptive**. These behaviors indicate that the misbehaving student is not participating in instruction, and is additionally preventing others from participating. These behaviors include excessive talking, standing or walking around at inappropriate times, calling out, touching or hitting others, making disruptive noises, and many others. These types of behavior are often addressed by the teacher when they occur and do not require serious disciplinary consequences unless the behaviors are repeated and the student does not respond to redirection.

Restorative Justice

Restorative justice is a practice in which students who have harmed their school community or an individual through their misbehavior are required to **repair the harm**. The first step is to facilitate a **conversation** regarding the offender's behavior. This is usually led by an adult in the school. The offender has the opportunity to provide his or her side of the story and give input on the consequences. Traditional consequences usually include detention, suspension, and expulsion, among others, whereas restorative justice provides an opportunity for a holistic approach to **correcting the misbehavior**, "righting a wrong" or "making it right" and preventing it from recurring in the future. There are **no predefined consequences**, as these might vary significantly, based on the individual incident. For example, if a student has a temper tantrum, flips a desk in a classroom, and overturns a supply table, a community of adults and peers may determine that the student must clean the classroom during lunch for a week in addition to offering a public apology to the teacher and classmates.

Classroom Management

Classroom management refers to the strategies that teachers use to maintain order in the classroom and establish an environment conducive to learning. Classroom management is effective in preventing and addressing **minor disciplinary problems**. A teacher who demonstrates effective classroom management considers student behavior and management in all aspects of the instructional process, including lesson planning, lesson delivery, room arrangement, procedures, and more. For example, a teacher may use **diverse instructional practices** to engage students and prevent disengagement or off-task behavior during a lesson. A teacher may also design a lesson so that students can get out of their seats and **move** to different areas of the classroom at various points. Classroom management also involves having clear **expectations** for student behavior, established **procedures** for all instructional activities, and strategies for effective **redirection** of students who misbehave. Teachers with effective classroom management also build **rapport** with students and utilize **parental communication** to preserve the learning environment.

Disciplinary Approaches

District discipline approaches range from lax to very stringent. A **lax approach** does not mean that school discipline does not exist; it means that discipline is often determined on an individual basis, reflective of the circumstances and individuals involved. This may include practices such as teen or peer courts and restorative justice models. Some discipline approaches combine **individualized disciplinary**

strategies with **set disciplinary policies**. These approaches may offer flexibility in disciplinary options for relatively minor offenses and more defined options for more severe offenses. The most **stringent discipline approaches** have strict, pre-determined consequences for student misbehaviors. The most common example of this type of discipline approach is a zero-tolerance policy. In **zero-tolerance policies**, the consequences associated with particular behavioral infractions are administered without regard to the individual offender, context, or other variables within the situation. Many districts implement discipline approaches that fall within the midrange of this continuum, but a district leader should determine the best discipline approach for the campuses based on student needs.

Parental Communication

Parental communication is an asset when addressing student discipline problems. It is important that parents are aware of their children's behavior while at school. This awareness, fostered through consistent and effective communication between the district and the parent, can help build a **positive relationship and rapport**. Additionally, the parent can support the district in disciplinary efforts and vice versa to establish **consistency** in behavioral expectations of the student. Finally, communication provides parents with the opportunity to **intervene** in a child's misbehavior before those behaviors escalate to more severe behaviors or have a negative impact on the student's academic progress. Failure to communicate with a parent regarding a child's behavior can cause **negative consequences** for the district, such as complaints about how the discipline was handled by district administration or contesting of assigned consequences. Parents or guardians should always be part of the disciplinary process.

Severe Disciplinary Problems

Role of Special Education Status in Addressing Disciplinary Problems

When a student who is identified as receiving special education services displays behavioral issues, it is important to take certain steps to meet the child's needs. Some students with this identification already have **behavioral plans** in place. Teachers and district leaders must abide by these plans, which may include specific strategies for correcting a student's behavior or predetermined disciplinary consequences decided by the special education committee, which may or may not be aligned to the general student code of conduct. If a student who receives special education services commits a **severe disciplinary infraction** that could warrant consequences such as suspension or expulsion, a special meeting must be held by the special education committee to determine if the behavior was a manifestation of the student's identified disability. If it is concluded by the committee that the behavior is a manifestation of the student's identified disability, that student would likely not be subject to the traditional disciplinary consequences outlined by the student code of conduct. On the other hand, if the committee determines that the student's behavior is not associated with the disability, the student would likely be subject to the outlined disciplinary consequences.

Disciplinary Alternative Education Programs

Suspension and expulsion are consequences for severe student behavioral infractions. **Suspensions** typically last one to three days, but for some offenses, students are removed from the traditional education setting for longer periods of time. The public school system provides a means of education for all students, even those who have been removed from their traditional school due to extended suspension or expulsion. Students in these situations may receive their education through an **alternative education program**. In these programs, students may be assigned to attend the program for a certain number of days, usually for no longer than a school year. School districts may establish alternative education programs within the district or work with a program operating in that region. Additionally, students who commit crimes punishable by law may attend a school operated by the local **juvenile justice department**. Like other alternative education programs, the assigned duration that a student must attend varies based on the offense, as determined by the courts.

Role of Law Enforcement in School Discipline

Some student behavioral infractions are not only violations of district codes of conduct, but also of the law. Consequently, **law enforcement** has the right and responsibility to administer **legal consequences** in addition to local disciplinary consequences. For example, if students engage in a physical altercation on campus, they are subject to local disciplinary consequences which may include suspension, but they are also subject to the law, which may warrant a citation. Many school districts and district leaders have opted to maintain a **police presence** on campus at all times. A school district may have its own police department dedicated to its schools. This police presence is established for the safety of everyone on campus, but if students break the law, the police exercise their authority by addressing the infraction. The involvement of law enforcement is discretionary, at times, depending on the offense. Law enforcement is not a replacement for school discipline, but it acts as a supplement.

Using Community Resources

Engaging Community Stakeholders

A district leader can take several steps to engage **community stakeholders** in order to utilize community resources and build partnerships. First, the leader should **communicate** effectively with stakeholders. This communication helps stakeholders to engage because they are aware of the activities happening at the school, the vision and goals for the school, and the accomplishments of the students and staff. When stakeholders are aware of these things, they are able to identify where they can support the district. Next, the district leader should invite stakeholders to **visit** the campuses and **participate** in school activities. This may include activities such as Career Day, awards assemblies, graduation, fairs, and more. Finally, the district leader should engage in **activities hosted by community stakeholders**. This will demonstrate that the district leader is supportive of their endeavor and is open to learning about the stakeholders' roles in the community. As the leader builds relationships with these stakeholders, he or she can identify individualized ways to further engage community stakeholders.

Community Resources

Almost all aspects of the district program can be supported with community resources. **Local community organizations** can prove to be valuable in a broad range of areas that benefit the district, its staff, and its students. These may include transportation, training, academic support, extracurricular activities, fundraising, clubs, sponsorships, internships for students, physical resources such as equipment, services, and much more. For example, community volunteers help to **maintain school safety** with services such as greeting visitors, monitoring halls, or assisting with arrival and dismissal. Some community organizations may be able to provide **school supplies** for students or classroom supplies for teachers, which can support the instructional program. Other organizations may have access to men and women who can serve as **mentors** to at-risk youth on campus. It is up to the district leader to identify community resources near the school and determine if and how those resources can benefit the school community.

Community Partnerships

Community partnerships are beneficial to the district and the community. Establishing **community partnerships** is a way of providing **resources** to students and their families, usually at little or no cost to them. This can be invaluable to low-income families who otherwise would not be able to afford the services. Additionally, establishing community partnerships creates **sustainability and stability** within the community. When the district and its families patronize the organizations in the community and utilize their services, this helps to ensure that the organization will remain operable in the community. Frequently, services disappear from communities because they are underutilized, especially in impoverished communities. Finally, when the district leader establishes partnerships within the community, this helps to **align** the district vision and goals with those of the community to garner more support and resources to accomplish the vision and goals.

Services for Students

Many community resources used to support schools are targeted toward students in need. Some community resources target **academic needs**. These include providing tutorial services, free or low-cost school supplies, free books, internships, training programs, and more. Other community resources target **physical health needs**. These resources may include free or low-cost immunizations, dental services, medical checkups, and more. These types of resources may also address other physical needs of students, such as food, clothing, toiletries, or haircuts and grooming. Additionally, some community resources cater to the **psychosocial needs** of students. These resources may include mentoring, counseling, therapy, peer mediation, and many others. Some organizations provide specific services while others offer a variety of services. District leaders need to coordinate access to and delivery of these services to best meet students' needs.

Services for Staff

Even though staff members of the district do not necessarily reside in the community associated with the district, some community organizations extend benefits and resources to staff because of their service to the community. These resources may include **memberships or discounts** to local business for purchasing food or supplies for the classroom, access to free **training or resources** that can aid in their professional development, or **partnerships** with local businesses to supplement instruction in the classroom. Many organizations in the community are willing to donate time, money, or resources and supplies for special events or activities hosted at the schools. Consequently, the district leader and staff members should keep community stakeholders informed about school events to help determine how these community partners can support the district.

Services for Parents

As residents of the community, parents often have access to certain resources. At times, these resources can be delivered through the schools to increase the likelihood of **parental engagement** in these resources. These services may include English as a Second Language (ESL) classes for non-native English speakers, GED or adult high school programs, technology courses, individual and family counseling, and more. Additionally, some community services assist adults with acquiring housing or meeting household expenses such as rent, utilities, and food. Other services may include childcare, parenting classes, and other supports for the adults and their families. For many of these community organizations, the rationale for providing support to parents is that the children will benefit, which in turn **positively affects their school life** in areas such as attendance and academic performance.

Partnering with Community and Recreational Centers

When schools partner with community and recreational centers, this is often an opportunity to provide students and their families with **resources** they may not normally have access to. Often, community members are unaware of services that these organizations provide at little to no cost, such as childcare, use of gym facilities, access to technology, and more. Similarly, these organizations can help to **expand the district program**. For example, an organization may partner with the district to provide childcare on the campuses for students whose parents cannot pick them up at school dismissal time. Similarly, a community center may provide GED preparation to adults and can offer these services on the school campuses to parents. These partnerships are **mutually beneficial** and often involve sharing services and facilities.

Memorandum of Understanding

A memorandum of understanding is a contract between two parties, outlining the details of an agreement in which no money is exchanged. It is an agreement of **services to be provided**. For example, an organization may offer to provide tutorial services for students in reading and math after school on the campuses at no cost to the district. The district and the organization would draft a **memorandum of understanding** that outlines the tutorial services to be provided and the district leader's promise to provide locations on campus for the services. Both parties would sign the document and receive an original copy. The verbiage of the memorandum of understanding can be the same as in a traditional contract, but often the language is simpler as the sole purpose of the document is to state the exchange of services with no monetary compensation. The purpose of the memorandum of understanding is to **document** the services that are to be provided. This type of documentation can be helpful for both parties in providing evidence that the services were agreed upon and delivered.

Collaborating with Community Members

Collaborating with members of the community can have long-term benefits for the district and the surrounding community. When there is collaboration and partnership between the community and the district, there can be an **alignment of vision and goals**. This fosters long-term, mutually beneficial **partnerships**. For example, community organizations and the district may identify a need for increased technology education within the community. They can collaborate to add technology programs in the district, programs for adults within the community, and an increase in Internet access for community members. Also, community programs can be integrated into the district program and even housed on the school campuses. For example, a GED program may be based on a school campus to increase accessibility to parents and encourage parental engagement at the school. Community support can sustain or boost student enrollment in the schools and participation in special school programs.

District and Local Employment Trends

The district provides education and training that make students **employable** in the community workforce. As a result, the district can supplement or adjust programming to respond to **community needs**, such as training students in particular fields that are experiencing an employment shortage within the community. For example, the district leader and community members may identify a need for more healthcare workers in their community. They can tailor a district program to offer healthcare courses and training that could lead to certifications and degrees in the healthcare field. These students could then enter the local workforce with the skills to fill the needs of local employers. Many districts, especially in their secondary schools, partner with their **local community colleges and community organizations** to identify employment trends to support the local community as well as to increase the likelihood that graduates can obtain employment.

Aligning Education Expectations with Employment Goals

It is beneficial to the district community, the community at large, and postsecondary education institutions to **align education expectations** between public school and college. Districts and students benefit when there is communication between area colleges and the district for the purpose of understanding local education trends and needs. For example, the local community college can communicate to district leaders that recently enrolled freshmen have significant deficits in math skills. This information can prompt a district leader to analyze and revise the current math program and make the needed adjustments to ensure that students are graduating with the knowledge and skills needed to be successful in college. Similarly, communication between postsecondary institutions and district leaders can help to identify the **soft skills** that students need to be successful in college, as well as **trends in degree programs and career paths**. This type of communication can also lead to the institution of **higher education programming** on school campuses, such as dual-credit enrollment or training and certification programs.

Maintaining a Safe School District

The first priority of a district leader is maintaining school safety. This benefits not only the students and staff, but also the community as a whole. When issues and conflicts identified at the schools are resolved promptly, this can prevent **escalation** of those issues outside the schools, which can ultimately prevent violence or other altercations in the community. Also, a safe school in the community becomes a **safe haven or refuge** within unsafe communities and neighborhoods. Community members are willing to engage in school events when they know that the schools are safe and organized. Additionally, community members and organizations are willing to support and invest in schools that are safe and well-run. In contrast, when a school is not safe, this can lead to decreased enrollment and a lack of parental and community support.

Relationships with Community Organizations

A district leader can build relationships with various community organizations through effective communication and active participation in community events. First, the district leader should effectively **communicate** to community leaders that he or she desires to partner and build a relationship. This communication can involve sharing the district vision and goals and learning about the vision and goals of the community organizations. This can lead to a discussion of how the district and community organizations can organize **mutually beneficial plans and activities**. Collaborating will help to establish relationships. Then, the district leader should be an **active participant in community events** so that he or she will be visible and recognizable, as well as to show support for the community. This participation may include attending events at other schools in the community, attending church services in the community, or participating in other community-sponsored events. Supporting the activities of community organizations demonstrates investment in the community and helps to build relationships.

Community Dynamics

It is important for a leader to understand the dynamics of a community to meet that community's needs and to establish productive relationships. These **dynamics** can be revealed in a variety of ways. Often, **community leaders and parents** in the community are willing to discuss the community's makeup and dynamics. The district leader can search for **publications**, such as community newspapers or bulletins, to stay up to date on community affairs. These newspapers often highlight community leaders, organizations, community needs, and upcoming community events. Additionally, the district leader can attend **community meetings** such as town hall meetings to learn about the concerns of the community. It is also important to learn who the **government officials** in the area are, as well as candidates running for office in upcoming elections.

Communication with Family and the Public

Communicating with Families and Public

A district leader should take advantage of multiple ways of communicating with families and the public. Communication can be facilitated through **technology**. Methods include emails, electronic newsletters, websites, social media, mass automated phone calls, and other forms of technology that can be used to share messages with large groups of people. The district leader can also communicate in ways that require **little or no technology**. This includes making personal phone calls, hosting community meetings, making public announcements at community events, mailing letters, and other methods. When hosting community meetings, the leader should ensure that these meetings are held at a **variety of times** that are convenient for parents and the community, such as early morning, late evening, or weekends. A leader can use a variety of ways to communicate and must identify the **most preferred and effective means of communication** for the district community. Additionally, the district leader can use **multiple modes of communication** while sharing the same message to reach as many people as possible.

Overcoming Language Barriers

In diverse communities, district leaders often encounter language barriers when attempting to communicate with parents of students or other community members. It is helpful when a leader is fluent in more than one language, but often a variety of languages are spoken in these communities. To **overcome language barriers**, a leader should be proactive in devising communication strategies. First, the leader should be **aware of all languages** that are spoken in the district community. Then, the leader should attempt to have school employees who are fluent in the languages spoken on each campus so they can **translate** when needed. Additionally, **district communications** can be translated into a variety of languages. Translators or translation machines can be available at community meetings, including sign language when appropriate. Many businesses offer translation services for documents, as well as for meetings and conferences held in real time.

Communicating with the Media

There are times that the district leader will need to communicate effectively with the **media**, for both positive and negative reasons. The district leader should first follow the protocols and procedures outlined by the school district when communicating with the media, especially in situations in which the media attention is negative for the district. Some school districts **centralize media communication** and do not permit staff to communicate with the media without express approval. When communicating with the media, district leaders should speak truthfully, communicate in alignment with the district vision and goals, and communicate according to school district regulations. A district leader can utilize media outlets to **positively highlight the district**, such as broadcasting upcoming events or spotlighting student and staff accomplishments.

Formal and Informal Communication

Formal communication is usually prepared in advance. The district leader knows what is to be communicated and how. **Formal communication** is typically **structured and controlled**. It is delivered in a formal way, such as in a presentation to the community or a speech at an event. Formal communication also involves **prepared print communication** such as a letter, email, or bulletin to the public. In contrast, **informal communication** is often **impromptu**. This often involves conversation with an individual or group, an unexpected phone call, or a text message. In informal communication, the topic may be unexpected or vary within the course of communication. Informal communication can occur before or after a formal meeting or event, as a result of an unexpected phone call, or in any variety of circumstances in which the district leader was not prepared for the communication or conversation.

Speaking Informally with Stakeholders

A district leader should take precautions when speaking informally with stakeholders to **protect** himself or herself, and protect the school district. **Informal conversation** can be used negatively by persons who do not have the best interest of the district or district leader in mind or who are seeking personal gain. As a result, a leader should take care to be professional even in informal speech and to speak in accordance with the district vision and goals. For example, a district leader may make a joke during an informal conversation after a parent meeting that the parent does not believe to be in good taste. That parent can then make a formal complaint to the school district regarding the leader's professionalism. Regardless of the leader's perception of his or her relationship with the stakeholder, it is imperative that he or she remembers his or her position as district leader when engaging in informal conversation. The leader should view all communication, formal or informal, as a **reflection** of the position of district leader and of the school district.

Communicating Through Email

When communicating via email, a district leader should make sure that the email communicates the message in the **intended way**. In order to do this, the leader should maintain a **professional tone**. Humor and sarcasm are not often conveyed well via email and should be avoided. The district leader should also review the email for proper spelling, grammar, and word use, as errors can cause the message to be misunderstood. The leader should use features such as *Reply All* and *cc* with caution, only sending the email to persons who need to be included in the conversation. Also, the district leader should confirm that any necessary attachments are included in the email, if applicable. It is also a good practice to confirm with the recipient that the email has been received. Emails with attachments or mass emails are sometimes redirected to the recipient's spam or junk mail folder and may not be received in a timely manner, if at all.

Scheduling Parent Meetings

When scheduling parent meetings for large groups of parents, the district leader should consider the time of day and day of the week that these meetings are to be held. The goal of these meetings is to effectively communicate with parents in a group setting, so the district leader needs to ensure that the scheduled day and time accommodate the majority of parents for **maximum attendance**. The ideal times for these events will vary based on the needs of parents in the community. In many communities, parents work during the day, so **evening meetings** are more favorable. In some communities, certain days of the week are dedicated to religious activities, sporting events, or other engagements, and this should be taken into consideration when scheduling a parent meeting. For example, a district leader would not want to schedule a parent meeting at the elementary school on the same evening as the high school football game, as this would put the two events in competition. The district leader can talk to parents and **survey families** to identify ideal times to host meetings and should be open to hosting meetings at a variety of times, such as early in the morning or on weekends.

Shared Decision-Making and Stakeholder Involvement

Shared Decision-Making Committee

The purpose of the Shared Decision-Making Committee (**SDMC**) in schools is to provide a structured process for the inclusion of **stakeholders** in the district decision-making process. This committee is made up of district leadership, school staff, parents, community members, and other key stakeholders that the district leader may choose to include. The committee meets regularly to discuss **key decisions** that the district leader will make. These decisions may involve district programming, fundraising, planning for school events, and other initiatives. In these meetings, participants are informed of **key details** that should be considered in making these decisions and are given the opportunity to **voice their opinions** on the decisions as well as to provide **recommendations**. The SDMC provides recommendations to the district leader but does not have authority to dictate decisions. However, the SDMC provides an opportunity for stakeholder participation in the school process and helps to build relationships between the district leader and stakeholders.

Family Involvement

District Decision-Making

The district leader should provide as many opportunities as possible to **include families** in district decision-making. First, the leader should **inform families in advance** of decisions that will be made. For example, the leader may alert the parents that he or she is considering converting a school playground into a garden. This gives families an opportunity to provide feedback prior to the decision. The district leader can use surveys to gather input from families regarding the district, providing data that can be used in decision-making. Additionally, the district leader can communicate with **parent organizations** on campus or form a **parent focus group** to gather feedback and opinions on decisions to be made at the school. Also, there should always be at least one parent representative on the **Shared Decision-Making Committee**.

Decisions Made About Their Child's Education

Each family should have the opportunity to be involved in decisions made about their individual child's education. These decisions may include course selection or district programming pathways, extracurricular activities like clubs and sports, opportunities for tutorials and extended learning, and many others. First, the district should provide clear and effective **communication** to the families, indicating areas of the district program in which they can help make decisions for their children. Then, the district leader can provide ways for parents to offer their **opinions**, such as through frequent parent meetings or holding one-on-one conferences. Also, phone calls and emails can be very effective in including parents in the decision-making process. Many schools send **informative letters or bulletins** home to parents to include them in the process. Some campuses have opted to staff a **parent liaison** who specializes in communicating with parents and encouraging their participation in the school decision-making process.

Benefits of Involving Families in Decision-Making

Involving families in decision-making is beneficial to both the families and the district. When families are involved in the process, this increases **buy-in** for the decisions that are made, which can lead to increased **support for district initiatives**. For example, if families help to decide which tutoring program to implement after school, they will be more likely to have their child participate in the tutorials. Involving families in decision-making also strengthens the **relationship between the district and families** and stimulates **parental engagement**. Also, when families are involved, they often share information and **perspectives** that can inform the district leader's decisions. This can help the leader make decisions that better address the needs of students and their families.

Two-Way Communication

Two-way communication is the process of sending and receiving messages. In two-way communication, a person who receives a message has an opportunity to **respond** or send a message back to the sender. When collaborating with stakeholders and families, it is important for the district leader to provide opportunities for **two-way communication**, in contrast to only sending **one-way messages**. Two-way communication helps the leader to confirm that the message or communication was received as intended. Sometimes a message can be unclear or misinterpreted, and this confusion can be identified in two-way communication. Additionally, two-way communication allows the district leader to learn more about the opinions, needs, and concerns of key stakeholders. Finally, two-way communication promotes involvement and engagement of the stakeholders, which can foster relationships between them and the district, and it can increase buy-in from the stakeholders in regard to the district leader's vision and goals.

Ensuring Two-Way Communication

A leader can ensure two-way communication takes place by providing many **opportunities** for stakeholders to communicate with him or her. For example, a district leader may host a community meeting and provide a time during the program for stakeholders to ask questions or voice their opinions. District leaders can also make themselves **accessible** to those seeking to communicate with them. This can be done in several ways, such as holding frequent meetings with stakeholders or choosing certain office hours with an "open-door policy." Other ways of promoting communication include sending out **surveys**, creating a **comment or feedback box** on campus, and being open to **phone calls and emails**. A district leader should be visible during parent and community events and display a willingness to engage in conversation with stakeholders, demonstrating **receptiveness** to two-way communication.

Contributions

Contributions of Stakeholders

The success of the school organization is dependent upon the contributions of many stakeholders, including employees, community members, local organizations, and other stakeholders. The superintendent can find opportunities to **publicly recognize** the contributions of stakeholders in order to demonstrate that he or she understands the value of their contributions and that the success of the organization depends on contributions like these. Public recognition could include recognizing a teacher of the month, principal of the month, or staff person of the month. Recognition may be given to organizations or businesses that support the academic programs on school campuses through volunteering, collaborations, or donations. Exceptional achievements and accomplishments can be recognized in public ways, such as at school board meetings, on the school district website, and in district publications. Additionally, the superintendent can take the time to **individually recognize** the contributions of others personally through verbal or written praise. When a superintendent fails to recognize the contributions of stakeholders, these persons may feel unappreciated, unnoticed, and less likely to contribute in a meaningful way in the future. Recognizing the contributions of others fosters continued collaboration and teamwork, which is necessary for the school organization to be successful.

Contributions of Individuals and Groups

It is beneficial for the superintendent to recognize and acknowledge the contributions of individuals and groups in goal attainment for several reasons. First, recognizing behaviors that have led to success will increase the likelihood that those behaviors will be **repeated**. For example, if a school campus was able to successfully earn an excellent rating on the state-mandated assessment, recognition from the superintendent would likely **reinforce** the behaviors that resulted in student success. Additionally, recognition from the superintendent can serve as an **incentive** for individuals and groups. Some are motivated by the prospect of being recognized publicly, receiving an award, or being invited to an exclusive function. Other recognition may include **monetary compensation** for exceptional performance. Positive praise and recognition related to the district's vision and goals will encourage individuals and groups of employees to strive toward these goals, which ultimately leads to student success.

Personal and Professional Ethics

Integrity

Integrity refers to being honest and trustworthy and exhibiting moral principles. A person with integrity is generally of good character. A district leader can demonstrate integrity by behaving in a **trustworthy** manner with district personnel, staff, students, parents, and community stakeholders. The district leader should behave **ethically** in regard to all aspects of the position, including finance, personnel issues, and student matters. A district leader with integrity will hold him or herself and others **accountable** for ethical behavior, will recognize when ethics have been breached, and will take appropriate action in response. A district leader will also implement systems and procedures to ensure that the **rights and confidentiality** of students and staff are maintained at all times.

Conflict of Interest

A conflict of interest is a situation in which the district leader can obtain personal gain or harm from a decision made as a leader. For example, a district leader may determine that a gymnasium needs to be repainted. A family member of the leader owns a company that provides such a service and offers a bid. This would present a **conflict of interest** for the leader because he or she would potentially derive a benefit from hiring a family member's business to complete the job. Other situations that could present a conflict of interest may include hiring or terminating staff, awarding or disciplining a student who is a family member, or voting in an official capacity for colleagues or family members. A district leader should be aware of potential conflicts of interest and **alert superiors** should such a situation arise.

Protecting Privacy and Confidentiality of Information

Laws and regulations have been enacted to protect the privacy and confidentiality of students and staff in schools. Specifically, the **Family Educational Rights and Privacy Act (FERPA)** is a federal law that protects the privacy of **student education records**. Any school that receives funds from the United States Department of Education is subject to this law. It provides guidelines for who can access or view student records, who can alter student records, and what student information can be disseminated without student or parental consent. District leaders must abide by this law and implement policies and procedures that ensure other district personnel also abide by this law. Additionally, districts have the obligation to **inform** parents and students aged 18 or older of their rights under FERPA.

Issues of Ethics and Integrity

A district leader will find that many of the situations they encounter involve **issues of ethics and integrity**. These situations may involve students, parents, personnel, and community members.

Situations regarding **students** may involve grades, retention or promotion, assigning consequences in discipline matters, awards and recognition, and others. Situations involving **parents** may be student-related or involve fundraising, elections to committees, or others. Situations regarding **personnel** may involve reprimands or other discipline, promotions, pay, or other elements. Additionally, situations involving **community members** may involve voting and elections, awarding contracts, exchanging services, and more. The leader must also demonstrate ethics and integrity in their own **decision-making processes** in regard to budgeting, district academic and extracurricular programming, and business and community partnerships.

Transparency in the Decision-Making Process

Some district decisions require input from stakeholders. In these decisions, it is important to have a **transparent decision-making process** so that all stakeholders can be assured that the decision is made ethically and with integrity. First, stakeholders must be **notified in advance** of the decision to be made. They should also have **access to relevant information** for making the decision, in accordance with any privacy or confidentiality regulations. They should be notified in advance of any **public meetings** related to the decision and documented meeting minutes should be made available. Any **voting** related to the decision should also be documented for transparency. Finally, when the district leader has made a decision, it should be **shared** with stakeholders along with the rationale for it, such as community input, votes, and other information.

Equitable Treatment of Students and Staff

The best way that the district leader can ensure equitable treatment of students and staff is to develop **policies and procedures** and adhere to them. When there are policies and procedures in place, the district leader can refer to these to determine the **best course of action** when dealing with students and staff. For example, if a student has excessive school absences, a district attendance policy should dictate when and how to address absenteeism. Similarly, if a staff member dresses unprofessionally for work, an employee handbook should outline how to address the staff member. In a situation with no guiding policy, the district leader should use **discretion** in handling the situation and subsequently develop a **guiding policy** for future incidents. This can be in the form of memorandums or addendums to existing student and staff handbooks. While there may be extenuating circumstances that require the district leader's discretion, policies and procedures ensure that all are treated equitably.

Acting Ethically

A leader can ensure that others are acting ethically by **communicating expectations** regarding ethical behavior. The leader can provide staff with **documents and training** that explain these expectations. Employees should acknowledge receipt of such documentation by signing to confirm that they have received them as well as signing in at training sessions to confirm participation. The leader can also **monitor employee behavior**. This can be done in person by walking around and observing performance or remotely by instructing others on the leadership team to observe employee behavior or monitoring with security cameras. Security cameras are useful in areas that are most prone to unethical conduct, such as places where money is exchanged, entrances and exits, records storage, and areas on the campuses that are not frequently trafficked. Additionally, the leader can implement **consequences for unethical behavior** and address such behavior swiftly. Employees are encouraged to behave ethically to avoid consequences for unethical behavior.

Review Video: Ethical and Professional Standards
Visit mometrix.com/academy and enter code: 391843

Consequences of Unethical Behavior

Consequences for an employee's unethical behavior can vary, depending on the severity of the offense. For a minor offense, the employee may receive a **verbal or written reprimand** to be included in his or her personnel file. This type of situation may require a formal conference with the district leader or other school district staff. More severe offenses can result in **suspension**, **reassignment**, or **termination of employment**. For example, if an employee has behaved in an unethical manner involving exchange of money, he or she may be reassigned to a position that does not require interaction with money. Severe offenses can result in the suspension or revocation of state licensure. Ethical offenses that involve breaking the law can also result in **legal consequences** such as fines, probation, or even imprisonment as determined by city, state, and federal law.

Ethical Violations

If a district leader has been made aware of an ethical violation, it is his or her responsibility to act immediately. In many cases, there are **procedures or guidelines** that a district leader should follow, as determined by the school district. These procedures may include notifying district personnel, initiating an investigation, conferencing with the offending employee, drafting a formal note of reprimand, or other actions. There should also be guidance from the school district on notifying outside **authorities or organizations**, such as law enforcement or Child Protective Services. It is important for a district leader to take reports of unethical behavior seriously and act quickly and appropriately. Additionally, the district leader should maintain thorough **documentation** of the events and timelines for audit purposes.

Social Justice

Social justice refers to the **fair and equitable treatment of all persons**, regardless of their status in society. Factors such as socioeconomic status, race, ethnicity, place of residence, and others influence the **privileges** that certain persons may have in society. These privileges, or lack thereof, can be reflected in the school system as well. The concept of social justice as it relates to education means that all students, regardless of their social status, socioeconomic status, race, ethnicity, religion, sexual orientation, or any other identifying factor, are entitled to an **equitable education** and access to **educational resources**. For example, it is considered a social injustice for children in poverty to have outdated textbooks and a lack of access to technology in schools. Social justice in education refers to advocating for children who are typically **marginalized and disenfranchised** so that they can receive the same educational opportunities as other children.

Advocating for All Children

A district leader is in a unique position to be an **advocate for all children on the campuses**. First, the district leader needs to ensure that the **academic and extracurricular programming** is accessible to all children and reflective of the needs of all children attending district schools. Next, the district leader should ensure that all **special programming** is properly funded and implemented on the campuses. This can include programs such as Title I, special education, gifted and talented programs, English as a Second Language programs, career and technology programs, and many others. Finally, some inequities are the result of **governmental policy**, which affect the district. The district leader can use his or her voice and authority to influence policy and promote social justice in the district. Examples of these types of policy issues include school finance and funding, school zoning, school vouchers, and many others.

Communicating Expectations

The district leader must communicate expectations to staff and students to increase the likelihood that staff and students will meet those expectations. It is difficult, if not impossible, for staff and students to meet expectations if they are unaware of them. This can result in **unintentional disregard of expectations**. For example, teachers may decide to leave campus during an instructional planning period. If the teachers are unaware that the district leader expects them to remain on campus even when they do not have class, it will be difficult for the district leader to hold them accountable for that behavior. Likewise, the district leader should communicate **expectations of behavior** to students before a presumed offense is committed. A district leader must effectively communicate expectations so that students and staff will know what behavior to demonstrate and so the district leader can hold them accountable for those behaviors.

WAYS TO COMMUNICATE EXPECTATIONS

A district leader has many opportunities to communicate expectations to staff and students. These expectations can be written and shared in **employee and student handbooks** or **codes of conduct**. These documents can be printed as well as made available online. The district leader may require that staff and students provide a signature acknowledging receipt of such documents. Additionally, expectations for behavior can be communicated or reinforced during **announcements**, in **assemblies or meetings**, and in **individual conversations**. Many district leaders post expectations for behavior on posters in school hallways and classrooms. These often take the form of classroom rules for behavior, hallway expectations, cafeteria expectations, and so on. When correcting behavior that does not meet expectations, the district leader should reinforce expectations for the offender. For example, the district leader may verbalize to an employee that he or she is late to work and remind him or her of the expected arrival time.

Transparent Decision-Making

TRANSPARENT DECISION-MAKING

Transparent decision-making is the act of making sure that the process, logic, and rationale used to make a decision are **clear and open** to others. When decision-making is transparent, any **critical information** used to inform that decision is also readily available to others for review. This transparency allows others to understand **how the decision was made**. For example, if a district leader were to decide whether to eliminate the art program, a transparent decision-making process would allow stakeholders and team members to observe and understand how the district leader makes the decision. The process may start with publicly making known that the decision needed to be made. Then, data relating to the art program would be provided, including data related to any other programming that may be compared to the art program. Additional rationale could be documented, such as evaluating the position of the art program in relation to the district vision and goals. Based on this relevant information, observers of the decision-making process would be able to **understand** and even **predict** the decision that the leader would make.

DATA-SUPPORTED DECISIONS

Data is essential to offering transparency in decision-making. Data is **objective**, which makes it less refutable. Stakeholders may question or contest a district leader's decisions in some cases, but they are less likely to question or contest the **data influencing those decisions**. Data that is shared may include financial data, student performance data, or data related to district demographics such as enrollment, attendance, or discipline. When data is shared with stakeholders, it is easier for them to understand the **basis and determining factors** for decisions. For example, if a district leader decides to eliminate a school program based on poor student participation, the district leader can be transparent and provide the attendance and participation data for that program to the stakeholders. As a result, the stakeholders will understand that the decision is based on objective data. Additionally, basing decisions on data will encourage the district leader to make sound decisions based on concrete data whenever possible because the district leader will be aware that the decision-making process will be observed by stakeholders.

SUPPORTING STAFF DECISIONS WITH DATA

Providing data is an essential component of transparency in decision-making. The district leader can share data such as **district performance data** and **individual student data** to demonstrate how a decision was made. Teachers and staff understand this data and, as employees working directly with students, are able to look at student data. This data can help them understand why decisions are made about certain curricular programs, district discipline procedures, and other aspects of the district program. Also, the district leader can use data to **support conversations with staff** regarding individual performance, which can lead to decision-making. For example, a district leader may determine that a third-grade reading teacher should be reassigned to a fourth-grade classroom. The leader can use student performance data and the teacher's performance evaluation data to explain the decision to the teacher. A district leader should always protect the **confidentiality** of students and personnel when applicable.

Supporting Community Stakeholders with Data

Providing data is an essential component of transparency in decision making. When being transparent with stakeholders, the district leader must be careful to protect the **confidentiality** of school, student, and personnel data. As a result, the district leader should be selective about the data that is shared with stakeholders and the manner in which it is shared. Data that is already public and is used to make a decision can be helpful when sharing data with stakeholders. The district leader should be prepared to **explain** the data, the measures used to obtain it, and its implications. Although the district leader cannot share individual student and staff data, the district leader can share **aggregates of the data**. For example, the district leader may provide data of third-grade student performance on a recent benchmark assessment. Data that is shared with stakeholders should be **clear, easy to understand, and purposeful** so that it adds to the transparency of the decision-making process.

Feedback and Reflection

Importance of Feedback

Feedback is the process of gathering information from an outside source to **evaluate** or **correct** a particular course of action. A district leader should seek feedback to ensure that he or she is on the **correct path** when making decisions. Without feedback, a district leader may proceed with a course of action, only to realize later that it was a mistake. For example, a leader may decide to host parent meetings on Wednesday evenings. After hosting the first meeting with poor turnout, the leader may find that many families in the community attend church on Wednesday evenings. Had the leader gathered feedback, a different time might have been chosen. Gathering feedback can help the district leader make corrections or alter a course in a timely manner. Additionally, gathering feedback from stakeholders demonstrates that the district leader is **humble** and **receptive to feedback**. Perceived humility in the leader can help in team building and relationship building with the staff and the community. Gathering feedback also increases **buy-in** from those providing the feedback, such as members of the leadership team, key community members, or school district office personnel.

Gathering Feedback

A district leader can gather feedback from stakeholders in various ways to aid in decision-making. A primary way of gathering feedback is presenting ideas and plans to the **district leadership team**. The leadership team may include assistant superintendents, deans, or other leaders on campus. This team is effective in providing feedback because they know the district, students, and community well and have demonstrated leadership skills and thinking. For example, the leadership team may provide feedback on a lunch schedule for one of the campuses based on their experiences from lunch duty in the cafeteria. Also, **supervising district personnel** are often available to provide feedback to the district leader, especially in confidential matters. The district leader can also solicit feedback from **students, parents, and community members**. This type of feedback can help the district leader see situations and potential decisions from other perspectives. For example, a student may provide feedback that the proposed after-school program does not interest the student body. Also, gathering and implementing feedback from **stakeholders** can increase stakeholder buy-in and support of the district's vision and goals.

Responding to Negative Feedback

When a leader solicits feedback from students, staff, or stakeholders, it is possible that some feedback may be **negative**. The negative feedback may be related to aspects of the district program or related to the leader directly. When a leader receives feedback, he or she must avoid an immediate **emotional response** to the feedback. First the leader must determine whether the feedback has **validity**. Persons providing feedback can sometimes speak out of anger or frustration and deliver the feedback in a harsh way. However, how feedback is delivered does not necessarily determine whether the feedback is valid. Consequently, the leader must reflect upon his or her own practices and identify whether the feedback identifies an area of improvement for the leader or the district program. If so, the leader must acknowledge this weak area and take steps to improve it. When improvements have been made, if possible, the leader should seek feedback once again to determine if the concerns of the stakeholders have been addressed.

Responding to Positive Feedback

Positive feedback from stakeholders can be encouraging for the district leader. Sometimes this feedback is solicited and other times it is volunteered. Positive feedback can be used for **reflection and improvement**. First, the leader needs to determine the **validity** of the feedback. Some people may feel the need to offer flattery or unsubstantiated positive feedback in an effort to favorably position themselves. Therefore, a leader must not assume that his or her performance or the district's performance is favorable just because one or two persons offered a compliment. Next, the leader must not become **overconfident** in the area that has received positive feedback. Instead, the feedback should encourage the leader to continue the actions that led to the favorable outcome to continue to achieve good results. Positive feedback can also be **shared** with other staff so they can be assured that they are performing well in the identified area.

Honest Self-Reflection

Honest self-reflection is a component of growth and efficacy as a district leader. A district leader should set aside time to reflect on **personal performance as a leader**, based on identified leadership **expectations and standards**. There are many models of leadership that the district leader can use for comparison, but most school districts select or develop a **tool for leadership evaluation**. These evaluation tools include the expectations for leadership skills, performance, and behaviors. District leaders can use the tools to identify their own strengths and weaknesses. Also, any time a leader is reading professional materials such as books or articles related to leadership, it is an opportunity to reflect on how he or she measures against the skills identified in the resource. Often, stakeholders such as parents or community members offer criticisms of the leader. The district leader should reflect upon the **validity of those criticisms** to determine areas for improvement. For example, during a parent conference, a parent may complain that the leader is a poor communicator. Even though the parent may have made the statement in a moment of frustration or anger, the district leader should take the opportunity to reflect upon his or her communication skills and how those skills were used in that situation and past situations.

Addressing Weaknesses

Once a leader has identified weaknesses through self-reflection, he or she can take several steps to **address** them. First, the district leader can read **books, articles, and other resources** related to the areas of weakness. For example, if the district leader has difficulty with time management, he or she can identify resources that can help to cultivate better time management skills. A leader can also participate in **training or professional development** related to the identified areas of weakness. A variety of professional organizations provide workshops and training related to various leadership competencies. The leader can also seek assistance from a **supervisor or other district staff person**. A supervisor can offer suggestions or guidance for improvement in a deficient area. Additionally, the district leader can obtain **mentors and coaches** outside of the district organization that can provide objective skill building in the district leader's deficit areas. Mentors may be retired superintendents or other types of leaders who are in the district leader's network and are willing to share their expertise. Mentors do not typically require payment. In contrast, coaches are often hired to help with targeted skill-building and professional growth.

Leader's Self-Reflection

Effect on the Leadership Team

A leader's self-reflection can affect the leadership team in a number of ways. First, it sets an example as a district leader that **self-reflection** should be a part of leadership practice. This also demonstrates to the leadership team that the leader is aware that he or she is not perfect and is making efforts to **address identified weaknesses**. The leadership team should be comprised of people who help to **compensate** for the leader's weaknesses. Therefore, when a leader identifies his or her weaknesses, this can lead to **adjustment** of the leadership team. For example, if the leader determines that his or her leadership in math and science is weak, the leader may identify a person who is strong in math and science to be a part of the leadership team. Additionally, a leader's self-reflection can lead to **shifting roles and responsibilities** on the leadership team and further reflection about the strengths and weaknesses of the entire team.

Effect on the Stakeholders

A leader's self-reflection can affect how he or she is **perceived** by stakeholders as well as the leader's **relationship** with stakeholders. When stakeholders observe the leader committing to self-improvement and making changes, they may conclude that the leader is humble and willing to improve the practice and the operation of the school district. This can build hope and trust among stakeholders. For example, the leader may communicate to stakeholders that he or she is working on improving communication skills and is committed to doing a better job of returning phone calls and responding to emails. Similarly, engagement in self-reflection and self-improvement demonstrates that the leader is **responsive to feedback**. It is difficult to engage with a leader who believes that he or she knows everything, does not need feedback, and cannot receive criticism. In contrast, a leader who reflects and improves can encourage stakeholders to engage with the leader and the district, and stronger relationships can be built between the leader and stakeholders.

Trends in Education

Technology

One-to-One Technology Model

The one-to-one technology model is the practice of providing a **technology device** to each student on campus. As technology use has increased in schools, access to technology has been a focal point to aid in student performance and growth. In many instances, district leaders calculate the **ratio** of computers or technology devices to students. For example, the district may purchase enough computers to ensure that there is one computer for every 10 students. When there are not enough technology devices on the campuses for every student, computer and Internet access may be limited due to the need to share technology devices on campus. This may be done by equipping classrooms with a limited number of computers, making laptop carts available, or creating computer labs, all of which must be shared by teachers and students. With the one-to-one technology model, the ratio of technology to students is **one device for each student**. This allows **maximum access to technology** on campus. These technology devices are usually personal laptop computers or tablets. In some instances, the students are entrusted with the technology and are permitted to take the devices home for technology access outside of school hours.

Bring-Your-Own-Device Technology Model

The bring-your-own-device technology model describes the practice of allowing students to bring their own **technology devices** to school for use in classroom instruction. Many families provide their children with computers, tablets, and phones that can access the Internet. When this model is implemented, students can bring these devices to school and use them to participate in computer-based or web-based activities. The bring-your-own-device model is **beneficial** because it saves the district from purchasing the number of technology devices necessary for every student to have access. The

downside of this model is that the district is not responsible for the care or repair of students' devices, not all students have a device, and there is often difficulty in designing lessons compatible with various types of technology. For example, there are different specifications for playing videos on tablets, laptops, and phones, which can be challenging to a teacher attempting to incorporate videos into the lesson. Also, this model has **limited efficacy** in impoverished communities, in which the majority of students do not have access to these devices.

Virtual School Model

The virtual school model is the practice of providing **online courses** to students, using a web-based platform or other computer-based program rather than physically attending a class. A student has access to instructional content online and participates in activities and tests to assess learning. In some virtual school models, students have **virtual access to a teacher**. In other models, the computer program is **automated** and student progress may be self-paced. Virtual school has been used in all grade levels as a supplement to traditional instruction or as a replacement. Virtual school can also be utilized for students who are home schooled. When used as a supplement to traditional classes, students may use virtual school to make up failed courses, participate in tutorials or interventions, or to access courses that are not offered on campus. The virtual school model requires that students have access to a technology device and Internet service. Many **businesses** also develop platforms and coursework for virtual schools. Most commonly, courses focus on the core content areas of reading, math, social studies, and science, but many learning platforms offer electives and tutorial programs.

Blended Learning

Blended learning is the process of incorporating **technology use** into **traditional classroom instruction**. In the blended learning model, teachers identify places in the lesson that can be **supplemented** with technology or in which technology can be used to drive the lesson. In this model, the teacher may use the technology in the lesson, but the focus is on students utilizing technology in the classroom. For example, a teacher may deliver content on a topic and then assess students' understanding with an online assessment tool. In the blended learning model, technology can be used to deliver content, such as accessing information through reading and videos or by creating slideshows or other presentations. Technology can be used to **assess** student learning as well. Blended learning models are often paired with **project-based learning models**. This allows students the freedom and opportunity to use the technology with limited guidance by the teacher to meet lesson objectives. In the blended learning model, technology use is **flexible**, so it may vary by content area or lesson as teachers still implement traditional instructional strategies.

Review Video: Benefits of Technology in the Classroom
Visit mometrix.com/academy and enter code: 536375

School Discipline

Role of Meditation in Schools

Meditation is the act of engaging in quiet and silent thought or reflection. This practice has been used in schools as a strategy for **redirecting poor student behavior**. When a student breaks a school rule or disrupts class, rather than discipline with in-school suspension, out-of-school suspension, or other traditional consequences, the student is instructed to **meditate**. When students are given the opportunity to meditate, they are placed in a quiet environment where they can focus on calming down, breathing, and thinking about appropriate behaviors to display. Districts that have implemented meditation as a discipline strategy have seen a decrease in suspension rates and fewer discipline referrals from teachers. The practice of meditation is thought to alleviate **emotional issues** such as anxiety, anger, depression, and frustration, which could be sources of student misbehavior.

Challenges of Promoting School Safety

It is a district leader's primary responsibility to keep students safe while at school. This responsibility can be challenging for a variety of reasons. Recent acts of school violence have caused educators and government officials to revisit laws, policies, and procedures relating to school safety. In some schools, **metal detectors** are used to promote school safety, but some deem that practice to be controversial. As schools are built or remodeled, **school designs** include limited entrances and exits to the school building and compartmentalized front office areas that can prevent unauthorized persons from gaining entrance into the school. Other strategies include staffing **uniformed police officers** on campus during school hours, implementing **standardized dress**, and limiting **backpacks and other large bags** on campuses. Additionally, many schools practice **drills** for emergencies, such as having an intruder on campus. Promoting school safety is challenging because not even the best preventative measures can guarantee the safety of students and staff.

Curricular Programming

Accelerated Learning

Accelerated learning is the practice of delivering content to students at an **accelerated pace**. For example, a traditional high school course that is delivered during an 18-week semester may be condensed into six or nine weeks. The purpose of accelerated learning is to provide students with **additional learning opportunities**. For example, if a student is already proficient in math, it can be reasoned that he or she should not have to sit through an 18-week course. Accelerated learning is also useful for students who have previously taken a course but were unsuccessful. These accelerated classes may be offered during summer breaks or built into the district's instructional program. Accelerated programs are often facilitated with **technology-based programs**, which can personalize and deliver content based on a student's needs. For example, a student enrolled in an accelerated course may take a pre-assessment online and then be assigned coursework based on assessment performance. A student would not have to complete coursework in areas of the course in which mastery is demonstrated.

School-Within-a-School Model

A school-within-a-school model describes the creation of a specialized school program to be operated on the **same campus** as the traditional school program. The students participating in the specialized program are still students of the school, but they may have limited or no interaction with the rest of the student body. For example, a high school may implement an engineering-based program on campus to which students may apply and be accepted. Students participating in this program will attend school on campus, but their classes, course pathways, and other activities are **separate** from the remainder of the student body. A school may have several schools within the school, or just one. Each of these schools may be designated with its own budget, programming, and administration. In most models, the schools are still identified as one school for state and federal accountability purposes. However, some school districts have extended the model and created an entirely separate school housed on the same campus. In these instances, the school programs are separate and only share the use of the school facilities.

Project-Based Learning

Project-based learning is the instructional practice of assigning projects to students as a means of driving instruction. In **project-based learning**, students are presented with a problem that must be solved. They are usually assigned to **groups or teams** for completion of the project. To solve this problem, students have to learn content, usually from more than one content area, and demonstrate **mastery of a variety of objectives and skills**. The teacher who has assigned the project delivers certain content to students and often provides access to designated resources. Students are responsible for extending their learning and conducting research, using the available resources and the Internet. The project is generally complex and can take as little as a few days to complete, or an entire school semester. With more complex project assignments, teachers expect students to demonstrate mastery of a greater number of learning objectives. Therefore, there may be multiple performance expectations for the project, such as papers, presentations, and more. Some school districts integrate some project-based learning into their curriculum, while others have designed their entire curriculum around project-based learning.

FLIPPED CLASSROOM MODEL

A flipped classroom model describes the instructional practice of changing the **delivery** of instructional content and the opportunities for **guided practice** within the lesson cycle. In a traditional classroom, a teacher delivers the content and may provide limited guided practice on an in-class assignment. The student may be assigned extended practice independently within the class or in the form of homework. In a flipped classroom model, the student is provided with the instructional content **electronically**, typically in the form of a recorded lecture or presentation video to watch outside of the classroom. In the classroom, the time that would have been dedicated to delivering content is used to support the student in **guided practice**. This allows the students more time and access to the teacher during the aspect of the lesson in which they are likely to need the teacher's guidance the most. This practice is considered a flipped classroom because, in essence, the lesson is done at home and the homework is done at school. Many districts have incorporated flipped lessons into their curriculum sparingly, while some have transformed their entire curricular program using the flipped classroom.

CHARTER SCHOOLS

A charter school is a specialized public school that operates according to a **charter** with a local or national organization. The charter may dictate how the school operates and whom it serves. Charter schools are **publicly funded**, which means they have to meet state and/or federal accountability standards. However, unlike traditional public schools, charter schools do not obtain funding from **local taxes**. Attending a charter school is free to students and their parents, but there may be an application or entrance requirements. Charter schools provide communities with additional options for educating their children. Some charter schools specialize in serving at-risk youth, a particular gender, certain career paths, or other niche areas. Proponents of charter schools view these schools as an additional option for students, especially if the community schools are not meeting their needs. However, opponents of charter schools believe that these schools take funding, enrollment, and support away from neighborhood schools.

MIDDLE COLLEGES

Middle colleges are **alternative high school programs** that are operated on community campuses. The purpose of a middle college is to provide an alternative environment for high school students and facilitate **independent student learning**. Students who attend middle colleges are given freedoms and liberty similar to college students and may even have a shorter school day or flexible school schedule. The school is operated by school district staff and students take their traditional high school courses, but they are also given the opportunity to take **college-level courses** taught by **community college professors**. Middle colleges often appeal to students who do not fit in with the environment or culture at their traditional school or who seek to earn college course credits while still in high school. Some middle colleges are designed and funded as charter schools while others are developed and operated as part of the traditional public-school system.

PERSONALIZED LEARNING

Personalized learning is the instructional strategy of tailoring academic content and instruction to students based on their individual needs. **Personalization** can be achieved based on a student's learning styles, personality, interests, career goals, and academic progress. Providing personalized learning can be complex, so it is often implemented with **computer programs**. Before personalization can occur, a student must be **assessed** on content relative to the type of personalization. For example, if learning will be personalized based on a student's learning style, he or she will take a learning style inventory. Based on the inventory results, a personal learning plan will be developed. The purpose of personalized learning is to address the **individual needs** of the student, with the goal of helping him or her achieve **academic growth and success**. Instruction may be differentiated based on the content the student receives, how the content is delivered, how the student is expected to engage with the content, the pace of progress through the content, and how students demonstrate mastery of the content. Personalized learning often accompanies **technology implementation models** such as one-to-one technology.

Flexible School Day

In a traditional school day, students report to school at a certain time in the morning, remain at school for nearly seven hours, and are then dismissed in the afternoon. A **flexible school day** modifies this traditional schedule to **accommodate** students and their families. There are many variations of the flexible school day, which may include attending a four-hour block of school at some scheduled time throughout the day, attending school in the evenings, or attending school at unscheduled times and accumulating hours over the course of a school week. A flexible school day is especially beneficial to students who are at risk of dropping out or have dropped out of school in the past. These students may have personal obligations that make it difficult to attend school on a traditional schedule, such as working full-time or caring for a child. Implementing a flexible school day is beneficial to the district and to students because students can attend school in a way that meets their individual needs and the school can help students complete their academic expectations for accountability purposes.

College and Career Readiness

Dual-Credit Enrollment

Dual-credit enrollment is a curricular program designed to give students the opportunity to earn **college credits** while they are still in high school. The program is called **dual-credit** because students enroll in high school and college at the same time. To participate, students must meet entry requirements for the **local community college**. This usually involves earning a specific score on an exam for math and reading. Once admitted to the college program, students take core courses that earn high school and college credits **simultaneously**. For example, a student may take a Freshman English 1301 course at the college level, which will also earn credit for the high school English year four requirement. The number of college credits that students may earn depends on the school-college partnership and availability of courses, but many districts offer the opportunity to earn an **associate's degree** while students are still in high school. This saves students and their families money in college tuition and also increases the likelihood that students will persist in college and earn degrees. These college classes can be taught on the high school campus by a qualified teacher or a visiting professor, or the students may travel to the local community college for part of the school day.

Advance Placement Courses

Advanced placement courses are college-level courses that are taught to high school students. **Advanced placement (AP) courses** contain the content of college-level courses and are taught with college-level rigor by teachers who meet certain qualifications. These courses are usually core content courses such as reading, math, science, or social studies. Students remain on the high school campus to take these courses and receive **high school credit** for successful course completion. However, students also have an opportunity to take an exam at the end of each course that can qualify them to earn **college credit**. If the student achieves an acceptable test score, he or she will earn college credit for that course, which is transferrable to most colleges or universities. Students may participate in a combination of AP and dual-credit courses to increase the number of college credits they can earn while still in high school. This saves students and their families money in college tuition and also increases the likelihood that they will persist in college and earn degrees.

International Baccalaureate Programs

An International Baccalaureate (**IB**) program is a rigorous school curricular program that has been implemented in schools across the world. In order to participate in this program and to be recognized as an IB school, schools must meet certain program requirements and be monitored and evaluated regularly. The authorization process can take two to three years. As an IB school, schools receive **professional development** and participate in the **international network** of IB schools. Additionally, students who attend IB schools often demonstrate higher levels of academic success when compared to schools without IB programs. This is due to the **specialized curriculum** offered as well as the **higher level of rigor** in IB schools. Students also have the opportunity to become more culturally aware and sensitive due to their acquisition of a **second language** as part of the program and their exposure to other students around the world.

Role of Career Pathways

Career pathways are specific tracks that students can participate in to prepare them for specific career fields or jobs. These tracks or pathways include **coursework** that is relevant to a student's chosen field. For example, if a student is interested in a career pathway for law and public office, his or her pathway may include more reading, writing, and social studies courses than students in other career pathways, as well as more elective courses related to the skills necessary to be successful in that career. **All school levels** can implement career pathways. In elementary schools, the delineation between the various pathways may not be as defined as in high schools, but it can lay the foundation for future studies. For example, a student in a fine arts career pathway from elementary school to high school would likely have an advantage over other students who are interested in fine arts but did not participate in the career pathway due to the career pathway providing general exposure to and participation in fine arts related coursework. Some state accountability systems require high school students to identify career pathways as part of **graduation requirements**.

Accountability

Student Growth

Student growth has become a focus in school accountability. In years past, **student performance** has been the sole focus. As a result, educators primarily focused on students who were likely to perform well on high-stakes tests. As a result, students who were not likely to pass these tests were **underserved**, along with students who would likely pass the test regardless of teacher intervention and support. In contrast, a focus on **student growth** and accountability for such growth means that educators must serve all students. Even if a student does not pass a state-mandated test, growth in performance must be demonstrated. This growth is often measured against a prediction of how the student is expected to perform, based on assessment data from previous years. To ensure that schools are adequately educating all students, **accountability standards** incorporate measures of student growth in addition to measuring student performance.

Student Performance

Student performance in school accountability describes how students perform on **state-mandated assessments**. A certain percentage of students must pass these tests for a district to be deemed acceptable. This performance is evaluated in each **core content area**, depending on the accountability system, but most frequently in reading and math. The performance standards and content areas evaluated can vary based on grade level and can also change with federal or state legislation. A district that performs well in one subject and not in another is still a failing district. Additionally, to ensure that all students are performing well and not just certain groups of students, district performance is evaluated for particular **subgroups** of students, based on demographics. These demographics may include race or ethnicity, socioeconomic status, special education status, limited English proficiency status, and more.

Federal Legislation Relating to District Accountability

Some of the most recent legislation related to public school accountability is the **Every Student Succeeds Act (ESSA)**, which was enacted in 2015 during President Obama's administration. This legislation replaced the **No Child Left Behind (NCLB) Act** of 2002, enacted during President Bush's administration. ESSA provides more flexibility to states by allowing individual states to provide plans for addressing **key educational goals** such as closing the achievement gap, ensuring and increasing equity in schools, improving the quality of instruction in schools, and improving growth and performance outcomes for all students. However, the basis of the law remains the same as that of NCLB. All students should have **full educational opportunity**. Consequently, there is a remaining focus on serving low-income students, students with special needs, and other students who have traditionally been marginalized in the public school system.

Failure to Meet Accountability Standards

Districts that do not meet accountability standards may be subject to local, state, or federal **sanctions**. For a first-time failure, consequences may not be severe. The district will likely have to provide notice to parents and the community that accountability standards were not met. The district may then have to develop a **formal plan** that outlines changes to help meet accountability standards the following year. Many school districts have strategies and supports in place for schools that do not meet accountability standards. Additionally, the state and federal government provide **resources** for these schools. The goal is not to punish school staff but to provide the resources and supports necessary to increase the likelihood of student success. This may include training and professional development, consulting staff, curriculum, and more. However, districts that **consistently fail to meet accountability standards** may experience more severe consequences. These may include changing or removing staff, changing the district leader, implementing specialized or more stringent school programming, or even closing some schools.

Decreasing Student Dropout Rates

A district's dropout rate is measured for district accountability. Dropouts miss their educational opportunity; consequently, many district leaders are developing creative ways to **decrease dropout rates**. To encourage students to remain in school, leaders are implementing more engaging **curricular programs** and featuring **career pathways** and opportunities to earn **college credit**. Other strategies include providing mentoring programs, offering a variety of extracurricular activities besides sports, and providing counseling and other mental health services. Also, some districts offer **accelerated school programming** to potential or recovered dropouts in an effort to help them to graduate more quickly. To encourage dropouts to return to school, districts are providing assistance, support, and resources to **families**. This type of support often requires partnership with other **organizations** within the community. District leaders and other staff often visit homes in the community to persuade students who have dropped out to return to school.

Chapter Quiz

Ready to see how well you retained what you just read? Scan the QR code to go directly to the chapter quiz interface for this study guide. If you're using a computer, simply visit the online resources page at **mometrix.com/resources719/osatsuper248** and click the Chapter Quizzes link.

OSAT Practice Test #1

Want to take this practice test in an online interactive format?
Check out the online resources page, which includes interactive practice questions and much more: **mometrix.com/resources719/osatsuper248**

1. After several occurrences of student misconduct within the district, a superintendent has decided to revise and update the student code of conduct. Which of the following measures should the superintendent take first to help ensure that the new code of conduct is equitable and addresses student behavior in a positive, fair, consistent, and unbiased manner?

a. Review a pre-existing student code of conduct from another district to gather ideas.
b. Delegate the responsibility of drafting the new student code of conduct to the principal of each school within the district.
c. Assign the task of developing the new student code of conduct to the district's legal team to ensure strict compliance with state and federal guidelines.
d. Engage a committee of administrators and school board members to collaborate in updating the student code of conduct.

2. This year, a superintendent is working closely with principals across the school district in crafting a strategic roadmap for success comprising the following initiatives:

1. Promote a collaborative atmosphere that encourages learning and development for educators
2. Integrate state-of-the-art technology to enhance teaching methods and student participation
3. Establish a systematic framework for continuous student assessment to inform instruction
4. Implement a series of tailored professional growth programs for educators

Which of the following is most likely the central objective guiding these initiatives?

a. Fostering stronger bonds among teachers and school administrators
b. Showcasing the school's modern educational practices to stakeholders
c. Positioning the school district as an exemplary educational institution
d. Creating a culture that actively promotes continuous improvement

3. The superintendent of a historically underperforming school district recognizes the potential for improving student achievement and well-being by cultivating meaningful and productive connections with families to create a comprehensive learning environment. However, many community members in the district are reluctant to engage in the educational program. Which of the following initiatives would be most effective in addressing this issue?

a. Collaborating with local businesses to offer incentives and rewards for family involvement in the education program
b. Conducting a comprehensive district-wide survey to determine the perspectives of families on ways in which the district can enhance engagement with them
c. Scheduling quarterly parent-teacher conferences to provide updates on student progress and address any concerns
d. Implementing a district-wide social media campaign to promote school events and encourage family participation

4. Upon realizing the budget limitations for acquiring technology resources in the district, the superintendent begins research to identify a national technology foundation that offers grants. With the intention of applying for a grant, the superintendent begins drafting a proposal. Which of the following elements should the superintendent ensure is included in this proposal?

a. A comprehensive overview of the district's academic programs and initiatives to showcase the overall educational environment
b. A brief overview of the district's history and accomplishments related to technology integration in the curriculum
c. A list of potential educational technology vendors that the district plans to work with to acquire resources
d. The district's goals, objectives, and a clear explanation of how the requested funds will be utilized to acquire specific technology resources

5. A superintendent of a historically underperforming district is reviewing student assessment data in mathematics from previous school years with the intention of developing strategies to increase engagement and improve academic performance in this subject area. Which of the following approaches would best facilitate informed decision-making for instructional improvement throughout this process?

a. Identifying specific mathematics concepts or skills within the assessments where students demonstrate the most growth and areas for improvement
b. Conducting a district-wide survey to gather student feedback on their preferred instructional methods in mathematics
c. Analyzing student attendance records to identify correlations between attendance and mathematics performance
d. Creating a test preparation program to improve student learning outcomes on mathematics assessments

6. In a school district that emphasizes promoting a culture of respect, inclusivity, and academic excellence, the superintendent has developed a mission that centers on providing a nurturing environment that supports every student's unique potential. To achieve a shared understanding of these principles, the superintendent recognizes the importance of modeling the district's core values in all aspects of her leadership. Which of the following actions would best exemplify this commitment?

a. Hosting monthly town hall meetings to discuss the district's mission and values with teachers, parents, and community members
b. Creating an annual district-wide event that showcases student achievements aligned with the core values of respect and inclusivity
c. Offering professional development sessions for teachers that emphasize the importance of academic excellence and fostering each student's potential
d. Demonstrating respectful and inclusive behavior during interactions with students, staff, parents, and community members

7. This school year, the district superintendent has established a comprehensive performance evaluation system that includes regular feedback and professional development opportunities for school leaders and staff members. Which of the following best describes the likely effect of implementing this strategy?

a. Lowering professional expectations to accommodate the varying skill and comfort levels of staff members
b. Allowing individual staff members to set their own professional goals based on personal preferences and teaching styles
c. Establishing clear and high expectations for professional practice at all levels within the district
d. Fostering autonomy and communicating a sense of trust that staff members will naturally meet professional expectations

8. A superintendent and the district board of education are working together to select a new principal for one of the district's elementary schools. Which of the following actions would best demonstrate the superintendent's understanding of their role while promoting openness, transparency, and accountability throughout this process?

a. Collaborating with educational experts to ensure that the selection process aligns with best practices
b. Allowing key stakeholders in the district to vote upon their preferred candidate
c. Consulting with teachers, staff, and parents to gather input and perspectives on the desired qualities and qualifications for the new principal
d. Appointing a principal from another school district to ensure that the elementary school receives a qualified and experienced candidate

9. The superintendent of a school district is dedicated to promoting equitable access to education and prioritizing the well-being of all students. Among the district's goals is the commitment to supporting students' nutritional needs through free and reduced-price breakfast and lunch programs. To achieve this, the superintendent must demonstrate effective management of both physical and financial resources. Which of the following actions best exemplifies the superintendent's understanding of acquiring and managing resources in alignment with this goal while specifically addressing the free and reduced-price breakfast and lunch program?

a. Conducting a comprehensive cost analysis to optimize the budget and allocate additional funds for free and reduced-price breakfast and lunch programs
b. Partnering with local farms to plant a school garden and incorporate fresh produce into school meals
c. Expanding the district's physical education programs to promote healthier eating habits among students
d. Hiring additional staff members in the food services department to manage the free and reduced-price breakfast and lunch program

10. In an effort to enhance teaching and learning in schools throughout the district, the superintendent has introduced a new initiative that provides every student with a personal tablet or laptop. As part of this initiative, all administrators and teachers have received professional development opportunities centered on integrating and applying new technology tools into the classroom. To further support educators in confidently and seamlessly integrating technology into their instructional practices, which of the following additional measures would be most effective?

a. Providing ongoing technical support and troubleshooting assistance throughout the school year
b. Having teachers log each time they incorporate technology resources into classroom instruction to promote accountability
c. Removing all traditional teaching methods and materials to rely exclusively on the new laptops and tablets
d. Hiring technology specialists to assist in daily classroom instruction to ensure that technology resources are utilized effectively

11. This year, the superintendent of a school district is committed to fostering stronger community engagement and improving communication with students' families. Their objective is to create a comprehensive public relations program that utilizes various communication channels to build community relationships, promote transparency, and increase stakeholder involvement. Which TWO of the following strategies would be most effective in achieving this goal?

a. Utilizing a popular social media platform to share regular updates on school events, important announcements, and achievements
b. Emailing weekly newsletters to parents and community members to highlight school news and upcoming events
c. Conducting an annual survey to gather feedback, suggestions, and insights related to the education program
d. Creating a website for the school district that provides contact details, academic calendars, and school policies

12. The superintendent of a school district has been working to build an educational environment focused on continuous and lasting improvement. To achieve this, she recognizes the importance of regularly evaluating and refining the district's mission, vision, and core values. As part of this effort, the superintendent has established a cross-functional team consisting of teachers, parents, community leaders, and students to collaboratively review the district's goals and values. Working together, the team analyzes data, gathers feedback, and identifies areas for enhancement to ensure that the district remains aligned with its mission. Which of the following options best captures the key benefit of this approach?

a. Improving the district's public reputation by highlighting the collaborative nature of decision-making processes
b. Enhancing the efficiency of administrative tasks to allow more time for curriculum development
c. Ensuring that the district's goals and values are relevant and responsive to evolving needs and expectations
d. Meeting regulatory requirements for annual reporting on district performance

13. In a school district with a vision of promoting sustainability and environmental consciousness, a superintendent aims to align the district's physical resources and support services accordingly. As part of this initiative, the superintendent plans to implement a waste reduction program that involves composting food waste from the school cafeterias and creating school gardens with the composted material. The harvested produce from the garden will then be used in the cafeteria, reducing the need for external sourcing. Which of the following actions best aligns with the superintendent's goal while effectively managing physical resources and support services?

a. Partnering with local food suppliers to purchase organic and locally sourced produce for the school cafeterias to ensure healthier meal options for students
b. Introducing a new after-school program focused on environmental education and sustainability
c. Implementing a district-wide recycling program for paper, plastic, and other recyclable materials
d. Collaborating with local waste management companies to establish a composting system that can efficiently handle the food waste generated by the school cafeterias

14. A school district is exploring the possibility of introducing a new STEM enrichment program for elementary school students that is designed to enhance learning through hands-on experiences and the integration of science, technology, engineering, and mathematics into daily instruction. However, there are some concerns among members of the board regarding the program's value, cost, and potential impact. Which of the following approaches would be most effective for the superintendent to advocate for the value of the STEM enrichment program and gain support among hesitant board members for its implementation?

a. Presenting only the positive aspects of the program in an effort to convince board members of its value and importance
b. Validating the board's hesitations and explaining that the positive outcomes of the program outweigh any potential negative aspects
c. Presenting research-based evidence and success stories from other districts or schools that have implemented similar STEM enrichment programs to showcase the positive outcomes and benefits for students
d. Collaborating with district board members to devise an alternative to a STEM enrichment program

15. A superintendent is preparing for an upcoming district board of education meeting to discuss the implementation of a new curriculum framework. Which of the following should the superintendent prioritize before the meeting to ensure compliance with state and federal laws regarding district board meetings?

a. Prepare a detailed presentation on the new curriculum framework to inform board members about its key components.
b. Ensure that all board members have access to meeting agendas and relevant documents.
c. Invite guest speakers from other districts to share their experiences with implementing similar curriculum frameworks.
d. Schedule the meeting at a convenient time for all board members to maximize attendance and participation.

16. A superintendent has a goal of increasing mental health support services for students across the school district. Faced with budget constraints, the superintendent is actively seeking strategies that maximize resources and promote cost-effectiveness. Which of the following strategies would be most effective in achieving this goal while considering financial limitations?

a. Implementing a district-wide professional development program for teachers and staff focused on mental health training
b. Collaborating with neighboring school districts to share licensed therapists and counselors
c. Hiring additional school counselors to provide individualized support to students
d. Collaborating with local community organizations to establish an after-school mental health program

17. In a school district with a significant English Language Learner (ELL) population, the superintendent has noticed that many ELL students are facing challenges in language acquisition and academic progress. Despite the presence of an English as a Second Language (ESL) program, these students are still struggling to comprehend class materials and actively participate in instruction due to challenges in communicating effectively in English. To address these issues, the superintendent is actively working on developing an intervention plan. Which of the following components should be incorporated into this plan to cater to the individual needs of these students and provide essential support for English Language acquisition?

a. Hiring additional administrative staff to oversee and manage the current ESL program
b. Increasing the availability of extracurricular activities to improve students' language skills outside of the classroom
c. Implementing a peer tutoring program where proficient English-speaking students are paired with ELL students
d. Focusing on improving students' academic performance across subjects with the intention of building academic language skills

18. A superintendent is leading an initiative to revise the district's discipline policies in order to promote restorative practices and reduce the use of punitive measures. Throughout the process, the superintendent intends to work collaboratively with the district board of education and involve them in decision-making. Which of the following initial actions would be most effective in promoting the development of consensus regarding decisions related to the revised discipline policies?

a. Conducting a comprehensive review of the current discipline policies to identify strengths and areas for improvement
b. Organizing a series of focus group workshops with board members to facilitate the exchange of ideas about restorative practices
c. Presenting board members with research-based evidence and case studies on successful implementation of restorative practices in other school districts
d. Facilitating collaborative decision-making sessions with board members to collectively analyze advantages and disadvantages of different disciplinary strategies and work toward devising new policies

19. A superintendent has recently noticed a decline in reading proficiency among elementary school students across the district. To address this issue, they are considering various approaches for implementing intervention systems to provide support and improve reading skills for each student. Which of the following initial steps would best align with the goal of developing effective intervention systems to address individual student needs and provide appropriate support?

a. Increasing the number of extracurricular activities related to literacy and English Language Arts
b. Establishing a school-wide reading assessment program that measures reading proficiency across all grade levels
c. Allocating additional funds for resources and materials to enhance language and literacy skill development
d. Providing teacher training workshops to improve instruction in English Language Arts

20. The superintendent of a school district is currently working on the development of a comprehensive district-wide policy regarding the sharing of student information on social media platforms. This initiative reflects the superintendent's understanding of the importance of adhering to which of the following federal laws?

a. The Every Student Succeeds Act (ESSA)
b. The Individuals with Disabilities Education Act (IDEA)
c. The Family Educational Rights and Privacy Act (FERPA)
d. The Health Insurance Portability and Accountability Act (HIPAA)

Refer to the following for questions 21–22:

> The superintendent of a school district has recently introduced a new comprehensive digital literacy program aimed at enhancing students' technological skills and fostering digital citizenship. After the initial implementation, it becomes apparent that the outcomes of the program are not uniformly successful across all grade levels and schools. Recognizing the benefits of a multifaceted approach, the superintendent plans to address this challenge from various angles. With the program's overarching goal in mind, they begin developing strategies to refine, adapt, and tailor the initiative to ensure that every student achieves success in the digital literacy program.

21. To evaluate the program's effectiveness and develop a strategic plan for improvement, which actions should the superintendent consider for gathering quantitative information? Select the TWO most effective options.

a. Forming a committee to review and redesign the entire program based on student engagement metrics to ensure alignment with students' interests and needs
b. Using digital tools to track student engagement, such as time spent on digital activities, completion rates of assignments, and interaction with online resources
c. Collecting data on the number of computers and devices used by students during the program's implementation
d. Implementing pre- and post-assessments to measure students' digital competencies relevant to the program's objectives
e. Distributing surveys to parents throughout the district to gather feedback regarding their opinions on the program's effectiveness to guide improvements

22. To evaluate the program's effectiveness and develop a strategic plan for improvement, which actions should the superintendent consider for gathering qualitative information? Select the TWO most effective options.

a. Conducting classroom observations to directly witness the program's implementation
b. Having students complete an online survey to provide feedback on their experiences with the digital literacy program
c. Holding a single focus group session with students from different schools throughout the district to gather their feedback on ways to improve the program
d. Conducting feedback sessions with teachers and parents to gather their insights into their experiences with the program
e. Analyzing data from attendance records to assess students' participation rates in the digital literacy program

23. A school district has recently experienced a rise in enrollment of students with special needs across all grade levels. Recognizing the importance of catering to the diverse learning needs of these students, the superintendent aims to promote instructional practices that align with students' learning and developmental stages while considering individual differences. The goal is to create an educational setting where students with special needs can actively engage in meaningful and relevant learning experiences that promote their academic growth, personal development, and overall achievement. Which of the following curriculum planning approaches would be most effective in achieving this?

a. Developing a standardized curriculum that maintains high academic expectations for all students and promotes inclusivity
b. Establishing a project-based learning curriculum that promotes hands-on learning to address students' diverse learning needs and preferences
c. Implementing a differentiated instruction approach that tailors instructional materials and practices to accommodate students with special needs
d. Adopting a technology-based curriculum to increase the availability of support and resources for students with special needs

24. A superintendent is seeking to identify potential partners to help achieve the district's goal of promoting career readiness among high school students through meaningful, real-world learning experiences. Which of the following would be most effective in achieving this goal?

a. Collaborating with local businesses to establish internship programs, mentoring, and job shadowing opportunities for students
b. Partnering with local colleges and universities to offer dual enrollment programs that offer college credits for completed courses
c. Connecting with nonprofit organizations in the community that offer vocational training for specific trades and industries
d. Coordinating with professionals in the community to hold career-focused workshops and guest speaker events to expose students to various career options

Refer to the following for questions 25–26:

> Dr. Hill, a superintendent, has recently learned that the staff of a culturally diverse high school within the district has been having trouble relating to and understanding students from backgrounds different than their own. The staff's limited cultural competence and understanding of diverse perspectives hinders their ability to effectively engage with and support students, leading to strained relationships and communication barriers. As a result, there is a disconnect between the staff and students that negatively impacts the overall school climate and student achievement. Upon learning this information, Dr. Hill sets the goal of improving the cultural

competence and responsiveness of the staff members of this high school to foster a more supportive and inclusive educational experience for all students.

25. Which of the following measures should Dr. Hill take first to address the issues presented in the scenario and work toward improving cultural competency and responsiveness among staff members of this high school?

a. Implement mandatory professional development focused on cultural competency for all staff members.
b. Establish a council in which students have the opportunity to express concerns and ideas, share experiences, and contribute to education-related decision making.
c. Examine student assessment scores to evaluate gaps in achievement between different cultural groups.
d. Conduct a comprehensive assessment of the school's current cultural competency and develop a targeted improvement plan.

26. Which of the following actions would best demonstrate Dr. Hill's commitment to improving cultural competency and responsiveness among staff members at this high school?

a. Emphasizing the importance of student academic achievement over cultural understanding
b. Facilitating professional learning communities in which staff can share ideas, instructional strategies, and experiences in working with students from different cultural backgrounds
c. Assigning a district-level cultural liaison to lead workshops where staff can learn about different cultural practices and perspectives
d. Assigning staff members to shadow and observe teachers who have successfully built strong relationships with students from diverse cultural backgrounds

27. A school superintendent becomes aware that a significant number of students in his district are experiencing food insecurity. While a free and reduced meal program has already been implemented during the school day, many students have limited access to nutritious meals outside of school hours. This situation is negatively impacting students' academic performances and overall well-being. Which of the following actions would be most effective in enhancing the community's support to advocate for the needs of these students?

a. Developing an informational campaign to raise awareness among families and community members about the impact of food insecurity on academic achievement and child development
b. Implementing a nutrition education program to teach students and their families about meal planning on a limited budget
c. Organizing a community fundraising event to provide financial assistance to food-insecure students and their families
d. Working with local food banks and community organizations to create a district-wide weekend meal program for food-insecure students

28. This school year, a district is facing budget cuts that have the potential to greatly affect the accessibility and quality of essential programs and resources for students. Recognizing the significance of the situation, the superintendent plans to work with the district board of education to confront these challenges. Which of the following would be the most effective approach for the superintendent to work alongside the board in addressing budgetary constraints and advocating for the value of public education?

a. Collaborating with board members to analyze budgetary challenges, prioritize impactful programs, and explore creative solutions for mitigating the impact of budget cuts
b. Requesting a meeting with the board to express frustration about budget cuts and insist that funding for essential programs and resources be restored
c. Harnessing community support to persuade the board into reversing their decisions and restoring the budget
d. Forming a committee of teachers, administrators, and parents to work with the board in developing strategies for addressing budget cuts

29. A school district has recently received a generous grant to support its STEM programs and initiatives. The grant comes with specific guidelines on how the funds should be used to enhance STEM education and opportunities for students. To maximize the impact of the grant, the superintendent has created a detailed budget plan to outline how the funds will be allocated. Which of the following additional measures would be beneficial in ensuring ethical and accountable management of the grant funds?

a. Using the grant funds to hire additional staff members to manage the implementation of STEM programs and initiatives
b. Working with the district's finance team to implement financial audits and performance evaluations of the STEM programs
c. Allocating grant funds to provide teachers with professional development opportunities focused on STEM instruction
d. Delegating the task of managing grant funds to principals at individual schools within the district

30. During a visit to a school in their district, a superintendent observes that students from diverse backgrounds are not actively engaged in extracurricular activities and do not feel a sense of belonging. This lack of representation and participation is negatively impacting the school's culture and climate. Which of the following actions would be most effective in helping the school create a more inclusive and supportive environment for all students?

a. Issuing a memo to all schools in the district about the importance of incorporating diversity into extracurricular activities
b. Allocating additional funds for teacher professional development focused on the benefits of extracurricular activities on student academic success
c. Collaborating with administrators, teachers, and staff to develop and implement a comprehensive plan for diverse and inclusive extracurricular activities that reflect the interests and backgrounds of all students
d. Implementing an incentive system to encourage student participation in extracurricular activities

31. In one of the district's middle schools, teachers have been noticing a concerning rise in incidents of bullying. Despite teachers noticing an increase in incidents, the number of reports of bullying from students has not changed. The superintendent acknowledges the importance of promptly addressing this ethical concern. Which of the following actions should the superintendent take first to establish a secure system for reporting and addressing bullying incidents?

a. Organizing assemblies across the district to raise awareness about the negative impacts of bullying
b. Implementing strict disciplinary measures against any students suspected of being involved in bullying to send a strong message about the unacceptability of such behavior
c. Reviewing and revising the student code of conduct to include strict policies regarding bullying behaviors
d. Establishing a confidential reporting system that allows students, parents, and staff to securely and anonymously report incidents of bullying

32. A school superintendent has initiated a program called Family Literacy Night, where parents and students can engage in interactive reading activities, storytelling sessions, and book clubs led by teachers and librarians. Which of the following best describes the primary purpose of this initiative?

a. Providing a space for parents and students to socialize and network with other families in the community
b. Providing an opportunity for parents and students to receive additional tutoring and academic support in reading and literacy
c. Fostering positive partnerships between schools and families to support student literacy development
d. Preparing students for the standardized assessment in English Language Arts by providing additional reading practice and resources

33. The superintendent of a school district has noticed a decline in student engagement and participation in extracurricular activities over the past year. The trend seems to be affecting students' overall sense of belonging and enthusiasm for their educational experience. The superintendent believes that adjustments may be needed in the district's mission, vision, and core values to address this issue and ensure the continued growth and well-being of all students. Which of the following strategies would be most effective in engaging stakeholders in the process of achieving this goal?

a. Organizing a public forum meeting to discuss the issue and develop new strategies for promoting extracurricular involvement
b. Conducting a district-wide survey to gather input from students, parents, teachers, and community members about their perceptions of the decline in student engagement
c. Sending a district-wide email to staff, parents, and students about the benefits of participation in extracurricular activities on academic achievement and development
d. Hosting a series of workshops led by teachers and administrators to educate parents and community members about the benefits of participation in extracurricular activities

34. The superintendent of a school district has noticed a decline in student engagement and motivation in high school science classrooms. She believes that incorporating real-world problem-solving and hands-on experiences will help students become more invested in learning. Which of the following actions are most consistent with this belief?

a. Standardizing the science curriculum across all high schools to ensure consistency in instructional practices
b. Encouraging teachers to incorporate formative assessments into science instruction to assess student engagement
c. Organizing collaborative workshops with local scientists and engineers to create authentic learning experiences for students
d. Allocating additional funds to high schools to purchase new textbooks and equipment for science instruction

35. When developing a student code of conduct, which of the following considerations should a superintendent prioritize to ensure compliance with the Individuals with Disabilities Education Act (IDEA) and address student discipline?

a. Applying the same disciplinary consequences to all students, regardless of individual needs or disabilities
b. Exempting students with disabilities from disciplinary actions to avoid potential conflicts with IDEA requirements
c. Incorporating clear provisions that outline how disciplinary actions will be tailored to the individual needs of students with disabilities in accordance with IDEA requirements
d. Adopting a positive behavior intervention and support (PBIS) system that encourages desired behavior among all students

36. This year, a school district's superintendent is focused on enhancing language and literacy instruction across all grade levels. To achieve this goal, the superintendent has introduced regular district-wide, grade-level team meetings in which educators can discuss literacy challenges, exchange successful teaching practices, and devise strategies to meet the diverse needs of students. In addition to improving literacy instruction, which of the following best describes the benefit of implementing these meetings?

a. Enabling educators to socialize and build stronger bonds, resulting in an improved staff morale throughout the district
b. Supporting staff development through job-embedded, collaborative professional learning opportunities
c. Providing a platform for educators to showcase their professional achievements and accomplishments
d. Differentiating professional learning opportunities to align with the interests and career goals of individual educators

37. The superintendent of a school district has been revising and developing an effective crisis response plan to address potential intruder situations. As part of this effort, they have been collaborating with local law enforcement agencies and security experts to assess and update the current plan, ensuring it incorporates the latest intruder response strategies. To further strengthen the effectiveness and efficiency of the district's crisis management plan in preparing for potential intruder situations, which of the following measures should the superintendent prioritize?

a. Assigning the responsibility of crisis management plan implementation to the district's security personnel
b. Allocating additional funds for purchasing surveillance cameras to monitor entrances and exits
c. Establishing an anonymous tip line for reporting security threats within the district
d. Conducting regular response drills in schools to familiarize students and staff with crisis management procedures and protocols

38. A school district is experiencing changes in demographics and student enrollment patterns due to population shifts in different neighborhoods. To address these shifts effectively, the superintendent seeks to cultivate collaborative relationships between feeder and connecting schools within the district through a vertical teaming approach. Which of the following actions best aligns with this objective?

a. Holding a meeting with administrators from feeder and connecting schools to discuss enrollment management and curricular alignment
b. Providing a professional development workshop for teachers from feeder and connecting schools to align instructional practices and curriculum
c. Assigning teachers from feeder schools to work at connecting schools to address enrollment imbalances
d. Implementing an online platform where teachers and administrators from feeder and connecting schools can share resources and collaborate on curricular and instructional matters

39. In a school district with a diverse group of administrators, teachers, and staff, the superintendent is committed to promoting professional growth and development through differentiated opportunities. One teacher in particular has expressed interest in enhancing his educational leadership skills. The superintendent aims to provide him with suitable research-based professional development to support this teacher's growth in this area. Which TWO of the following professional learning opportunities should the superintendent consider providing?

a. An online course on classroom management strategies
b. A workshop on implementing technology in the classroom
c. A mentoring program with an experienced administrator
d. Attendance at a conference on student engagement techniques
e. A training program focused on educational leadership and school management

Refer to the following for questions 40–42:

> This school year, a district is implementing a new project-based learning curriculum designed to enhance student engagement and promote the development of critical thinking skills across all grade levels. This curriculum focuses on hands-on learning experiences that require students to apply their knowledge and skills to solve problems in real-world scenarios. Throughout the year, the superintendent intends to employ multiple strategies to continuously monitor the implementation of the new program and evaluate its effect on student learning and academic success.

40. Which of the following strategies would be most beneficial in evaluating the effectiveness of the project-based learning curriculum and its instructional practices?

a. Analyzing student performance data on project-based assessments to determine their ability to apply knowledge and skills in real-world contexts
b. Communicating with teachers to gather their input on the alignment of instructional practices with project-based learning targets
c. Consulting key stakeholders to gather feedback regarding the practicality and relevance of project-based learning experiences
d. Researching the effectiveness of project-based learning in neighboring districts that have adopted similar programs

41. To measure the impact of project-based learning on students' growth in critical thinking skills, the superintendent plans to administer pre- and post- assessments at the beginning and end of the school year, respectively. This strategy will allow the superintendent to do which of the following?

a. Measure the effectiveness of project-based learning in promoting student engagement and collaboration.
b. Evaluate the impact and effectiveness of the project-based curriculum on student learning and growth.
c. Gather feedback from students regarding their perceptions of project-based learning.
d. Evaluate teachers' overall competency in implementing a project-based learning curriculum.

42. In addition to the superintendent's previous actions, which of the following approaches would be most helpful in evaluating the overall effectiveness of the project-based learning program in promoting student growth and achievement?

a. Conducting student satisfaction surveys regarding their overall experience with project-based learning
b. Analyzing student attendance records to assess their engagement with project-based learning activities
c. Leading regular reflection and collaboration meetings with school administrators and teachers to discuss student progress, engagement, and overall achievement
d. Communicating with superintendents from neighboring districts to seek input on best practices for implementing a project-based learning curriculum

Refer to the following for questions 43–44:

> The superintendent of a school district is responsible for approving contracts with vendors for various educational services and supplies. One of the vendors under consideration is a close personal friend of the superintendent. This vendor offers a significant discount on their services compared to other vendors in the market. The services provided by this vendor are aligned with the district's needs and would offer potential cost savings for the district.

43. Which of the following best describes the potential ethical concern with considering a contract with this particular vendor?

a. The superintendent's personal relationship with the vendor may cause a conflict of interest, which could compromise impartial decision-making.
b. The vendor's discount may indicate a lack of quality or reliability in their services.
c. The superintendent should prioritize supporting local businesses and organizations, regardless of personal relationships.
d. The superintendent may accept sub-par services in favor of prioritizing their personal relationship with the vendor.

44. Which of the following actions would be most effective for the superintendent to avoid a potential conflict of interest in this scenario?

a. Proceed with approving the contract, as the vendor offers a significant discount and meets the district's needs.
b. Seek guidance from the school board on whether to proceed with the contract.
c. Recuse herself from the decision-making process and assign the responsibility to another administrator or committee.
d. Disclose the personal relationship with the vendor to the appropriate stakeholders and seek their input before making a decision.

45. The superintendent of a school district aims to enhance communication and collaboration among teachers to foster a more cohesive and supportive educational community. Currently, teachers face challenges in sharing resources efficiently, leading to unnecessary extra work and limited access to teaching materials. To address this issue, the superintendent is seeking a solution that can streamline resource sharing and promote a collaborative culture among educators in the district. Which of the following strategies would be most effective in achieving this goal?

a. Establishing monthly meetings for teachers to exchange physical copies of teaching materials and resources
b. Implementing an online repository where teachers can easily upload, access, and download teaching resources and materials
c. Providing teachers with a set of USB drives containing various teaching resources to share among grade-level teams
d. Encouraging teachers to communicate and collaborate through email and file attachments to exchange teaching resources and materials

46. A superintendent receives a report from a concerned parent regarding an incident of bullying in one of the schools within the district. The parent claims that his child has been subjected to verbal and physical harassment by her peers. Which of the following responses would best exemplify dedication to creating a safe, caring, and healthy environment for all students?

a. Issuing a school-wide statement about the importance of respectful behavior without directly addressing the incident
b. Assuring the parent that the school will investigate the matter and implement appropriate disciplinary measures
c. Organizing an assembly in which the School Resource Officer and guidance counselor speak to the school about the negative impacts of bullying
d. Collaborating with teachers, counselors, and administrators to develop and implement a comprehensive anti-bullying program that includes education, prevention, and intervention strategies

47. A newly appointed superintendent is actively working to craft a new district mission with a clear focus on cultivating both inclusivity and academic excellence, aimed at equipping students for success in a globalized society. The superintendent is determined to create a strong bond between the district's mission, vision, and core values, all while ensuring that this understanding is shared throughout the educational community. To achieve this, the superintendent recognizes the importance of communicating the mission to key stakeholders, including students, parents, educators, and community members, through multiple avenues to foster a united commitment toward a common goal. Which TWO of the following approaches would be most effective in accomplishing this?

a. Conducting quarterly meetings where parents, teachers, and students can collectively discuss and reflect upon the district's effectiveness in promoting inclusivity and academic excellence and preparing students for a globalized society
b. Publishing an annual newsletter that highlights student success stories, showcasing the positive impact of the district's new mission and its influence in preparing students for success in a globalized society
c. Hosting a monthly webinar for students, parents, educators, and community members to discuss information, updates, and accomplishments related to fostering inclusivity and academic excellence and preparing students for a globalized society
d. Distributing a handbook to students, parents, and district staff that outlines the district's mission, vision, and core values, along with examples of practical strategies for promoting inclusivity and academic excellence and preparing students for a globalized society
e. Conducting an anonymous online survey for parents, teachers, and students to gather feedback on their preferences regarding the district's mission, vision, and goals

48. In a district comprising several schools with diverse student populations, one elementary school in particular, located in a low-income neighborhood, stands out due to its limited and outdated collection of books and other media in the school library. In contrast to other schools within the district, this elementary school lacks the resources necessary to provide a comparable selection of reading materials for its students. While the superintendent acknowledges the importance of equitable resource access for every student, budget limitations impede the allocation of additional funds for library and media resources at this specific school. Considering these circumstances, which of the following measures would be most appropriate for addressing this imbalance and fostering equity among all students?

a. Transferring a portion of library resources from other schools in the district to the elementary school in need
b. Asking families from the elementary school in need to donate unwanted books from home to the school library
c. Seeking donations or sponsorships from local businesses and community organizations to fund library and media resources for the elementary school in need
d. Encouraging teachers and staff at the elementary school in need to develop innovative strategies for utilizing limited library media resources

49. In a school district facing increased demands for student support services and limited financial resources, the superintendent aims to optimize district efficiency while ensuring that teachers and staff are assigned roles that leverage their professional expertise to effectively meet student learning needs. The district is currently experiencing a surge in students requiring individualized support, such as counseling, special education, and English language instruction. Despite budget constraints, the superintendent aims to implement strategic resource allocation and staff assignment to maintain a high standard of learning for all students. Which of the following would be most effective in achieving this goal?

a. Developing a job-rotation program that allows teachers and staff to gain experience in different roles within the district
b. Conducting regular teacher and staff evaluations to identify individual strengths and areas for growth and allow for strategic staff assignment
c. Forming collaborative teams of teachers, specialists, and support staff to identify student learning needs and design comprehensive, tailored intervention plans
d. Reducing the number of support staff positions to save on costs and allocating additional funding for instructional resources and materials

50. A newly appointed superintendent has a goal of fostering a cohesive and collaborative educational environment that prioritizes student success. To achieve this goal, the superintendent is committed to building strong and productive partnerships with key stakeholders in the district, including members of the district board of education. Which of the following approaches would be most effective in successfully establishing and maintaining these relationships?

a. Sending out weekly newsletters to inform board members about important information and updates regarding the education program
b. Facilitating regular meetings with the district board of education to discuss key issues, provide updates, and align priorities to achieve shared goals
c. Engaging in collaborative sessions with teachers and staff members across the district to negotiate contracts, working conditions, and benefits
d. Organizing regular town hall meetings where members of the school community can express concerns and discuss matters related to the education program

51. Which of the following measures by a superintendent would be most effective in addressing the academic and social needs of students with disabilities while fostering a sense of active engagement in the school community?

a. Maintaining the same high academic expectations for all students, regardless of disability status
b. Establishing a support center in all schools within the district in which students can access academic assistance, tutoring, and social-emotional learning programs
c. Mandating district-wide staff professional development focused on instructional strategies for increasing student engagement
d. Implementing a before-school and after-school tutoring program that is available to all students

52. A school district recently renovated its science labs and acquired new equipment, including chemistry tools, biology instruments, and physics apparatus, to enhance students' hands-on learning experiences. The superintendent is dedicated to prioritizing the safety and well-being of students and staff within the district while ensuring compliance with federal laws and regulations. Which of the following actions best demonstrates a focus on Occupational Safety and Health Administration (OSHA) compliance and effective management of physical resources, particularly in relation to ensuring the safe and proper usage of the newly acquired science equipment in the school district?

a. Implementing a new district-wide science curriculum to optimize the usage of the new equipment
b. Hiring additional custodial staff to manage the maintenance and upkeep of the science labs and equipment
c. Providing teachers and staff with professional development opportunities focused on best practices for integrating the new science equipment into instruction
d. Conducting regular safety inspections of the newly renovated science labs to identify and address potential hazards and ensure OSHA compliance for staff and students using the new equipment

53. The superintendent has received a report from a concerned parent of a high school student that one of her children's teachers is text messaging her child using his personal cell phone number. The texts are personal in nature and are not related to the teacher's class. Which of the following responses would be the most appropriate course of action in this situation?

a. Assigning an investigation to the school's principal to maintain confidentiality and minimize disruption in the school
b. Engaging in a thorough investigation by gathering evidence and interviewing the teacher, student, and any potential witnesses
c. Advising the parent to address the issue directly with the teacher first to avoid any potentially false allegations
d. Suspending the teacher without pay

54. A superintendent has decided to organize and implement a program called the "Student Success Team" in each school within the district. These teams will consist of teachers, counselors, and support staff who collaborate to identify, create, and implement targeted interventions and supports to meet the individual academic and socioeconomic needs of students. Through this initiative, the superintendent likely intends to:

a. Manage staff involvement in addressing students' needs by relying on pre-determined intervention programs.
b. Promote independent initiatives by individual staff members.
c. Establish a collaborative culture where staff collectively address students' diverse academic and socioeconomic needs.
d. Delegate all responsibilities for meeting students' needs to teachers and support staff.

55. A superintendent has recently become aware of a concerning rise in behavioral issues among students at one of the middle schools in the district. Some students are displaying disruptive behaviors in classrooms, while others are involved in conflicts and bullying incidents. To tackle these challenges, the superintendent is focused on creating intervention plans tailored to address the individual behavioral needs of each student and providing the necessary support. Which of the following actions best aligns with the superintendent's goal of effectively addressing these behavioral issues?

a. Expanding the school's sports programs and extracurricular activities to provide more options for students to engage in positive and constructive activities
b. Organizing a student support team consisting of teachers, counselors, and behavior specialists to create personalized behavior intervention plans
c. Installing new security cameras throughout the school to deter misbehavior and maintain a safe environment
d. Providing teachers and staff with professional development opportunities focused on classroom management techniques

56. A school district has recently hired a group of enthusiastic new teachers and promoted several veteran teachers to leadership roles. To address the varied needs of these educators and ensure their continuous professional growth, the superintendent recognizes the importance of providing several differentiated opportunities for learning and development. Which measures from the list below would be effective in addressing the needs of both the veteran and new teachers? Select all that apply.

a. Hosting a district-wide conference with various sessions on innovative teaching methods and classroom management techniques
b. Developing a mentorship program that pairs experienced administrators with new teachers to provide personalized guidance and support
c. Implementing a new evaluation framework and rubric to assess teacher performance in the classroom
d. Establishing a reward system that recognizes the accomplishments and achievements of both novice and experienced staff to encourage continuous improvement
e. Conducting workshops on effective leadership strategies and decision-making skills exclusively for experienced administrators to foster their professional growth
f. Offering specialized training sessions on technology integration to enhance classroom instruction
g. Organizing a single training session for all educators that covers a broad range of topics
h. Providing financial support for administrators and staff to attend professional conferences and workshops that focus on areas relevant to their individual growth and development

57. As part of a plan to improve student learning outcomes in English Language Arts across elementary schools in the district, the superintendent plans to continuously evaluate instructional practices and student progress throughout the school year. Which of the following approaches would be most effective in achieving this goal?

a. Attending a conference on educational leadership to enhance his knowledge of instructional improvement strategies and best practices in English Language Arts instruction
b. Collaborating with English Language Arts teachers to develop common formative assessments aligned with the English Language Arts curriculum and standards, which are administered regularly to monitor student learning and identify areas for improvement
c. Establishing a committee of parents, teachers, and community members to review and analyze student math portfolios to assess their progress and growth over time
d. Conducting a district-wide survey to gather feedback from students and teachers regarding their perception of English Language Arts instruction

58. The superintendent of a school district has a goal of improving students' reading proficiency in elementary grades. To achieve this, the superintendent has implemented a data collection system focused on students' reading comprehension levels, fluency, and vocabulary metrics. This process also includes gathering feedback from teachers and classroom observations. The collected data is then carefully analyzed and shared with teachers and stakeholders to guide decisions and develop targeted strategies to effectively enhance students' reading proficiency skills. Which of the following options best captures the superintendent's approach in using data to improve reading proficiency in the district?

a. Streamlining the data collection process by relying solely on quantitative metrics to increase efficiency
b. Analyzing general reading proficiency levels across the district rather than targeting specific skills to determine the effectiveness of the reading program
c. Creating a comprehensive data collection and analysis system through quantitative and qualitative feedback
d. Relying primarily on personal observations and anecdotal evidence to guide the improvement process

59. Following a significant cybersecurity breach that compromised sensitive student and staff data, the superintendent is collaborating with local IT experts to assess and identify vulnerabilities in the district's current cybersecurity infrastructure and develop a remediation plan. Which of the following additional measures should the superintendent take to help prevent future potential breaches in cybersecurity?

a. Conducting regular cybersecurity training sessions for administrators, teachers, and staff to raise awareness about cybersecurity best practices and risk mitigation
b. Allocating additional funds to purchase advanced cybersecurity software to prevent future breaches
c. Issuing a public statement about the cybersecurity breach detailing remediation measures to protect student and staff data security
d. Assigning crisis management in response to cybersecurity breaches to the district IT team

60. Over the past few years, a school district has experienced a steady increase in the student dropout rate. After careful analysis, the superintendent has identified the need for a targeted improvement strategy to address this concern. Which TWO of the following strategies would be most effective in facilitating both incremental and transformational change?

a. Launching a district-wide campaign promoting the importance of education and the consequences of dropping out to create an immediate impact
b. Implementing an initiative to improve the school's infrastructure, including facilities and technology, with the expectation that better physical resources will reduce the student dropout rate
c. Establishing a mentorship program where experienced teachers work closely with at-risk students to provide individualized support and guidance
d. Overhauling the curriculum and teaching methods to incorporate real-world applications and hands-on learning experiences that make learning more relevant and engaging
e. Holding regular meetings with parents and students to gather feedback and insights, then adjusting school policies and resources accordingly

61. The superintendent of a school district has recently implemented a new district-wide assessment system that will play a significant role in evaluating student performance and determining school rankings. However, some administrators and teachers in the district have expressed concerns about the integrity of the new assessment process, as they suspect that it may be easy for staff members to tamper with student test scores to improve the overall performance of their schools. Which of the following actions would be most effective in ensuring ethical and professional behavior within the district and maintaining the integrity of the assessment process?

a. Implementing stricter security measures to prevent tampering with student test scores, such as assigning independent proctors or using secure online assessment platforms
b. Communicating with administrators and teachers to encourage them to report any observed or suspected instances of tampering with student test scores
c. Conducting an investigation to identify teachers and administrators who express concerns about the new assessment system, as they may be more likely to tamper with student test scores
d. Reviewing the district's assessment policies and procedures and making necessary revisions to enhance transparency, accountability, and the prevention of potential manipulation of student test scores

62. This school year, the superintendent of a school district wants to emphasize technology integration and 21st century skills. The district is planning a new mission focused on equipping students with the skills they need to thrive in a digitally interconnected world while fostering a sense of global citizenship. The superintendent recognizes the importance of developing a shared vision of this goal among teachers, students, parents, and community members. Which of the following approaches would be most effective in supporting the superintendent's aim of cultivating a shared vision among stakeholders?

a. Conducting quarterly focus group discussions with parents, teachers, students, and community members to gather diverse perspectives on how the district's mission and values can be integrated into daily educational practices
b. Initiating a program that pairs students from various grade levels with local businesses to collaborate on projects aligned with the district's core values
c. Distributing a monthly newsletter that features success stories of teachers and students who have demonstrated the district's core values through their projects, initiatives, and contributions to the community
d. Organizing an annual community event where teachers, parents, students, and community members come together to participate in hands-on activities that reflect the district's mission

63. The superintendent of a school district believes that staff morale and student achievement can be improved by increasing opportunities for educators to engage in reflection, study, and professional development. Which of the following strategies would be most effective in achieving this goal?

a. Implementing a strict performance evaluation framework and developing an action plan for underperforming staff members
b. Creating a rigid curriculum framework and measuring teacher effectiveness based on standardized assessment scores
c. Assigning professional development workshops based on staff strengths and weaknesses and enforcing regular mandatory department meetings
d. Establishing a mentorship program and creating a discussion platform for teachers and staff to communicate

64. A superintendent is developing a vision for the district that revolves around community engagement and service. The focus is on creating a holistic educational experience that not only imparts academic knowledge but also cultivates a sense of social responsibility among students. In developing this strategy, which of the following actions best aligns plans to the components of this vision?

a. Initiating partnerships with local nonprofits to integrate service-learning projects into the curriculum
b. Creating a school garden to teach students about plant growth and sustainability
c. Collaborating with local businesses to provide student internships for career exploration
d. Introducing a cultural awareness curriculum to broaden students' awareness of diversity in the community

65. A superintendent has recently recognized the need to address student tardiness in the district's high schools, as it is adversely affecting classroom instruction and overall student success. To create a comprehensive policy that effectively tackles this issue and promotes student achievement, which of the following initial actions should the superintendent prioritize?

a. Assigning additional staff in the high schools to monitor student arrival times
b. Increasing disciplinary actions for tardiness to deter students from arriving late to school
c. Delegating the responsibility of enforcing tardiness policies solely to teachers in the school buildings
d. Collaborating with teachers, administrators, and parents to gain an understanding of the underlying causes of student tardiness

66. A new superintendent has just been appointed to serve in a culturally diverse school district. One of her first priorities is to foster a learning environment that values inclusivity and embraces the unique backgrounds of all students. Which of the following initiatives would best exemplify this commitment?

a. Establishing a program where students from different cultures and backgrounds are paired up to support and learn from one another
b. Organizing a one-time cultural celebration event at the end of the school year in which students can showcase traditional foods, music, and clothing from their cultures
c. Adopting a district-wide bilingual immersion program to promote second-language acquisition among native English-speaking students
d. Providing a diverse range of extracurricular activities to encourage students of all backgrounds to participate and interact with one another

Refer to the following for questions 67–69:

> The superintendent of a school district known for its commitment to fostering equity and inclusiveness is dedicated to ensuring that all students are provided with equal opportunities for success. They believe that the district's core values of equity, inclusiveness, caring, and trust must be reflected in the district's approach to education. Recently, the superintendent has been presented with a chart that displays the academic performance data for various populations of students over the past three years. The

data includes information about students' test scores, attendance rates, and participation in support programs.

Student Group	English Language Arts Test Scores (Average %)	Math Test Scores (Average %)	Average Attendance Rate (%)	Participation in Support Programs (Average %)
English Language Learners	57	60	88	60
Special Education	72	70	84	58
Low-Income	75	68	72	50
General Student Population (Excluding Special Populations)	85	88	90	45

67. Based on the information presented in the chart above, which of the following measures would be most effective in enhancing equity and inclusivity among low-income students in the district?

a. Offering an after-school tutoring program to help improve low-income students' academic performance
b. Implementing a district-wide reward system for students with consistently high attendance rates
c. Allocating additional funding for instructional materials and resources to improve test scores in English Language Arts and Mathematics
d. Providing targeted support initiatives—such as mentoring and family engagement strategies—to improve the attendance rates of low-income students

68. The superintendent is actively seeking strategies to foster a more supportive, equitable, and inclusive learning environment to ultimately improve academic achievement and overall well-being for all student groups. Based on the information presented in the chart above, which of the following actions should the superintendent prioritize?

a. Establishing communication channels between teachers, parents, and students about the availability and benefits of support programs in the district
b. Hiring additional staff to provide students in need with increased individualized instruction
c. Providing teachers in the district with professional development opportunities focused on improving their knowledge in their subject areas
d. Allocating additional funding to purchase new technology equipment to enhance classroom instruction and learning

69. To effectively address the specific needs of English Language Learners (ELLs) and foster an equitable, inclusive, caring, and trusting environment for these students, which of the following actions would be most appropriate based on the information presented in the chart above?

a. Initiating a district-wide campaign to enhance parental engagement among ELL students
b. Increasing the availability of extracurricular activities to provide ELL students with opportunities for social interactions
c. Establishing specialized language support programs designed to promote ELL students' academic language acquisition and proficiency
d. Implementing a reward system to recognize ELL students with high attendance rates, aiming to boost their overall engagement in the learning process

70. Teachers within a particular school district have reported growing concern about a lack of communication and collaboration between teachers and students. They have expressed that students often feel disconnected and disengaged from learning, resulting in a steady decline in academic performance. Which of the following actions could the superintendent take to most effectively address this issue and promote positive relationships between students and staff?

a. Establishing a system in which students can provide anonymous feedback to their teachers about their learning experiences
b. Creating a student advisory council in which students can voice their opinions and actively participate in decision-making processes within their school
c. Organizing regular professional development opportunities for teachers to improve their skills in communicating with students
d. Establishing a mentorship program where teachers are paired with students to provide guidance and support

71. A school district has recently implemented a new reading intervention program aimed at supporting struggling readers in elementary schools. Throughout the school year, the superintendent wants to ensure that administrators and teachers are continuously monitoring student progress and the effectiveness of their instructional practices related to the program. Which of the following strategies would be most effective in achieving this goal?

a. Collaborating with school librarians to create a reading log system for students to track their daily reading progress
b. Conducting regular school visits and classroom observations to ensure that the program and assessments are being correctly implemented
c. Providing administrators and teachers with professional development opportunities focused on data analysis and interpretation techniques
d. Creating a system for teachers to regularly collect and analyze student reading data to identify areas for instructional improvement

72. A superintendent has recently conducted a formal observation of a high school science teacher in the district. To provide valuable feedback and support this teacher's professional development, which of the following steps should the superintendent take next?

a. Follow up with the teacher via email after the observation to acknowledge her efforts and express gratitude for the invitation to her classroom.
b. Ask the teacher to complete a series of reflection questions after the observation to self-assess her effectiveness.
c. Encourage the teacher to adopt a daily reflection practice by journaling about the effectiveness of each lesson, instructional strategies, and overall student engagement.
d. Schedule a post-observation meeting with the teacher to discuss her performance, identify strengths, and work together to set professional development goals based on the rubric and indicators used in the observation.

73. A large outdoor playground with diverse equipment and open spaces has recently been installed at an elementary school in the district. Currently, the playground is only accessible for use during school hours, but the superintendent believes that opening it beyond those hours would have a positive impact on students, families, and community members. Which of the following strategies would be most effective in achieving this goal?

a. Allowing extended access to the playground, but utilizing surveillance measures to ensure safety and proper use of equipment and spaces
b. Implementing policies to ensure that only students and their families have access to the school playground
c. Collaborating with local organizations and community centers to organize supervised recreational activities on the playground during non-school hours
d. Allowing full and open access to the playground equipment and spaces at all times

74. The superintendent of a school district has a goal of creating and implementing a research-based evaluation system that is designed to provide targeted and constructive feedback to support teachers' development. To ensure its successful implementation, which of the following should the superintendent prioritize as a key initial step?

a. Hiring external evaluators to conduct observations independently, ensuring objective assessments aligned with the evaluation framework
b. Communicating the new evaluation system to teachers, staff, and administrators, emphasizing the importance of adherence to the predetermined criteria
c. Developing a set of evaluation guidelines and rubrics based on administrative perspectives to provide consistent feedback across the district
d. Engaging teachers in the design and piloting of the evaluation system, integrating their input and insights to ensure relevance and accuracy

75. Through a comprehensive district-wide survey of administrators, teachers, and staff members, the superintendent discovered concerning evidence indicating that a particular group of students is disproportionately perceived as academically deficient due to their ethnicity and socioeconomic background. Which TWO of the following strategies would be most effective in addressing this issue to mitigate the prevalence of deficit-based education?

a. Collaborating with community organizations and parents to host cultural events and activities that celebrate diversity
b. Establishing tutoring programs that specifically target the identified group of students to provide academic support
c. Establishing a strengths-based framework for instruction that recognizes and builds upon the skills and abilities of the identified group of students
d. Providing professional development opportunities for educators to build cultural competence and develop strategies to counter implicit biases

76. In a middle school within your district, there are several students who exhibit challenges in their social interactions with peers, which results in these students feeling excluded and struggling to form positive relationships. Which of the following responses best showcases a superintendent's dedication to promoting positive relationships and academic learning, as well as healthy social and emotional development for these students?

a. Developing and implementing a social-emotional learning (SEL) curriculum focused on building empathy, effective communication, and relationship skills
b. Implementing an assigned seating arrangement during lunch to encourage students to interact with peers outside of their normal social groups
c. Hosting regular school-wide events that promote collaboration and teamwork
d. Assigning peer tutors to struggling students to provide academic support and foster positive social interactions

77. A newly appointed superintendent is confronted with a multifaceted challenge. Student test scores throughout the district have been consistently low, teacher turnover is high, and community involvement is minimal. Which of the following strategies would be most effective in addressing these issues? Select all that apply.

a. Collaborating only with a select group of veteran teachers to identify the most critical areas for improvement and implement improvements based on their recommendations
b. Developing a comprehensive five-year plan that involves a complete overhaul of the curriculum, introducing innovative teaching methodologies, and restructuring administrative roles to address the district's issues holistically
c. Introducing small, targeted changes to the existing curriculum and teaching methods each academic year to ensure steady progress in student performance while minimizing disruption
d. Allocating a significant budget for acquiring state-of-the-art educational technology and resources, anticipating that these tools will drive positive change across the district
e. Holding regular town hall meetings with teachers, parents, and community members to gather diverse perspectives and then refining the improvement strategy based on community input
f. Prioritizing public relations efforts to highlight the district's strengths and achievements with the expectation that an improved public image will address the underlying academic and community-related issues
g. Establishing a cross-functional task force comprising district officials, teachers, and representatives from community organizations to periodically assess challenges, allowing for an adaptive approach to improvement

78. A newly appointed superintendent in a culturally diverse school district is developing strategies to enhance student learning outcomes in English Language Arts (ELA) across all grade levels. To achieve this, the superintendent has been actively working with a curriculum committee, which includes administrators and teachers, to assess and update the current ELA curriculum. The committee's primary focus is ensuring the curriculum aligns with academic standards, reflecting high expectations for student learning, and promoting cultural responsiveness. Which of the following TWO actions should the superintendent and committee prioritize to achieve this goal?

a. Researching various ELA textbooks and learning materials from different vendors to select books that best align with academic standards and offer rigorous, culturally responsive content
b. Conducting focus groups with students to gather their input and perspectives on the ELA curriculum to ensure that it is culturally responsive and academically rigorous
c. Identifying experienced ELA teachers to individually design and deliver lesson plans that incorporate culturally responsive content
d. Creating professional development workshops focused on culturally responsive teaching methods to help teachers integrate these practices into ELA instruction

79. The superintendent of a school district has identified a significant need for improving mathematics proficiency among middle school students. The current assessment data indicates that performance in mathematics has been consistently below the desired standards. To initiate the process of addressing this challenge, the superintendent has completed a thorough examination of the district's mathematics education goals and objectives. Which subsequent step should the superintendent prioritize in crafting a strategic plan for improving mathematics proficiency across the district?

a. Conducting a needs assessment to determine high-leverage areas of need in mathematics education
b. Aligning goals with the district's vision and overall educational objectives
c. Developing a plan of action to improve mathematics proficiency based on district and school needs
d. Establishing a task force to address the identified gap in mathematics proficiency

80. A school district is in the process of implementing a new formative assessment strategy to monitor student progress and inform instructional practice. Which TWO of the following approaches would be most beneficial in allowing the superintendent to determine the effectiveness and validity of this new assessment method in evaluating student learning?

a. Administering end-of-year standardized assessments to evaluate overall student achievement
b. Conducting regular classroom visits to observe the implementation of the new formative assessment strategy
c. Analyzing student work samples and portfolios to assess their growth and development over time
d. Conducting teacher evaluations based on students' standardized assessment scores

81. In a school district known for its cultural diversity, the superintendent has a vision of cultivating an environment where every student's unique background is not only acknowledged but also integrated into their learning experience. To achieve this, the superintendent aims to implement a comprehensive cultural awareness curriculum throughout all grade levels. Which of the following actions would be most strategic in acquiring the necessary human resources to support the development and implementation of this vision?

a. Hiring a team of technology experts to review and make improvements to digital resources that will be used in the new curriculum
b. Collaborating with local musicians and dancers to organize school assemblies to showcase various cultures through performance
c. Establishing a team of culturally knowledgeable educators, including bilingual instructors, to design and deliver the new curriculum
d. Hiring more counselors and school psychologists who are familiar with different cultures

82. A school district has recently undergone a significant growth in student enrollment, resulting in an increased administrative workload. Consequently, the existing organizational structures have been less efficient in managing the district's growing needs. Administrators and staff members have been facing challenges in coordinating resources, implementing timely decisions, and maintaining smooth operations within the schools. Which of the following TWO strategies would be most effective in addressing these issues to improve efficiency and prevent disruptions to teaching and learning throughout the district?

a. Hiring additional administrative personnel to support the growing demands and responsibilities
b. Engaging in a comprehensive analysis of existing organizational structures to identify areas for improvement and streamline administrative tasks
c. Establishing a weekly communication forum to facilitate collaboration among administrators, teachers, and staff
d. Implementing a task management system that allows administrators and staff to prioritize and track their responsibilities efficiently

83. A superintendent is collaborating with administrators and teachers from elementary schools throughout the district to establish comprehensive strategies that embody the following core principles within curriculum planning and instruction:

- Embracing the individuality of each child and acknowledging their distinctive developmental pace
- Fostering optimal learning through active engagement and exploration of the environment to utilize sensory experiences
- Recognizing the intrinsic value of play as a primary and effective mode of learning for children
- Understanding the interconnectedness and mutual reinforcement of cognitive, physical, social, and emotional development

Which curriculum planning framework do these principles align with?

a. Developmentally Appropriate Practice
b. Culturally Responsive Teaching Framework
c. Evidence-Based Curriculum Model
d. Experiential Learning Approach

84. The superintendent of a school district facing budget constraints is actively seeking new funding opportunities to provide the infrastructure and resources necessary to foster digital literacy and technological competency among students. Which of the following measures should the superintendent take first to achieve this goal and ensure the ethical and accountable management of fiscal resources?

a. Assessing technology needs in schools across the district and allocating existing technology resources accordingly
b. Seeking state aid opportunities that are available for general school programs to allow for flexibility in how the funds are utilized
c. Identifying federal, state, and local grants explicitly designated for technology infrastructure and resources
d. Utilizing surplus funds from previous budget years to purchase technology resources and equipment

Refer to the following for questions 85–87:

> A newly appointed superintendent of a large school district is faced with managing staffing needs across various schools and departments. The district has historically experienced a high turnover rate among administrators and staff, impacting the stability and continuity of educational services. There have also been concerns raised about the effectiveness of the current recruitment and hiring processes, leading to challenges in retaining highly qualified personnel. The superintendent must develop a comprehensive plan for staffing management that addresses these challenges and ensures that the district's recruitment, support, and retention processes are efficient and effective. Additionally, the superintendent must implement procedures for staff discipline, remediation, and dismissal while strictly following due process procedures. The superintendent's ability to navigate these complexities will play a critical role in shaping the district's workforce and maintaining a positive and supportive work environment for administrators and staff.

85. In response to the high turnover rate among administrators and staff in the school district, the superintendent is seeking to establish a more effective system for retaining talented educators. Which of the following strategies would be most effective for achieving this goal?

a. Implementing a standardized recruitment process for all positions within the district to streamline hiring procedures and ensure consistency
b. Increasing the use of temporary contracts for staff members to offer more flexibility in staffing and adapt to changing needs
c. Conducting periodic performance evaluations for all educators and staff members to identify areas for improvement and determine retention strategies
d. Establishing a mentorship program for new administrators and staff members to provide guidance and support during their initial period of employment

86. Which of the following strategies would be most effective in addressing high turnover and retention of administrators and staff for the school district?

a. Partnering with local universities and colleges to establish internship programs that allow aspiring educators to gain experience within the district
b. Conducting in-depth background checks and reference verifications for all candidates
c. Delegating the recruitment and hiring responsibilities to the Human Resources department
d. Implementing an online application program that streamlines the hiring process

87. While developing their staffing management plan, the superintendent encounters a situation involving an employee accused of misconduct that could potentially lead to dismissal. In handling this matter, what is the most appropriate course of action to ensure compliance with required due process procedures?

a. Immediately suspend the employee pending the investigation and disciplinary proceedings.
b. Conduct an internal investigation into the matter to determine the need for disciplinary action.
c. Provide the accused employee with a written notice of the allegations and the evidence supporting the claims.
d. Dismiss the accused employee based on the allegations to avoid a formal investigation and risk to the district's reputation.

88. A newly appointed superintendent has a goal of improving evaluation practices to enhance teacher professional growth in the district. To achieve this, they have introduced two distinct research-anchored evaluation systems: the Peer Collaboration Evaluation (PCE) and the Classroom Observation Feedback (COF). In the PCE, teachers collaborate as partners to provide feedback on one another's teaching approaches and use this feedback for their own self-reflection and self-assessment. The COF system employs trained instructional coaches to observe and provide feedback to teachers. Each system is grounded in research and aims to support the development of teachers and staff. Which of the following statements best describes the difference between these two evaluation systems?

a. The PCE system involves self-reflection and self-assessment, while the COF system focuses on instructional coaching and external observation.
b. The PCE system involves pairing teachers with experienced mentors for feedback, whereas the COF system relies on a rubric-based approach.
c. The PCE system tracks teachers' progress over time, while the COF system involves monthly feedback cycles.
d. The PCE system involves individual teacher goal-setting, while the COF system focuses on collaborative improvement strategies.

89. In a historically underperforming school district, the superintendent aims to enhance student assessment scores across grade levels, focusing on mathematics. The superintendent's goal is to involve stakeholders in evidence-based inquiry to formulate strategic improvement plans. Which approach below aligns best with this commitment?

a. Conducting a survey among administrators, teachers, and community members in the district to gather personal anecdotes about their experience with the current mathematics curriculum
b. Organizing a town hall meeting with teachers, administrators, parents, and community members to brainstorm strategies for improving assessment scores in mathematics
c. Holding quarterly meetings with math teachers, curriculum experts, parents, and researchers to review student assessment data, identify trends, and develop focused improvement strategies
d. Facilitating workshops for teachers, administrators, parents, and community members to learn strategies for improving student learning outcomes in mathematics

90. A school district has just adopted a new curriculum framework that will be implemented in the upcoming school year. To prepare, the superintendent has provided administrators, teachers, and staff across the district with professional development opportunities aimed at supporting them in aligning instructional practices with this new framework. Which of the following additional actions should the superintendent prioritize to accurately measure student learning and gather meaningful feedback regarding the new curriculum?

a. Conduct regular school visits and classroom observations to gauge student engagement and participation in the new curriculum
b. Review and revise existing assessment methods to align with the new curriculum
c. Assign teachers to observe and document student progress throughout the school year
d. Conduct district-wide student surveys to gather their feedback regarding the new curriculum

91. One of the high schools in a school district has a high population of socioeconomically disadvantaged students. Many of these students are unable to afford the large participation fee required to engage in school athletics. The fee is necessary to cover the cost of transportation, uniforms, and athletic equipment. This financial barrier limits these students' ability to participate in school sports, thus hindering the overall educational experience. Which of the following measures should the superintendent take to most effectively address this disparity and ensure equitable access to resources and school activities for all students?

a. Eliminate the participation fee entirely and reduce the budget allocated for school athletics.
b. Implement a tiered fee structure based on students' family income, with lower-income students paying a reduced or waived participation fee.
c. Provide alternative extracurricular activities that do not require a participation fee.
d. Create a scholarship program that pays the participation fee for students that demonstrate exceptional talent in their chosen sport.

92. A historically underperforming school district is aiming to improve student learning outcomes in mathematics. The superintendent has decided to collaborate with administrators and teachers in the district to review and revise the current assessment methods to ensure they align with the curriculum and instructional practices. Which of the following actions should be prioritized in order to achieve this goal?

a. Researching various vendors to determine which new mathematics textbook series would be most effective in improving student learning outcomes on assessments
b. Revising the yearly budget to allocate additional funds for investing in new technology for assessment purposes
c. Creating professional development workshops to help teachers align instructional practices with mathematics assessments
d. Analyzing the mathematics curriculum and identifying the specific learning outcomes to be assessed

93. The newly appointed superintendent of a school district has identified a persistent achievement gap between English Language Learners (ELLs) and their native English-speaking peers in the district and recognizes the need for additional support to ensure their academic success. Which of the following actions would best demonstrate the superintendent's commitment to promoting and safeguarding equitable education for these students?

a. Encouraging teachers to incorporate linguistic supports into instruction, such as visual aids and modified assignments
b. Creating a program in which ELL students are paired with native English-speaking peers to provide linguistic support
c. Adopting a standardized curriculum to ensure that all students are held to the same high academic expectations
d. Implementing a comprehensive English as a Second Language (ESL) program that provides targeted language instruction and support to ELL students at various proficiency levels

94. The superintendent of a forward-thinking school district has been actively working to refine and update the district's mission, vision, and core values to stay aligned with the evolving expectations and needs of students, parents, teachers, and the community. As part of this effort, the superintendent has been leading quarterly town hall meetings, conducting surveys among parents and members of the educational community, and leading focus groups to gather valuable insights. Which of the following best describes how these approaches will benefit the superintendent in achieving his goal?

a. Streamlining administrative processes to reduce operational costs and optimize human resource allocation within the district
b. Engaging stakeholders in the process of evaluating and adjusting the district's mission, vision, and core values
c. Delegating the responsibility of refining and updating the district's mission, vision, and core values to stakeholders within the educational community
d. Educating stakeholders about the importance of reflecting the district's mission, vision, and core values in daily practices

95. A superintendent discovers that an administrator in their district has been manipulating student attendance records to improve the school's Average Daily Attendance rate. This behavior directly violates the district's policies and compromises the integrity of the educational system. Which of the following courses of action would be most appropriate in this situation?

a. Consult with other administrators to determine the most appropriate response, taking into account the potential impact on the district's reputation.
b. Immediately address the issue with the administrator in question and initiate appropriate disciplinary actions.
c. Schedule a meeting with the administrator in question to review the district's policies, emphasizing the importance of honesty, legality, and ethical conduct.
d. Review the attendance records for all schools in the district to ensure accuracy and consistency.

96. The superintendent of a historically low-performing school district wants to implement a program in the upcoming school year to promote staff collaboration, support, and shared responsibility for student success as a measure to improve overall school achievement. Which of the following would be most effective in addressing this goal?

a. Assigning teachers and staff members to work independently on specific tasks
b. Establishing a teacher evaluation system based on student assessment scores
c. Establishing a system for peer observation and feedback to encourage collaboration and professional growth
d. Instituting a competitive reward system where individual staff members are recognized for their performance

97. A superintendent is leading a new initiative that aims to elevate academic performance as well as the practical relevance of education in high schools across the district. This effort seeks to bridge classroom learning with real-world applications to prepare students for the challenges of a rapidly changing job market. To aid in the implementation of this initiative, the superintendent seeks to bring together teachers, parents, and local business leaders. Which of the following actions would be most effective in fostering alignment among these stakeholders to ensure collective commitment to realizing this vision?

a. Highlighting the district's accomplishments in extracurricular activities and sports
b. Creating marketing campaigns to increase the district's enrollment numbers
c. Building shared understanding through regular meetings, workshops, and joint projects
d. Establishing an online platform for addressing concerns related to the education program

98. The superintendent of a culturally diverse school district has been actively working toward promoting a professional culture focused on ethical and equitable practices. One recent initiative has been the implementation of a comprehensive equity policy that aims to eliminate achievement gaps and provide equal opportunities for all students. Which of the following next steps would be most effective in further promoting ethical and equitable practices across the district?

a. Conducting district-wide training sessions for staff members on cultural responsiveness and implicit bias
b. Revising the curriculum to include diverse perspectives and experiences
c. Creating a student-led committee to provide input on school policies and practices
d. Establishing partnerships with organizations in the community to provide access to resources and support for students

99. Parents and community members within a school district have recently expressed growing concern regarding the fair distribution of funds for technology resources across schools. In light of these concerns, which of the following actions by the district superintendent would be most effective in promoting transparency and building trust among stakeholders in the district?

a. Publishing an annual report on the district's technology budget that outlines the specific allocation of technology resources across schools
b. Establishing a technology advisory committee comprising district staff, parents, students, and community members to review and provide recommendations on the allocation of funds for technology resources
c. Conducting periodic surveys to collect feedback from staff, parents, and community members about their perceptions of the district's financial decisions regarding technology resources
d. Creating an online platform in which parents and community members can track the district's expenditures on technology resources for each school

100. A superintendent has recently identified inconsistencies in the science curriculum across different grade levels in the district, with variations in topics covered and the depth of content presented. To address this issue, the superintendent's goal is to establish a coherent system that facilitates a seamless transition for students from one grade level to another while building upon the foundational knowledge and skills specified in the academic standards. Which of the following actions would be the most effective in achieving this objective and ensuring alignment of curriculum and instruction with the academic standards?

a. Allocating additional funds to schools in the district to purchase the latest science textbooks and resources
b. Establishing a district-wide curriculum mapping process to ensure alignment of curriculum and instruction with academic standards
c. Implementing project-based learning across all science classes in the district to enhance student engagement and critical thinking skills
d. Conducting a district-wide survey of students and parents to gather feedback about their preferences for science topics and content

101. In a school district with a strong commitment to community engagement and holistic student development, the superintendent's vision focuses on fostering a sense of empathy and active citizenship among students. This vision is encapsulated in the district's core values of compassion, collaboration, and social responsibility. The superintendent believes in leading by example to ensure that these values are ingrained within the district's culture and shared by both the school and the local community. Which of the following actions best aligns with the superintendent's commitment to modeling the district's core values throughout their leadership role?

a. Hosting monthly town hall meetings where district leaders, parents, students, and community members engage in discussions about how the district's core values are reflected in various educational initiatives
b. Organizing and participating in a series of district-wide community service events where students, teachers, administrators, and local residents collaborate to contribute to the betterment of the community
c. Establishing a platform for students to nominate teachers who demonstrate the district's core values in their teaching approach
d. Launching a district-wide multimedia campaign that highlights the achievements of students and staff who exemplify the district's core values

Refer to the following for questions 102–103:

The superintendent of a school district in a busy urban community is dedicated to fostering a more inclusive and equitable educational environment. The district's vision is to introduce a comprehensive program aimed at integrating social and emotional learning (SEL) into its curriculum to address the diverse needs of its student population and ensure a more holistic educational experience. However, this ambitious change also comes with its fair share of uncertainties, potential risks, and complexities in managing the transition effectively.

102. With the implementation of a social and emotional learning (SEL) component into the existing curriculum, the superintendent faces a notable uncertainty: the potential impact of this change on existing teaching methodologies. To properly manage this uncertainty, which of the following actions should the superintendent prioritize?

a. Developing a comprehensive communication plan to inform parents about the upcoming curriculum change
b. Choosing a well-suited change management model to guide a gradual integration process
c. Implementing the new curriculum immediately to gauge its real-time effects on teaching methods
d. Conducting a survey among students throughout the district to gain feedback about their thoughts on the new curriculum and teaching strategies

103. The implementation of the new social and emotional learning (SEL) curriculum has prompted resistance from teachers and parents, stemming from concerns about potential disruptions to the current educational structure. How can the superintendent effectively address these challenges while ensuring that the change process remains aligned with the district's overarching goal of providing a comprehensive education that addresses students' diverse needs?

a. Proceeding with the curriculum implementation, assuming that the benefits of the program will naturally become evident over time
b. Establishing a committee of teachers, parents, and administrators to collaborate in addressing concerns, sharing insights, and co-creating solutions
c. Holding separate meetings with teachers and parents to discuss their concerns individually and attempt to address them one-on-one
d. Providing a written explanation of the new curriculum to teachers and parents in the district and asking them to submit their feedback via an online form

104. Upon analyzing student assessment data across the school district, a superintendent identifies a significant achievement gap in mathematics between a specific group of historically underperforming students and their peers. Which of the following initiatives would be most effective in addressing this achievement gap and promoting equitable access to learning opportunities?

a. Allocating additional funds to purchase new mathematics software and digital resources for all classrooms
b. Implementing a comprehensive district-wide mathematics review and revision process to ensure alignment with best practices and provide targeted support for underperforming students
c. Conducting monthly professional development workshops for mathematics teachers to improve their instructional strategies
d. Providing all mathematics teachers in the district with an instructional aide in the classroom for additional support

105. In developing a new vision and mission for the school district, a superintendent has a goal of creating a collaborative culture in which staff are collectively dedicated to student success. Which of the following strategies would be most effective in achieving this goal?

a. Assigning individual teachers to handle specific subject areas and establishing specialized teams to handle specific student needs
b. Conducting evaluations to assess individual performance and offering incentives to motivate staff members
c. Enforcing a strict top-down leadership approach for decision-making and emphasizing the importance of hierarchical structures
d. Establishing professional learning communities and providing professional development opportunities focused on meeting students' holistic needs

106. The superintendent of a school district aims to increase the percentage of graduating seniors attending higher education institutions and believes this can best be achieved by forging community partnerships to expand student learning opportunities. Which of the following strategies would be most effective in accomplishing this goal?

a. Encouraging students to attend a career fair at the local community college to explore different career paths and options for pursuing higher education
b. Collaborating with the local community college to provide a dual enrollment program that allows high school seniors to earn college credits
c. Creating a merit-based academic excellence scholarship award for students pursuing higher education
d. Establishing a career center in all high schools in the district and hiring career specialists to offer guidance, support, and resources for students pursuing higher education

107. A teacher in a school district has applied for an extended medical leave of absence due to a chronic and serious health condition. The teacher has provided all necessary medical documentation and meets the eligibility requirements for medical leave under the Family and Medical Leave Act (FMLA). Which of the following actions should the superintendent take to ensure compliance with state and federal laws related to employment in this situation?

a. Request additional medical documentation from the teacher to further verify the seriousness of their health condition before making a final decision.
b. Grant the teacher's request for medical leave, ensuring that her job is protected during her absence and that she receives the appropriate benefits and accommodations.
c. Temporarily delay the teacher's request, citing the need to maintain staffing levels at the school.
d. Send an email to staff members within the district to inquire if anyone would be willing to donate sick leave to the teacher in need.

Refer to the following for questions 108–110:

The superintendent of a school district aims to provide professional development opportunities that motivate and foster continuous learning and growth for all administrators, teachers, and staff in the school district. The chart below represents the level of participation in several professional development programs, as well as their impact on participants' pedagogical knowledge and skills. The effectiveness of each program was measured by comparing scores between pre-assessments and post-assessments, resulting in an overall improvement score.

Professional Development Program	Number of Participants District-wide	Pre-Assessment Score	Post-Assessment Score	Improvement Score
Data-driven Instructional Methods	40	60	75	15
Technology Integration Training	35	65	80	15
Culturally Responsive Teaching	50	50	70	20
Classroom Management Strategies	45	55	65	10

108. Based on the data provided in the chart, which of the following professional development programs should the superintendent focus on improving to promote continuous learning and growth for staff in the district?

a. Data-driven Instructional Methods
b. Technology Integration Training
c. Culturally Responsive Teaching
d. Classroom Management Strategies

109. The superintendent recognizes the importance of implementing research-based practices to foster the personal and professional growth of the district's staff. Based on the information presented in the chart above, which professional development program shows the most promising improvement in supporting the continuous personal and professional growth of staff members?

a. Data-driven Instructional Methods
b. Technology Integration Training
c. Culturally Responsive Teaching
d. Classroom Management Strategies

110. Considering the data provided in the chart regarding staff participation, which future professional development opportunity would best foster staff motivation for continuous learning and growth?

a. "Equity and Access for All: Empowering Diverse Learners"
b. "Unlocking Student Potential with Differentiated Instruction Strategies"
c. "Cultivating Emotional Intelligence: Implementing Social and Emotional Learning (SEL) in Schools"
d. "Empowering Learners Through Project-Based Learning"

111. Recently in a school district, a superintendent has been receiving reports from concerned parents about inconsistent bus timings and delays that are impacting student punctuality and attendance. In response, the superintendent is seeking an approach to identify and address issues related to bus routes and schedules. Due to budget constraints, the superintendent is unable to hire additional bus drivers to alleviate the problem. Which of the following alternative strategies would be most effective to achieve this goal and optimize the district transportation system to ensure smooth daily operations?

a. Reducing the number of school bus stops to minimize route distances and save time
b. Forming a committee of teachers and administrators to conduct regular surveys on bus services and gather feedback from parents
c. Organizing professional development workshops for bus drivers focused on improving time management and route planning skills
d. Reviewing and rearranging existing bus routes to improve efficiency

Refer to the following for questions 112–113:

> For the upcoming school year, a newly appointed superintendent is developing a new vision for the district. Central to this vision is increasing student engagement and fostering inclusivity by aligning the curriculum and learning experiences with students' diverse backgrounds. The district is located in a community known for its rich cultural tapestry and diverse immigrant population, and as such, the superintendent recognizes the value of embracing and celebrating students' heritages to enhance the educational experience. To achieve this, the superintendent is actively seeking to tap into community resources to enrich learning and promote a sense of belonging and pride among students.

112. Which of the following strategies would be most effective in leveraging the community's cultural resources to enrich student learning for all students?

a. Offering professional development opportunities for teachers and staff to improve their cultural competency in the classroom
b. Allocating additional funds to increase the availability of extracurricular activities offered in schools
c. Collaborating with local artists, musicians, and performers to offer workshops and performances at schools
d. Partnering with cultural centers to develop after-school programs that showcase and celebrate diverse traditions, arts, and heritage of the community

113. As part of the superintendent's efforts to shape the new vision for the district, the superintendent has decided to create an advisory council comprising community members, parents, and educators to participate in decision-making processes related to the education program. Which of the following best describes how this strategy will effectively improve the school environment and student learning outcomes?

a. Gathering multiple perspectives to review the district's decisions related to the education program
b. Creating a positive public image of the school district by including individuals from various backgrounds in decision-making processes
c. Streamlining the overall decision-making process to increase efficiency and productivity
d. Leveraging the diverse perspectives of various stakeholders to gain a better understanding of the community's strengths and needs

Refer to the following for questions 114–116:

In a progressive school district located in a culturally diverse community, a newly appointed superintendent is actively engaged in developing a new mission, vision, and core values to address the evolving needs of the student body and the community at large. The district aims to cultivate a culture of academic excellence while also nurturing students' social and emotional growth in an inclusive environment. The superintendent recognizes that these guiding principles must be a collaborative effort, drawing insights from various stakeholders to ensure a comprehensive and impactful transformation.

114. To effectively engage stakeholders in shaping the district's mission, vision, and core values, which of the following actions should the superintendent prioritize?

a. Asking parents, teachers, administrators, and community members to vote on the district's new mission, vision, and core values through an online poll
b. Engaging parents, students, educators, community members, and representatives from cultural organizations in collaborative discussions
c. Delegating the process of engaging stakeholders in shaping the district's mission, vision, and core values to administrators in the district
d. Sending out a brief email to educators, parents, and community members in the district asking for their input on the district's mission, vision, and core values

115. As part of the process of involving stakeholders in redefining the district's mission, vision, and core values, which of the following actions would be most effective in allowing the superintendent to ask crucial questions and solicit input to employ effective decision-making strategies?

a. Distributing a survey to all students and staff members asking for their individual preferences and suggestions on revising the district's mission, vision, and core values
b. Assigning a small committee of senior administrators to draft a new mission, vision, and core values based on their expertise and experiences
c. Convening focus groups with teachers, parents, students, and community representatives to gather insights and address concerns
d. Organizing a single town hall meeting to present the district's new mission, vision, and core values to the community and allowing attendees to provide immediate feedback

116. After completing the process of redefining the district's mission, vision, and core values, the superintendent would like to express genuine appreciation for the contributions of stakeholders. Which of the following approaches would be most appropriate in doing so?

a. Publicly acknowledging the insights of parents, students, teachers, and community members during town hall meetings and district-wide events
b. Sending a standardized district-wide email recognizing the efforts of all individuals involved in the process
c. Posting a message of appreciation on the district's website
d. Hosting a virtual meeting with stakeholders to discuss the outcomes of the redefined mission, vision, and core values

117. The superintendent of a rural school district has recently learned that many parents and community members are unaware of the district's academic programs and initiatives. This lack of awareness is hindering the district's ability to engage families and the community in the education program and support the achievement of district goals. Which of the following strategies would be most effective in addressing this issue and promoting a comprehensive understanding of the district's offerings?

a. Hosting a district-wide open house event where parents and community members can explore the various academic programs and initiatives offered by the district
b. Leading quarterly town hall meetings to present information and updates about the district's academic programs and initiatives
c. Sending out printed brochures and pamphlets that provide information about academic programs and initiatives within the district
d. Creating an online portal on the district's website that provides a discussion forum and information about academic programs and initiatives

118. A superintendent is leading a school district that has recently experienced a significant rise in its immigrant student population, with a substantial number of these students identified as English Language Learners (ELLs). The superintendent strongly believes in harnessing students' diverse cultures and backgrounds as valuable assets for teaching and creating an enriching and inclusive educational environment. Which of the following actions best aligns with this philosophy?

a. Organizing regular district-wide cultural celebrations where students can share their traditions and customs
b. Working closely with teachers and language specialists to develop culturally responsive and linguistically appropriate learning materials that incorporate students' backgrounds and languages into the curriculum
c. Establishing a comprehensive language support program for ELLs focused on accelerating English language acquisition and proficiency development
d. Providing teachers and staff with professional development opportunities focused on bilingual immersion techniques

119. In a middle school within the district, an incident occurs in which a group of students vandalizes school property by painting walls and lockers with graffiti. Which of the following actions by the superintendent would best ensure that this misconduct is addressed fairly and consistently?

a. Pursuing legal action against the responsible students for destruction of property to ensure that they are held accountable for their actions
b. Having the students participate in a restorative justice program that involves repairing the damage they caused, engaging in dialogue with affected staff members, and reflecting on the impact of their actions
c. Expelling the responsible students from the school to send a strong message about the consequences of vandalism
d. Implementing a universal discipline policy where any form of student misconduct results in the same predetermined consequences, regardless of specific circumstances

120. A newly appointed superintendent has the goal of developing workplace conditions that promote effective instructional practice and student learning while simultaneously prioritizing staff well-being and work-life balance. Which of the following strategies would be most effective in achieving this goal?

a. Providing regular and comprehensive professional development opportunities for teachers to enhance their pedagogical knowledge and skills
b. Implementing strict performance evaluations to identify underperforming staff members
c. Increasing teacher workload to maximize productivity and instructional time
d. Focusing solely on student achievement outcomes before addressing staff needs

Answer Key and Explanations for Test #1

1. D: Developing an effective code of conduct that adequately reflects the unique needs, values, and expectations of a school district requires the superintendent to engage in collaborative efforts with school administrators and members of the school board. Collaboration helps to ensure that the code of conduct promotes equity, addresses student behavior fairly and consistently, and avoids biases. School administrators possess invaluable insights into the specific needs and challenges within their respective schools. Their experience allows them to provide a comprehensive understanding of student and staff needs, which is essential in drafting a code of conduct that fosters positive behavior, maintains consistency in disciplinary actions, and ensures fairness when addressing misconduct. Involving members of the school board in the development of a new student code of conduct is equally important. As representatives appointed by the community, their participation ensures that the code of conduct aligns with the district's values and expectations while considering the diverse perspectives, needs, and interests of the community. Through collaborative efforts with school administrators and members of the school board, the superintendent fosters transparency and inclusivity in the development process. This approach promotes a shared sense of responsibility for upholding the student code of conduct, ensuring that it effectively addresses student behavior, promotes fairness, and supports a positive school climate.

2. D: Encouraging continuous professional improvement throughout a school district is essential for the district's growth and success. Doing so fosters ongoing learning, adaptation, and development, which ultimately results in improved student learning outcomes. Achieving steady, ongoing professional development requires a comprehensive strategy that aligns various initiatives with the district's broader goals. In this scenario, the initiatives outlined by the superintendent are beneficial in cultivating a culture that emphasizes and supports continuous improvement. By encouraging collaboration among educators, the superintendent creates an environment that promotes open dialogue and the exchange of ideas and experiences, fostering a shared sense of growth. Integrating new technology materials and resources into teaching methods encourages innovation and helps educators adapt to modern trends to promote continuous development. A systematic framework for continuous student assessment allows educators to consistently analyze learning outcomes, thus facilitating targeted improvements over time. Further, providing tailored professional growth programs communicates the district's dedication to staff development, reinforcing the importance of continuous improvement. By integrating these initiatives into a cohesive approach, the superintendent can actively create a professional environment in which staff members are motivated to engage in continuous improvement, learning, and growth.

3. B: Family involvement in the education program plays an integral role in promoting student success and cultivating a comprehensive learning environment. However, for a variety of reasons, some families may be hesitant to become active participants in their children's education. This may stem from factors such as unfamiliarity with the educational program, previous negative experiences, or ineffective family engagement strategies within the district. In this scenario, the superintendent could effectively address this issue by conducting a comprehensive district-wide survey to determine how to best encourage family engagement in the school community. A survey would be a systematic and inclusive approach for gathering valuable insights directly from families regarding how they would most like to participate in the education program. By actively seeking their perspectives, the superintendent can identify areas for improvement and tailor engagement strategies to meet families' specific needs and preferences. Such an initiative would foster a stronger sense of collaboration, trust, and mutual respect between families and schools, ultimately leading to greater family participation and enhancing the overall learning experience for students.

4. D: While the procedure for applying for grants may vary depending on the specific grant program and organization, a superintendent is typically required to draft a comprehensive proposal as part of the application process. When crafting a grant proposal, it is essential to provide a detailed account of the district's goals, objectives, and of how the requested funds will be utilized to enhance the educational experience for students. Structuring a proposal in this way demonstrates a strong alignment between the requested funds and the district's overall vision for improving student learning outcomes. This approach exhibits an understanding of the challenges faced by the district and outlines the desired outcomes to be achieved with the grant funds. Highlighting how the grant funds will directly address the district's needs helps the proposal become more focused and compelling, thus significantly increasing the likelihood of securing grant funds. Incorporating all these elements in a grant proposal effectively communicates the district's strategic planning and conveys a strong commitment to utilizing the grant funds to meet the specific needs of students and support their academic success.

5. A: Effective instructional improvement relies on evidence-based decision-making informed by student assessment data. In the given scenario, the superintendent aims to enhance engagement and improve academic performance in mathematics within a historically underperforming district. To facilitate informed decision-making for instructional improvement, the superintendent should prioritize identifying specific mathematics concepts or skills within the assessments where students demonstrate the most growth and areas for improvement. By analyzing student assessment data in this manner, the superintendent can gain valuable insights into students' performance levels, identify areas where they have shown growth, and pinpoint specific concepts or skills that require additional support for improvement. This data-driven approach would allow the superintendent to make informed decisions regarding instructional strategies and interventions tailored to address the identified areas for improvement. By focusing on these specific concepts or skills, the superintendent can align instructional practices and allocate resources effectively to support and improve student learning outcomes in mathematics.

6. D: Creating an educational environment that prioritizes respect, inclusivity, and academic excellence requires active leadership that resonates with the district's values. In this context, the superintendent's role in embodying these principles is essential to fostering a shared understanding within the school community. To best model the district's core values, the superintendent must conscientiously demonstrate respectful and inclusive behavior during interactions with students, staff, parents, and community members. Doing so authentically promotes an understanding of these core values while setting an example for others to follow in their own roles, contributing to a cohesive and aligned school community.

7. C: Quality learning and whole-child development occur when school leaders, teachers, and staff members are held to clear and high professional expectations. Establishing these expectations increases engagement, commitment, and accountability from all individuals within the school building while ensuring that instructional practices align with the district's goals for student achievement. The superintendent can achieve this by establishing a comprehensive performance evaluation system that includes regular feedback and professional development opportunities. This establishes a standard for professionalism that can guide educators to continuously reflect on and improve their practice for enhanced student learning. By implementing a comprehensive system for professional evaluation, the superintendent establishes a culture focused on professional excellence, continuous improvement, and dedication to whole-child development and the shared vision, goals, and objectives of the district.

8. C: Openness, transparency, and accountability are integral aspects of the superintendent's role that help foster trust, inclusivity, and the effective governance of a district. In this scenario, the superintendent can best exemplify these characteristics by consulting with teachers, staff, and parents to gather input and perspectives on the desired qualities and qualifications for the new elementary school principal. By acknowledging the value of gathering diverse perspectives and insights from individuals who will be directly affected by the selection of a new principal, the superintendent fosters transparency, openness, and accountability. Engaging teachers, staff, and parents in the process allows these individuals to contribute to decision-making, thus ensuring that the selection of a new principal reflects a collaborative effort and represents the needs of the school community.

9. A: Cost analysis is an integral process in effectively managing financial and physical resources in a school district, as it provides invaluable insights into how funds are allocated and utilized. Understanding the financial implications of various programs and initiatives allows superintendents to make informed decisions and optimize resource allocation to support the district's goals effectively. In this scenario, the superintendent aims to promote equitable access to education and prioritize students' well-being, specifically through free and reduced-price breakfast and lunch programs. To achieve this, the superintendent must conduct a comprehensive cost analysis to strategically manage the budget, review expenses to identify potential areas for optimization, and allocate additional funds for the breakfast and lunch programs. This approach would help to ensure that the nutritional needs of all students are met while making the best use of available financial resources to promote equity and inclusivity within the district's educational programs.

10. A: Offering educators professional development opportunities is essential to fostering their knowledge and confidence in integrating technology into the classroom. However, to ensure that technology resources are effectively utilized and applied to enhance teaching and learning outcomes, it is also important to offer continuous support. Providing educators with access to technical experts who can assist with troubleshooting, resolving issues, and answering questions would facilitate a smooth integration of student laptops and tablets into daily instruction. This approach would enable teachers to focus on their instructional goals without feeling overwhelmed by technical challenges, creating a supportive environment for experimenting with technology tools and trying new instructional approaches. By offering ongoing technical support, the superintendent can help ensure a seamless integration of student laptops and tablets, ultimately enhancing the overall teaching and learning experience in the district.

11. A, B: Establishing positive public relations plays a vital role in helping a school district build strong relationships with the community and students' families by fostering a sense of trust, credibility, and transparency. To achieve this, the superintendent should employ various communication channels to ensure comprehensive outreach that meets the needs of all stakeholders. In today's digital society, utilizing social media and email is integral for establishing and maintaining communication with students' families and community members. Social media platforms provide powerful tools for efficient, effective, and open communication. They enable real-time updates on important school news, events, and achievements, thus promoting transparency and showcasing the district's accomplishments. The interactive nature of social media platforms allows for active participation and dialogue, which serves to strengthen involvement and create a positive perception of the district. Additionally, emailing weekly newsletters provides targeted and consistent communication while accommodating families who may not utilize social media. This approach keeps families informed while demonstrating the district's commitment to transparency and open communication. In contrast, creating a school website, while useful for providing information, lacks the interactive nature necessary for fostering open dialogue and therefore may not be as effective in promoting community engagement and communication as social media and email. By combining these strategies, the superintendent can address diverse communication preferences by engaging individuals through real-time interaction and delivering personalized updates via email. Implementing both approaches would establish a comprehensive public relations program that fosters increased community engagement and improved communication with families.

12. C: A well-structured system for evaluating and adjusting a school district's mission, vision, and core values is a fundamental component of effective educational leadership. This regular evaluation and adjustment ensures that the district remains aligned with its goals while staying responsive to the changing needs and expectations of its stakeholders. In this scenario, forming a cross-functional team is a beneficial strategy for engaging stakeholders to help achieve this goal. By involving teachers, parents, community leaders, and students in the evaluation and adjustment of the district's goals and values, the superintendent fosters a sense of ownership and collaboration. Stakeholders feel that their perspectives are valued and that their voices contribute to shaping the educational direction of the district. This engagement enhances transparency while simultaneously building trust among stakeholders, reinforcing a shared commitment to the district's success. Further, aligning the district's mission with the changing needs of students, parents, educators, and the community helps create a more relevant and impactful educational experience. This adaptability ensures that the district's initiatives remain current, meaningful, and effective, ultimately leading to improved student outcomes and community satisfaction.

13. D: Effective management of physical resources and support services is essential for the smooth operation and success of various programs and initiatives in a school district. Part of this responsibility includes ensuring efficiency, practicality, and cost-effectiveness to optimize the use of resources while achieving the district's goals. In this scenario, the superintendent's vision of promoting sustainability and environmental consciousness aligns with the waste reduction program aimed at composting food waste from the school cafeterias and using it in school gardens. To ensure the program's effectiveness, the superintendent must demonstrate skillful management of physical resources and support services. By collaborating with local waste management companies to establish a composting system, the superintendent can implement a sustainable waste disposal system without significant upfront costs, ensuring the waste reduction program's financial viability while fostering environmental consciousness within the school community. This action would reduce the district's environmental impact while creating a sustainable cycle by using composted material to grow produce for the cafeteria, therefore reducing external sourcing needs. By implementing a cost-effective waste reduction program through collaboration with local waste management companies, the superintendent can demonstrate effective resource management while promoting a sustainable and eco-friendly learning environment that aligns with the district's goals.

14. C: Effectively advocating for students' needs and the value of public education will often require a strategic approach when working with the district board of education to garner support and engage all stakeholders. In this scenario, the superintendent could best gain support among hesitant board members regarding the implementation of a STEM enrichment program by presenting them with research-based evidence and success stories from other districts or schools that have adopted similar programs. This would allow the superintendent to provide factual information that supports the positive outcomes and benefits of a STEM enrichment program. Such evidence could include data on increased student engagement, improved critical thinking skills, and enhanced academic performance. Through this approach, the superintendent could effectively address the concerns of hesitant board members and demonstrate the benefits of the program for students, thus building confidence in its value and effectiveness and garnering greater support for its implementation.

15. B: Adhering to state and federal laws when planning and conducting district board meetings is essential for a superintendent to ensure the proper functioning and governance of the education system. Upholding legal requirements is necessary for ensuring transparency, accountability, and fairness in decision-making processes while also protecting the rights and interests of stakeholders. An important component of upholding these laws includes ensuring all board members have access to meeting agendas and relevant documents prior to the district board meeting. This allows board members equal opportunity to review pertinent information in advance and arrive at the meeting prepared to make informed decisions, thus facilitating a productive session that complies with regulations related to the distribution of meeting agendas and materials.

16. B: "Shared services" in school districts refers to the collaborative utilization of resources, personnel, and expertise among multiple schools or districts to maximize efficiency and effectiveness in providing various services. Rather than each school or district independently providing these services, shared services allow for consolidation and collaboration, resulting in cost savings, improved quality, and increased access to resources for all students in the district. In this scenario, the superintendent could best achieve their goal to increase mental health support services for students by partnering with neighboring districts to share licensed therapists and counselors. Doing so would allow the superintendent to pool resources and expertise from licensed mental health professionals to provide a wider range of services without incurring additional costs. This approach would help ensure a comprehensive and cost-effective means of meeting students' mental health needs within the constraints of the budget.

17. C: Developing and implementing effective intervention systems requires understanding each student's unique learning needs to allow for tailored support for academic success. Prioritizing individual learning needs means that interventions are targeted and student-centered, enabling students to overcome challenges and reach their full potential. In this particular school district, English Language Learner (ELL) students facing challenges in language acquisition and academic progress will require an intervention system that aligns with their individual proficiency levels and linguistic needs. Incorporating a peer tutoring program in which proficient English-speaking students are paired with ELL students would allow for such personalization while fostering a supportive and collaborative learning environment. Peer tutors can provide one-on-one language support and help foster language development through meaningful interactions and academic collaboration. This approach would serve to improve ELL students' language skills while promoting social integration and increasing students' confidence in communicating in English, ultimately helping them overcome language barriers, actively participate in classroom activities, and succeed academically.

18. D: Establishing consensus on decisions concerning the district's education program requires proactive steps by the superintendent to cultivate partnerships and promote effective communication. To achieve this, the superintendent can facilitate collaborative decision-making sessions with board members. In this scenario, doing so would allow the superintendent to directly work with board members to analyze a range of disciplinary strategies, discuss their respective advantages and disadvantages, and collectively work toward a consensus on the revised policies. This approach would encourage active engagement and involvement from board members, thus fostering an environment of open dialogue and shared decision-making. Further, through these collaborative sessions, board members can express their viewpoints, raise concerns, and contribute their expertise, leading to well-informed and balanced decisions while increasing the likelihood of achieving consensus regarding the revised discipline policies.

19. B: To implement instructional interventions that effectively address the diverse learning needs of each student, the superintendent must prioritize gathering and analyzing the appropriate data. Learning this necessary information about students' skills, abilities, and areas for improvement enables the superintendent to implement specialized support that meets students' individual needs. In this scenario, implementing a school-wide reading assessment program would allow the superintendent to gather comprehensive data on students' reading proficiency across all grade levels. This information will help the superintendent identify students who are struggling with reading and develop targeted intervention strategies tailored to their specific needs. By utilizing the data provided from a school-wide reading assessment program, the superintendent can ensure that interventions are based on objective and reliable data, therefore increasing effectiveness in supporting student growth and improvement in reading proficiency skills.

20. C: The Family Educational Rights and Privacy Act (FERPA) is a federal law designed to protect the privacy of student information. This includes academic, disciplinary, and medical records, as well as any personally identifiable information. According to this mandate, schools may not disclose students' education records without consent from parents, legal caregivers, or from the student upon turning 18. In an increasingly digital age, it is important to recognize that these regulations extend to sharing student information on social media, as these platforms are often easily accessible by the public and doing so could compromise students' and families' rights to privacy. To ensure professional conduct and adhere to guidelines established by FERPA related to sharing student information on social media, the superintendent should develop a district-wide policy that clearly outlines expectations for doing so. In this scenario, by developing and implementing such a policy across their district, the superintendent demonstrates an understanding of FERPA as it relates to social media and takes proactive measures to protect the privacy rights of students and families. Although The Health Insurance Portability and Accountability Act (HIPAA) (choice D) also deals with privacy concerns, HIPAA protects the privacy of one's medical information and does not apply to most student information.

21. B, D: Implementing multiple strategies for gathering data is essential for effectively evaluating and making necessary adjustments to educational programs in a school district. Doing so allows for a comprehensive approach to addressing challenges and responding to students' evolving needs. In this scenario, the superintendent should employ various methods for gathering quantitative data to make informed decisions about improvements to the digital literacy program. One effective strategy involves utilizing digital tools to monitor student engagement, such as tracking the time students spend on digital activities, their completion rates of assignments, and their interactions with online resources. This approach would provide quantifiable metrics that offer insights into student involvement and interaction with the program. With this information, the superintendent can identify trends, patterns, and areas of concern, enabling data-driven decision-making to enhance the program's effectiveness. Additionally, the superintendent should consider conducting pre- and post-assessments to measure students' digital competencies relative to the program's objectives. By assessing students' skills before and after the program's implementation, the superintendent can gather quantitative data that illustrates the impact of the program on students' abilities. This data would be beneficial in pinpointing areas of success and areas that require adjustments, allowing for a focused and targeted strategic plan. By combining these strategies, the superintendent can ensure a holistic approach to data collection, leveraging quantitative information to craft a well-informed strategic plan for program improvement that addresses disparities in learning outcomes across grade levels and schools.

22. A, D: Effective evaluation and adjustment of strategic plans for educational programs in a school district requires a multifaceted approach that encompasses both quantitative and qualitative data. Gathering information from multiple sources provides a comprehensive understanding of program dynamics. In this scenario, combining quantitative data with qualitative insights will be beneficial in highlighting the nuances of the digital literacy program's implementation and impact to effectively evaluate and enhance its success. By conducting classroom observations to witness the digital literacy program in action, the superintendent can assess student engagement, teacher effectiveness, and the overall learning environment. These observations can provide contextual insights, allowing for informed adjustments to the program. In addition, conducting feedback sessions with teachers and parents would be beneficial in gathering first-hand qualitative information. Teachers interact with the program daily and possess unique perspectives on its strengths and challenges. Gathering their insights through feedback sessions would enable the superintendent to identify specific strengths and areas for improvement and to make necessary adjustments. By combining classroom observations with teacher and parent feedback, the superintendent can gain a comprehensive view of the program's efficacy, enabling informed strategic planning and adjustments that address diverse aspects of program implementation and student outcomes.

23. C: All students will inevitably arrive in the classroom possessing a distinct set of learning needs. As such, it is important to adapt the curriculum to meet these learning needs to promote growth, development, and academic achievement for all students. Approaching curriculum planning through the lens of differentiated instruction is an effective strategy for achieving this, as it involves aligning the curriculum and instructional methods to the varied needs of students, particularly those with special needs. This approach allows educators to offer multiple avenues for learning, accommodating differences in learning styles, abilities, needs, and preferences. By identifying each student's strengths and challenges, educators can design and implement appropriate learning tasks, adjust the pacing of instruction, and provide the support necessary to ensure that the curriculum aligns with each student's developmental stage. By planning the curriculum using differentiated instruction as a framework, educators can employ a variety of strategies, such as flexible grouping, tiered assignments, and varied assessments to effectively engage and challenge students with special needs. Doing so would promote engagement and active participation in meaningful learning experiences while fostering an inclusive learning environment in which students of all abilities feel valued and capable of achieving their full potential.

24. A: Establishing productive partnerships with stakeholder groups in the community is invaluable for acquiring the necessary resources, networks, and expertise to achieve district goals and promote student success. By identifying and fostering partnerships with local businesses to create internship programs and job shadowing opportunities, the superintendent can offer students experiences that integrate classroom learning with real-world applications. These partnerships would provide students with the opportunity to develop practical skills, explore various career pathways, and benefit from the insights of professionals across different fields. Furthermore, collaborating with local businesses aligns the district's educational goals with the needs of the local community, thus fostering a connection between academic learning and real-world relevance. Such partnerships would significantly enhance students' career readiness by equipping them with hands-on experiences, relevant skills, and industry perspectives. This approach would foster a sense of engagement, motivation, and preparedness among high school students, ultimately leading to their overall success in future careers.

25. D: To effectively enhance cultural competency and responsiveness within a school, it is important to identify specific areas for improvement and implement targeted strategies for addressing them. In this scenario, the most effective approach for supporting Dr. Hill's goal of improving cultural competency and responsiveness among staff members while advocating for the success of all students would be to conduct a comprehensive assessment of the school's cultural competency and develop a focused improvement plan. This systematic and data-informed process would enable Dr. Hill and the school to proactively address cultural competency gaps among staff members. By conducting the assessment, Dr. Hill would gain valuable insight into specific areas requiring improvement and could tailor professional development opportunities to align with the unique needs of both staff and students. Doing so would establish a solid foundation for improving cultural competency and responsiveness throughout the school, thus fostering an inclusive and supportive learning environment for all students.

26. C: To create an equitable, supportive, and inclusive learning environment, it is imperative that staff members develop their understanding of the cultural backgrounds and experiences of their students, as well as how those differences might impact teaching and learning. In this scenario, Dr. Hill's commitment and advocacy for cultural competence and responsiveness in this high school would be best demonstrated by assigning a district-level cultural liaison to lead workshops for staff to learn about different cultural practices and perspectives. This action would ensure targeted support, guidance, and resources to enhance staff members' understanding of their diverse student population's cultural needs. The workshops could focus on cultural awareness, sensitivity, and understanding, allowing staff members to develop effective interpersonal and communication skills with students from different cultural backgrounds. By fostering cultural competence and responsiveness, the school would establish stronger connections, promote positive staff-student relationships, and create an inclusive and supportive environment where students feel valued, supported, and understood in their academic and personal growth. If Dr. Hill took this proactive approach, it would exemplify his dedication to equity and the success of all students, demonstrating his advocacy for fostering cultural competency and responsiveness among the school staff.

27. D: Advocating for the needs of students requires a comprehensive approach to support their well-being both within and outside of school hours. A superintendent's role includes not only recognizing and addressing these needs but also garnering community support to do so. In the case of food-insecure students, the superintendent can enhance community awareness and support by collaborating with local food banks and community organizations. Together, they can establish a district-wide weekend meal program that provides nutritious meals to students during non-school days. Such an initiative would address the immediate challenge of food insecurity among students while deepening the community's understanding of the prevalence and impact of the issue. By fostering support and advocacy for the needs of food-insecure students beyond the existing free and reduced meal program, this collaborative effort helps ensure equitable access to nutrition through proactive community engagement.

28. A: Advocating for students' needs and the value of public education is an integral aspect of the superintendent's role and requires effective and productive collaboration with board members to address challenges that may occur within the district, such as budget cuts. Working together with board members in this situation will help all parties gain a comprehensive understanding of budgetary challenges and develop creative solutions accordingly. Through collaboration, the superintendent and board members can analyze budgetary challenges, prioritize the continuity of programs and resources that most significantly impact student success, and explore strategies for mitigating the impact of budget cuts. This approach allows the superintendent and board members to engage in creative problem-solving, to minimize the effects of budget cuts, and to ensure the continuation of essential programs.

29. B: Implementing systems to manage fiscal resources is essential for ensuring ethical practice and accountability while maximizing the impact and efficiency of funds throughout a school district. In this scenario, creating a detailed budget plan will be beneficial in helping the superintendent adhere to the grant's guidelines while enhancing STEM learning for students within the district. To ensure ongoing effectiveness and grant compliance, the superintendent would benefit from collaborating with the district's finance team to conduct regular and comprehensive audits and performance evaluations of the STEM programs and initiatives. By actively engaging the finance team in monitoring the financial accounts and conducting audits, the superintendent can promote a responsible and transparent approach to managing fiscal resources. Financial audits would serve to ensure that the grant funds received for supporting STEM programs are utilized efficiently and in alignment with the district's goals. Audits would also provide a detailed assessment of how the funds are being allocated and spent, allowing the superintendent to identify any discrepancies or potential areas for improvement. Additionally, performance evaluations of STEM programs and initiatives would allow the superintendent to assess their effectiveness and impact on student learning and engagement. These evaluations would provide valuable data to drive decision-making, thus allowing the district to make informed choices about resource allocation and program improvements. With this proactive approach to financial planning and monitoring, the superintendent can promote transparency and responsibility in handling fiscal resources while ensuring that the district optimizes the grant funds to increase STEM learning opportunities for students.

30. C: Collaborating with professionals in the school building is essential to identifying and improving upon areas of need to promote an inclusive and supportive learning environment for all students. In this situation, acknowledging and addressing the lack of representation and participation in extracurricular activities will help build a positive culture and climate in which all students feel valued and included in their school community. By actively working with administrators, teachers, and staff in the school, the superintendent can help develop and implement a comprehensive plan for creating diverse and inclusive extracurricular opportunities that meet the needs of all students. This would help ensure that extracurricular activities reflected the interests and backgrounds of all students, thus increasing engagement and participation and fostering a sense of belonging for all students.

31. D: Instances of bullying within a school district can present significant ethical concerns. It is therefore imperative that the superintendent enact procedures to address these issues promptly and comprehensively, beginning with providing effective avenues for reporting bullying incidents. Often, reporting bullying concerns can be challenging for many individuals who fear retaliation or ridicule. In this scenario, establishing a confidential reporting system would address this issue by providing a secure and anonymous system for students, parents, and staff to report instances of bullying without the risk of repercussions or exposure. A secure reporting system would foster an environment of trust and open communication, thus facilitating the identification and resolution of bullying incidents. Such a system would establish the foundation for further actions to reduce bullying, including investigations, interventions, and prevention strategies. By creating a secure and anonymous reporting system, the superintendent empowers individuals to come forward and enables the school to take appropriate and effective action against bullying.

32. C: Fostering positive and productive partnerships between schools and students' families has significant benefits that enhance overall learning experiences. Doing so creates a collaborative and supportive environment that fosters engagement, positive attitudes toward learning, and greater academic achievement. In this example, the superintendent most likely intended to establish such partnerships by initiating Family Literacy Night. Such a program provides a space in which schools and families can come together to collectively enhance students' literacy skills. Through interactive reading activities, storytelling sessions, and book clubs, parents and students can actively participate in literacy-focused learning experiences. Holding regular Family Literacy Nights strengthens the positive connection between schools and families, thus promoting a sense of shared responsibility in supporting students' literacy development. Cultivating positive partnerships by implementing Family Literacy Night encourages active family involvement, communication, and collaboration between family members, teachers, and school librarians, which will ultimately result in greater literacy skill development.

33. B: Continuously reviewing and revising a district's mission, vision, and core values is an important part of ensuring that the educational experience remains relevant, meaningful, and aligned with the evolving needs and expectations of students. By regularly revisiting these foundational elements, the superintendent can address emerging challenges to facilitate an environment in which students excel both academically and personally. Engaging stakeholders in this process is integral, as it brings forth the diverse perspectives of students, parents, teachers, and community members. In this scenario, their feedback can provide valuable insights into the nuances of student engagement and participation in extracurricular activities. By conducting a district-wide survey, the superintendent can gain a comprehensive understanding of the decline in student engagement and can tailor adjustments to the mission, vision, and core values that reflect the actual experiences and expectations of those directly affected. The collaborative nature of engaging stakeholders through surveys ensures that any changes made to the district's guiding principles are well-informed, inclusive, and genuinely responsive to the changing dynamics of the education landscape. This approach would empower the superintendent to lead the district with insight and foresight, ultimately improving student engagement and participation in extracurricular activities.

34. C: Implementing authentic learning tasks in the classroom is an effective strategy for promoting student engagement and fostering intellectually challenging experiences. These tasks mirror real-world situations, allowing students to apply classroom knowledge in practical contexts while promoting critical thinking and creative problem-solving. By immersing students in hands-on experiences that resonate with their interests, educators foster a deeper understanding of the subject matter, and students become active participants in their own learning. This student-centered approach cultivates a sense of ownership and motivation, as students can see the relevance and significance of what they are learning. In this scenario, organizing collaborative workshops with local scientists and engineers would help the superintendent provide students with authentic and intellectually challenging tasks that extend beyond the classroom. Interacting with professionals from the field not only enhances students' understanding of scientific principles but also makes their learning experiences more relevant, engaging, and meaningful. Such workshops would introduce students to the practical applications of science, allowing them to see how the knowledge they gain in the classroom can be applied in real-world situations. By promoting such authentic learning experiences, the superintendent can encourage instructional practices that are both intellectually stimulating and effective. This approach fosters curiosity, critical thinking, and problem-solving skills, ultimately leading to improved student engagement and academic performance in science.

35. C: To create a fair, equitable, and legally compliant educational environment, all school districts must adhere to state and federal guidelines when developing a student code of conduct. For example, all policies and procedures related to student behavioral expectations and disciplinary action must align with guidelines established by the Individuals with Disabilities Education Act (IDEA). Under this mandate, students with disabilities must be given the individual support and resources necessary to facilitate a free appropriate education in the least restrictive environment. When developing a student code of conduct, a superintendent should prioritize including explicit language that addresses how behavioral expectations and disciplinary actions will be adapted to meet the unique needs of students with disabilities. This may include stating that a student's Individualized Education Program (IEP) will be considered when enacting any disciplinary measures, and that Behavior Intervention Plans (BIPs) will be developed as necessary to provide support to effectively address behavioral challenges. This approach fosters an equitable and inclusive school environment in which students with disabilities receive the necessary support and accommodations to navigate behavioral challenges while ensuring compliance with IDEA requirements.

36. B: Providing educators with collaborative, job-embedded professional development opportunities helps foster a culture of continuous improvement and collective learning. By working together with colleagues and embedding learning in daily work, educators can engage in relevant experiences that directly relate to their classroom practice. This allows them to apply new knowledge and strategies immediately to enhance teaching effectiveness and improve student learning outcomes. By introducing regular district-wide, grade-level team meetings, the superintendent can provide a collaborative space for educators to participate in continuous, job-embedded professional development to enhance language and literacy instruction across grade levels. Educators can use these meetings to discuss language and literacy challenges, share successful teaching practices, and work together in developing strategies for effectively meeting students' learning needs. Collaborative learning encourages educators to learn from one another, drawing on their collective expertise to develop innovative approaches that can positively influence student learning outcomes. This form of professional development empowers educators by creating a supportive and cohesive community committed to enhancing language and literacy instruction across the district.

37. D: Protecting the safety of students and staff in a school district requires effective, efficient crisis response plans in the event of an emergency. In this scenario, working with local law enforcement and security experts is an essential first step in enhancing preparedness for potential intruder situations, as it allows the superintendent to update the district's procedures to align with the most current response strategies. To further strengthen the crisis management plan for intruder situations, it is important that the superintendent ensures that all schools throughout the district hold regular intruder response drills. Drills would allow students and staff to actively engage and familiarize themselves with the crisis management procedures, instilling a sense of readiness and confidence during potential intruder situations. By regularly practicing these drills, the superintendent can ensure that everyone is well-equipped to respond efficiently in times of crisis. The combination of updating the plan and conducting drills is a comprehensive approach to crisis management that will enable the school community to act swiftly and effectively in the event of a potential intruder.

38. D: Vertical teaming refers to coordination and collaboration between feeder and connecting schools to help facilitate smooth transitions as students advance through their academic careers. By implementing a vertical teaming approach, districts can address changes in demographics and student enrollment patterns more effectively while supporting successful transitions between schools. One strategy for vertical teaming includes implementing a centralized online platform where teachers and administrators from feeder and connecting schools can collaborate. Such a platform would serve as a space for educators from these schools to share resources, discuss ideas, and work together to align curriculum and instruction. This approach would be effective in fostering a cohesive learning experience for students as they transition from one school to another, ensuring they receive consistent and coordinated instruction throughout their educational journey.

39. C, E: An important component of promoting continuous professional growth in a school district includes providing administrators, teachers, and staff with differentiated learning opportunities that align with their interests, needs, and career aspirations. In this scenario, a teacher has expressed interest in enhancing his educational leadership skills. To meet this teacher's specific needs, the superintendent should consider offering a mentoring program with an experienced administrator coupled with a training program focused on educational leadership and school management. Pairing the teacher with a seasoned administrator in a mentorship program means the teacher can receive personalized guidance and valuable insights into educational leadership. Through this mentorship, the teacher can benefit from practical strategies and advice to develop his leadership skills. Further, by enrolling the teacher in a training program focused on educational leadership and school management, the superintendent can provide targeted instruction on best practices in leading educational initiatives and managing school operations. This approach would help to ensure that the teacher gains the necessary knowledge and skills to excel in an educational leadership role, therefore enabling him to make informed decisions within the school community. By offering these differentiated learning opportunities, the superintendent can empower this teacher to engage in meaningful professional development that aligns with his career goals and fosters growth in educational leadership.

40. A: Assessments that align with both the curriculum and instructional practices provide valuable insight into students' overall understanding and progress toward mastering learning goals. In this scenario, analyzing students' performance on project-based assessments would allow the superintendent to gather direct feedback regarding their ability to apply learned knowledge and skills in real-world contexts, which is the primary goal of project-based learning. By evaluating students' performance on assessments that are specifically designed to align with project-based learning objectives, the superintendent can determine the effectiveness of the curriculum and instructional practices in promoting critical thinking and problem-solving skills. This would allow the superintendent to identify strengths and areas for improvement within the project-based learning curriculum and make necessary adjustments to the program to continuously promote student learning and academic success.

41. B: Evaluating student performance on assessments provides valuable insight into the effectiveness and alignment of instructional practices with the curriculum and learning targets. Specifically, administering pre- and post- assessments allows for a comprehensive analysis of student growth and development over time. In other words, pre- and post- assessments help educators measure the impact of instructional practices on learning outcomes. In this scenario, conducting pre- and post- assessments allows the superintendent to establish a link between student performances and the instructional practices employed in the project-based learning program. By evaluating student growth in critical thinking skills, the superintendent can gather feedback on how effectively the instructional practices associated with project-based learning are fostering the desired outcomes. This connection helps the superintendent assess the effectiveness of instructional practices by determining whether they are supporting student learning and academic success in the context of project-based learning. A comprehensive analysis of the impact of the curriculum on students' development of critical thinking skills provides valuable information to guide future instruction, refine teaching strategies, and make adjustments to continuously improve the project-based learning program and enhance student success.

42. C: Gathering both quantitative and qualitative data is beneficial in helping a superintendent develop a comprehensive perspective regarding the effectiveness of instructional programs. Analyzing student performance through various assessments, including pre- and post- tests, will provide the superintendent with objective, measurable feedback on the effectiveness of the project-based learning program in promoting student growth and academic achievement. By coupling this strategy with conducting regular reflection and collaboration meetings with school administrators and teachers, the superintendent can gain a holistic view of the daily functioning of the program and its impact on student engagement and success. The superintendent can use these meetings to gather firsthand qualitative feedback about the implementation of the project-based learning program while facilitating open dialogue to share insights, discuss challenges, and identify areas for improvement. This will allow the superintendent to make well-informed decisions and make necessary adjustments to continuously improve the quality of the project-based learning program and enhance student learning.

43. A: An effective superintendent consistently upholds ethical standards in all aspects of their role. This commitment fosters professionalism, fairness, and integrity within the school district while promoting ethical and professional relationships and decision-making among administrators and staff. This includes acting ethically by demonstrating impartiality when making decisions that impact the district and its educational programs. In this situation, considering a vendor contract with a close personal friend creates a potential conflict of interest. The superintendent's personal relationship with the vendor introduces biases and the possibility of preferential treatment, which undermines fundamental principles such as fairness, transparency, and equal opportunity within the district. Prioritizing the personal relationship over an objective evaluation of other vendors jeopardizes the integrity of the procurement process. Avoiding conflicts of interest is integral to ensuring impartial decision-making and upholding the district's commitment to ethical and transparent practices. By adhering to ethical standards and prioritizing the best interests of the district, the superintendent maintains the trust of the community and fosters equal opportunities for all vendors.

44. C: A superintendent must act ethically and professionally in all situations. This includes recognizing and appropriately addressing potential conflicts of interest during decision-making processes so as to avoid any potential biases and maintain impartiality. In the given scenario, the superintendent's personal relationship with the vendor introduces the risk of bias, which could influence the decision-making process. To uphold ethical standards, the most appropriate course of action would be for the superintendent to recuse herself from the vendor selection process. In doing so, the superintendent acknowledges the implications of her relationship with the vendor and takes proactive steps to avoid perceptions of favoritism or personal influence and to ensure fairness in the selection process. By assigning this responsibility to another administrator or committee, the superintendent ensures objectivity in the vendor selection process, thus upholding fairness, equal opportunity, and ethical integrity.

45. B: Promoting a culture of collaboration and resource sharing among educators significantly enhances teaching and learning outcomes within a school district. By tapping into the wealth of collective knowledge and expertise, educators can create a more enriching learning experience for students. An effective strategy to achieve this is implementing an online repository, which would provide teachers with the ability to upload, access, and download teaching resources and materials. With this streamlined approach, teachers can efficiently share lesson plans, activities, and multimedia resources, reducing redundant work and saving time. The accessibility of an online repository fosters a collaborative environment where teachers can contribute to and benefit from a shared pool of knowledge, thus expanding their repertoire of instructional materials and strategies. Teachers can continuously update an online repository with new materials, therefore ensuring its adaptability to evolving needs and encouraging ongoing collaboration and communication among educators. Through the implementation of an online repository, the superintendent can create a supportive educational community where teachers can exchange ideas and leverage collective knowledge to enrich students' learning experiences. The integration of technology in this manner enhances communication and collaboration, leading to improved teaching practices and student learning outcomes throughout the district.

46. D: A superintendent is responsible for creating a safe, caring, and healthy learning environment for all students. This includes addressing instances of bullying within the school district swiftly and thoroughly. In this situation, collaborating with key stakeholders, such as teachers, counselors, and administrators to develop and implement an anti-bullying program would best demonstrate commitment to addressing the reported incident and preventing future occurrences. Such a program should include education to raise awareness about bullying, prevention strategies to promote a positive school climate, and intervention techniques to support victims and address bullying behaviors. This proactive and multifaceted approach effectively addresses the immediate concern while establishing a long-term framework for fostering a safe, caring, and healthy environment across the school district.

47. C, D: In the realm of educational leadership, crafting and communicating a district mission is essential in uniting stakeholders around common goals. By effectively conveying the district's mission to promote inclusivity and academic excellence while preparing students for success in a globalized society, the superintendent can help ensure that all members of the educational community share a clear and cohesive understanding of its purpose. This understanding ultimately fosters unity and commitment toward realizing the district's goals. To achieve this, employing multiple means of communication is vital, as it accommodates a diverse range of needs and increases the likelihood of reaching all stakeholders. By hosting a monthly webinar for students, parents, educators, and community members, the superintendent can leverage the power of technology to engage stakeholders in meaningful discussions about strategies promoting inclusivity and academic excellence while preparing students for a globalized society. Webinars provide an interactive platform to share information, updates, and accomplishments related to the new district mission. This approach facilitates real-time communication while encouraging open dialogue and enabling participants to share their insights and experiences, thus fostering a stronger sense of connection. The superintendent can further ensure that communication about this initiative reaches key stakeholders by distributing a comprehensive handbook outlining the district's new mission, vision, and core values. This tangible resource would serve as a reference guide, ensuring that students, parents, and district staff have easy access to the foundational principles of the district's mission. By supplementing this with practical strategies for fostering inclusivity, academic excellence, and preparing students for success in a globalized society, the handbook equips stakeholders with actionable insights to infuse elements of the mission into daily practices, therefore promoting a shared commitment to its fulfillment.

48. C: Ensuring equitable education for all students includes providing access to essential learning materials and resources, including library and media resources. However, budget constraints can sometimes pose challenges in meeting these needs. In this scenario, the district faces limited financial resources to allocate library and media resources for the elementary school in need. To address this effectively, the superintendent can work with local businesses and community organizations to seek external support. By fostering partnerships and securing donations or sponsorships, the superintendent can acquire new and updated library and media resources specifically for the elementary school in need, thus ensuring equitable access across the district. This strategic approach harnesses community engagement to bridge the resource gap and promote equal educational opportunities for all students.

49. C: Amidst budget constraints, school districts can face significant challenges in efficiently organizing and allocating staff resources to meet students' learning needs, particularly when there is a surge in demand for student support services. To address this issue, the superintendent must implement strategic measures to optimize district efficiency and ensure that teachers and staff are assigned roles that leverage their professional expertise. One effective approach to this challenge would be to form collaborative teams of teachers, specialists, and support staff to identify student learning needs and design comprehensive, tailored intervention plans. This strategy would bring together educators with diverse skill sets, enabling the district to harness their collective knowledge to effectively address individual student needs. These collaborative teams could capitalize on each member's strengths to create targeted intervention plans that cater to the specific needs of students requiring personalized support. Through this approach, the district can optimize staff resources while ensuring that each student receives the support necessary to thrive academically and emotionally. By working together, teams can maximize the impact of limited resources, providing efficient and effective support services that align with the district's budget constraints while fostering a supportive learning environment focused on quality learning experiences for every student.

50. B: Establishing and maintaining productive relationships with members of the district board of education is essential in achieving the district's mission and goals to promote student success. This can be achieved by facilitating regular meetings with members of the district board. Such meetings would provide a space to openly discuss important matters related to the education program, provide updates on initiatives and progress, and ensure alignment between the district's objectives and the board's vision. Fostering a sense of collaboration and shared responsibility would enable the superintendent to garner support from the board and work together with them toward the common goal of enhancing student achievement. By maintaining open and transparent communication, the superintendent can cultivate a sense of trust and strengthen relationships with members of the board, thus allowing for more effective decision-making and the successful implementation of district-wide initiatives.

51. B: Promoting the academic and social well-being of students with disabilities requires that the superintendent understand how to implement strategies and programs that adequately address students' unique sets of needs. By establishing district-wide student support centers that offer academic assistance, tutoring, and social-emotional learning programs, a superintendent can effectively meet a range of needs and foster a sense of active engagement in the school community. Such a program would provide students with access to the necessary resources, support, and tools to overcome barriers to learning and achieve academic success while helping them develop important social skills such as effective communication, relationship-building, and empathy. When these needs are properly addressed, students are more likely to become actively engaged in the school community.

52. D: Effectively managing physical resources in a school district includes adhering to federal laws and regulations to protect the safety and well-being of students and staff. One such set of regulations is mandated by the Occupational Safety and Health Administration (OSHA), which establishes and oversees safety standards in the workplace. In this scenario, the superintendent must ensure that the new science labs and equipment, along with their use by students and staff, strictly adhere to OSHA guidelines. To do so, it is important that the superintendent conduct regular safety inspections of the science labs and equipment. This would allow the superintendent to identify any hazards and ensure OSHA compliance, therefore protecting the safety of teachers, staff, and students using the new equipment. Regular safety inspections would allow for safety concerns to be addressed quickly while fostering a conducive environment for students to actively participate in hands-on learning experiences in science. By upholding OSHA standards through consistent inspections, the superintendent can ensure a safe learning environment that aligns with federal regulations and protects the well-being of teachers, staff, and students.

53. B: Recognizing and responding appropriately to potential ethical issues in the school district is integral to ensuring a safe and secure educational environment. The superintendent must be prompt and thorough when addressing such matters; this includes following established procedures and immediately conducting an investigation when ethical issues are reported. In this scenario, a thorough investigation will allow the superintendent to gather evidence and communicate with the individuals involved, including the teacher in question, the student, and possible witnesses. Gathering evidence will help the superintendent to determine the nature of the communication while considering all perspectives, thus ensuring an objective assessment of the situation. By following established procedures and diligently collecting evidence, the superintendent can make informed decisions and take appropriate actions based on facts. This proactive approach fosters transparency and accountability within the district while demonstrating a commitment to maintaining ethical integrity. Although suspending the teacher without pay (choice D) may be an appropriate action depending on the nature of the texts, investigating the situation should be the first step.

54. C: Learning and whole-child development are most effective when school leaders, teachers, and support staff collaborate to address students' individual academic, social, and emotional needs. In creating a "Student Success Team," the superintendent intends to establish such a collaborative culture among staff members by encouraging them to work together to develop targeted interventions and support systems that address the unique academic, social, and emotional needs of students. This approach promotes a shared responsibility for student success by empowering staff to take ownership of interventions and contributes to a supportive and nurturing learning environment that promotes student success and wellbeing.

55. B: Behavioral issues among students can vary significantly, making personalized and comprehensive intervention plans essential in cultivating a positive learning environment and supporting the well-being of all learners. Behavior Intervention Plans (BIPs) are personalized and systematic approaches aimed at addressing behavioral challenges and supporting students in educational settings. These plans involve identifying specific behaviors requiring attention, understanding their underlying causes, and devising tailored strategies to address them effectively. BIPs serve as valuable tools for promoting positive behavior, improving social interactions, and providing targeted support to students facing behavioral difficulties. The development of BIPs typically involves a student support team consisting of educators, counselors, and behavioral specialists who work together to ensure that interventions align with the individual needs of each student. In this scenario, organizing such a team to create personalized BIPs would be most effective in addressing the increased prevalence of behavioral issues among students in the identified middle school. By forming a dedicated team, the superintendent can ensure that the development of BIPs is collaborative and incorporates insights from multiple perspectives. Each student's unique behavioral needs can be thoroughly assessed, and individual strategies can be devised to address their specific challenges. This student-centered approach would foster a positive learning environment in which students receive the necessary support to succeed academically, socially, and emotionally.

56. A, B, F, H: In a diverse educational environment, providing differentiated avenues for professional learning and growth is essential to supporting the unique interests, needs, and career goals of all staff members. Recognizing that educators, both novice and experienced, possess varying levels of expertise and areas of focus is an important part of creating a comprehensive approach that caters to all educators' professional development. In the above scenario, answer choices A, B, F, and H each represent differentiated opportunities that support the needs of both novice and experienced educators. Hosting a district-wide conference on innovative teaching methods and classroom management techniques allows educators to select sessions aligned with their interests, fostering engagement and growth in specific areas. By implementing a mentorship program, the superintendent acknowledges the importance of personalized guidance—experienced administrators can offer valuable support to new teachers as they navigate their roles. Such mentorships are often beneficial both to the mentor and the mentee. Further, offering specialized training sessions on technology integration provides a pathway for both novice and experienced teachers to enhance their instructional practices and meet students' evolving learning needs. Lastly, providing financial support for attending relevant professional development events helps to ensure that administrators and staff can access tailored opportunities that align with their individual growth trajectories. By providing differentiated pathways for professional learning and growth, the superintendent can foster continuous improvement and empower educators of all experience levels to excel in their roles.

57. B: Conducting regular formative assessments throughout instruction is a valuable strategy for gathering and analyzing data to evaluate the effectiveness of instructional practices and monitor student progress. Such assessments can be formal or informal, and they can occur throughout instruction to measure student engagement, understanding, and the overall effectiveness of instructional strategies. Educators can use the data gathered to identify areas for improvement and make continuous adjustments throughout the learning process to promote student success. In this example, collaborating with English Language Arts teachers in the district to develop a set of common formative assessments aligned with the curriculum and academic standards would help provide the feedback necessary to improve student learning outcomes. District-wide collaboration would ensure consistency and alignment in assessing student learning, therefore promoting a sense of shared responsibility and understanding of expectations and instructional goals. This approach would facilitate targeted interventions and support for students while simultaneously providing feedback to continuously refine teaching practices, leading to improved student learning outcomes in English Language Arts.

58. C: A well-structured data collection and analysis system is indispensable in guiding informed decisions and driving improvements within a school district. This systematic approach empowers educators to base their choices on relevant, objective information and accurate insights. In this scenario, the superintendent has implemented a multifaceted data collection and analysis system that fosters a comprehensive and data-driven approach to continuous improvement in literacy. This method ensures a comprehensive understanding of students' reading proficiency, integrating an array of data sources. These encompass both qualitative data, such as teacher assessments and observations, and quantitative sources, including reading fluency and vocabulary metrics. The superintendent's strategy recognizes the dynamic nature of educational improvement, acknowledging that progress is not uniform. The varied facets of data, gathered and meticulously analyzed, provide the district with the flexibility to adapt and customize instructional strategies to cater to the diverse and evolving needs of students. Ultimately, this comprehensive data-driven strategy equips educators with the means to make informed adjustments to curriculum and instruction that effectively enhance reading proficiency among elementary students in the district.

59. A: Maintaining cybersecurity in an increasingly digital era is essential in protecting the safety of students and staff within a school district. In this scenario, collaborating with local IT experts after a cybersecurity breach that compromised student and staff data is an important first step in assessing the district's current cybersecurity infrastructure and identifying weaknesses to improve security and prevent future occurrences. The superintendent can further prevent future breaches by conducting regular training sessions for administrators, teachers, and staff that focus on best practices and risk mitigation related to cybersecurity. Regular training would help ensure that educators are informed and equipped to identify potential breaches and respond effectively in the event of a cybersecurity threat. These trainings would help teachers, administrators, and staff understand how to protect sensitive data while promoting awareness of common strategies used by cybercriminals. With increased awareness and knowledge of how to identify and prevent breaches to cybersecurity, the district can reduce the likelihood of threats and protect student and staff data more effectively.

60. C, D: Effective educational leadership requires the implementation of both incremental and transformational strategies to achieve continuous and lasting positive change. Incremental adjustments allow for targeted, immediate improvements, while transformational shifts bring about holistic and lasting changes. Balancing these strategies is essential for district and school improvement, as it is important to address both immediate concerns and long-term progress goals. When addressing an increasing student dropout rate, establishing a mentorship program would provide an incremental change that offers personalized support. By pairing experienced teachers with students at risk of dropping out, this strategy provides individualized guidance and promotes immediate improvement in student engagement and performance. This approach acknowledges that, while long-term changes are necessary, offering targeted support can result in immediate positive effects. To drive a transformational change for lasting improvement in student retention, the superintendent should work to overhaul the curriculum and teaching methods used in the school. This strategy would fundamentally change how instruction is delivered, incorporating real-world, hands-on experiences to increase student engagement by making learning more relevant and meaningful. Through the integration of both incremental and transformational changes, the superintendent can ensure that the school experiences immediate positive change while laying the foundation for sustained, meaningful improvement over time.

61. D: To cultivate a culture of ethical and professional conduct among administrators, teachers, and staff, it is important to establish clear policies that outline expectations, promote accountability, and incorporate safeguards against misconduct. By thoroughly reviewing the district's assessment policies and procedures in this scenario, the superintendent can identify any potential gaps or vulnerabilities that may enable the manipulation of student test scores. Doing so would allow the superintendent to address any shortcomings within the policies, therefore helping to ensure that assessments are conducted in a standardized and ethical manner. Further, by implementing necessary revisions, the superintendent can enhance the prevention of any potential tampering with student test scores. This proactive approach sends a clear message to administrators, teachers, and staff about professional expectations regarding the new assessment system and communicates that any efforts to compromise student test scores will not be tolerated. Taking these steps would establish a framework for consistent and equitable assessment practices to ensure that student performance is accurately and honestly represented.

62. A: Another integral component of the superintendent's role is understanding strategies for cultivating a shared vision among various stakeholders within the school district. This shared vision helps align everyone involved toward a common goal and ensures that all perspectives and needs are considered. In this scenario, the superintendent aims to emphasize technology integration and 21st-century skills through a new mission that will focus on preparing students for the digital world while fostering a sense of global citizenship. To effectively develop a shared vision and understanding of this mission, the superintendent should conduct quarterly focus group discussions with parents, teachers, students, and community members. By engaging in these discussions, the superintendent can gather diverse perspectives and insights from different stakeholders. This inclusive approach would allow for a comprehensive understanding of how the district's mission and values can be integrated into daily educational practices. By creating a space for open dialogue and collaboration, the superintendent can tap into the collective wisdom of the educational community, thus helping to ensure that the vision is well-rounded and considers the needs and goals of everyone involved. Further, the insights gained from these focus group discussions can provide valuable guidance in refining the district's mission, vision, and core values to better resonate with the stakeholders it serves and increase the likelihood of successful implementation.

63. D: Staff morale and, ultimately, student achievement benefit when educators are provided with ample opportunities to engage in self-reflection, study, and professional development. Providing such opportunities communicates that educators are valued and respected in their field and demonstrates a commitment to their continuous growth. Establishing a mentorship program in which experienced educators can guide new or less-experienced colleagues is a highly effective strategy for encouraging staff to develop their pedagogical knowledge and skills. A mentorship program provides a collaborative, supportive environment for reflection and guidance. Mentors can share experiences, professional knowledge, and constructive feedback to help new colleagues improve their practice. Further, establishing a platform for teachers to share and discuss reflections, insights, and best practices is also beneficial in promoting continuous professional learning and development. Such a platform can provide a space in which educators can openly exchange ideas, seek advice, discuss instructional strategies, and learn from one another.

64. A: Driving meaningful change in education requires the development of effective strategies that uphold the district's vision and mission. An important part of this process involves ensuring that actions intended to reach the district's goals align seamlessly with the various components of the established vision. In the context of community engagement and services, such alignment ensures that each action contributes cohesively to the comprehensive educational experience aimed at fostering students' sense of social responsibility. By forging partnerships with local nonprofit entities to integrate service-learning projects into the curriculum, the superintendent can directly align actions with the mission of fostering community involvement and social responsibility. This approach would encompass a holistic educational philosophy, merging academic knowledge with hands-on projects that strengthen students' understanding of their roles and responsibilities within the community.

65. D: Effectively addressing issues presented within a school district requires the superintendent to first gain an understanding of the underlying causes. Doing so allows the superintendent to develop and implement policies and procedures that adequately meet the needs of schools and students in the district. In this scenario, working with key stakeholders, including teachers, administrators, and parents, would help the superintendent gain insight into the root causes of student tardiness among high schools in the district. Through this collaborative and student-centered approach, the superintendent can develop a comprehensive understanding of the unique circumstances that may be contributing to student tardiness. Potential challenges could include transportation, family circumstances, or other factors that may impact punctuality. By identifying the underlying causes of tardiness in the district, the superintendent can tailor interventions and policies that directly address the root of the issue in a manner that is responsive to students' specific needs, thus fostering a supportive environment that promotes student success.

66. A: Providing students with the opportunity to learn about one another's cultures, backgrounds, and experiences is an integral component in creating a safe, welcoming, and inclusive environment that embraces diversity. Doing so helps students build understanding and appreciation for different perspectives while allowing them to discover similarities among themselves. Implementing a program where students from different cultures are paired up to support and learn from one another would provide students from different backgrounds with the opportunity to connect, share traditions and customs, and collaborate, thus fostering a sense of support, mutual respect, and inclusivity within the school community. Such an initiative would promote a safe environment for all students while simultaneously integrating the cultures and languages of the school community into the learning environment for a more diverse educational experience. A celebration event would also provide students with the opportunity to learn about other students' cultures and share their own experiences, but a one-time event would not show as strong of a commitment to this initiative as an established program.

67. D: Fostering inclusivity and equity in a learning environment requires a conscientious effort to advocate for and address the specific needs of all students, including those from low-income backgrounds. The data presented in the chart above highlights disparities among student groups, particularly those from low-income backgrounds, who exhibit lower test scores, engagement in support programs, and—most notably—attendance rates. Lower attendance rates can significantly hinder students' academic achievement and overall learning experience and therefore must be explicitly and thoroughly addressed. The superintendent in this scenario can mitigate this challenge by advocating for initiatives that directly target attendance issues among low-income students. These initiatives—such as mentoring programs and family engagement strategies—would be beneficial in addressing the root causes of the attendance issues while promoting collaborative relationships between schools and families to enhance the overall learning experience for all students. By addressing attendance barriers, the superintendent can positively influence students' academic outcomes and overall well-being, thus contributing to a more equitable and inclusive learning environment.

68. A: Cultivating an environment of inclusivity, care, equity, and trust is integral to students' holistic development and success. To achieve this, it is imperative that students of all backgrounds have access to the necessary support to meet their unique learning needs. The chart provided highlights the challenge of low participation rates in support programs across all student groups in the district, thus indicating a gap in meeting their learning needs. Such a gap in support is likely to hinder students' academic performance and overall learning experience. By establishing effective lines of communication among teachers, parents, and students to inform them about the availability and advantages of support programs, the superintendent can effectively begin addressing this area of concern to foster a more equitable, inclusive, and supportive learning environment. Prioritizing clear communication would help to ensure that all stakeholders are well-informed about resources that can aid students in their learning. This proactive approach would enhance the likelihood of students' success by providing them with the support they need while demonstrating a strong commitment to fostering an inclusive, equitable, and caring learning environment.

69. C: In cultivating an educational environment that is truly equitable, inclusive, caring, and built on trust, it is essential to recognize and address the distinctive learning needs of all students. English Language Learners (ELLs), in particular, may face specific challenges related to academic language acquisition, which can significantly influence their performance. The chart provided highlights this concern, indicating lower test scores in English Language Arts and Math compared to their peers in other groups. These students often struggle with deciphering intricate academic language, which is a challenge that warrants targeted support. By establishing specialized language support programs, the superintendent can provide ELL students with the necessary tools and resources to enhance their command of academic language in English. Doing so would help to enhance ELL students' comprehension of subject material and, ultimately, their academic achievement, thus fostering a more equitable, inclusive, and caring learning environment.

70. B: The quality of relationships among students, teachers, and staff in a school plays a significant role in fostering academic achievement and supporting social-emotional development. When students feel engaged and included in the learning process, they are more likely to form positive connections with the adults in the school. A superintendent could effectively address the issue in the given scenario by establishing a student advisory council. Doing so would provide students with a platform to express their opinions and concerns, share experiences, and actively participate in decision-making processes that directly affect their education. Using this strategy, the superintendent creates an environment of open dialogue and collaboration in which students feel acknowledged in their perspectives, empowered to take ownership over their own learning, and included in the school community. Involving students in decision-making ensures that their voices are heard and their contributions to the school community are recognized, thus resulting in enhanced engagement and stronger relationships with adults in the building. This promotes a culture of collaboration and mutual respect, ultimately creating a thriving environment for academic achievement and social-emotional development.

71. D: Regularly gathering and analyzing data to evaluate the effectiveness of instructional practices and monitor student progress is essential for ensuring the success of educational programs. This process enables stakeholders to identify program strengths, pinpoint areas that require improvement, and make necessary adjustments to enhance student learning outcomes. As such, it is important to ensure that administrators and teachers are engaged in collecting, analyzing, and utilizing student data to make informed instructional decisions. Implementing a structured system for administrators and teachers to collect and analyze student reading data would serve as an effective approach. Establishing a systematic process for gathering relevant assessment data would promote efficiency and consistency in data collection and ensure all stakeholders collect the same types of information from students in the reading intervention program. In addition, this approach encourages collaboration among administrators and staff, as it enables them to collectively examine and interpret the data, discuss students' reading progress, and identify which instructional strategies have proven effective and which may need adjustments to better support struggling readers. Implementing a system for administrators and teachers to regularly collect and analyze student data promotes their active involvement in utilizing assessment data. Implementing this system would also foster collaboration, informed decision-making, and instructional improvement, ultimately supporting student learning and success within the reading intervention program.

72. D: In a school district, conducting formal evaluations is essential for providing actionable feedback to support the growth and professional development of staff members. Superintendents must offer meaningful guidance to educators based on their instructional practices to promote continuous instructional improvement and enhance student learning outcomes. For example, after observing a teacher in her science class, the next step should be to schedule a meeting with the teacher for a comprehensive discussion. During this meeting, the superintendent can identify the teacher's strengths and discuss areas for improvement based on the observation, using a rubric and relevant performance indicators. This collaborative approach empowers the teacher to take ownership of her professional growth and sets clear, attainable professional development goals. By utilizing a rubric, the superintendent can ensure that the evaluation process is rooted in objective criteria, making it an effective method for providing specific and constructive feedback that will further enhance the teacher's instructional practices.

73. C: Opening school facilities and resources to students, families, and community members beyond regular school hours can greatly enhance community engagement and yield positive outcomes. By partnering with local organizations and community centers to coordinate supervised recreational activities on the new playground during non-school hours, the superintendent can effectively extend its accessibility to the community. Doing so would allow students, families, and community members to make use of the playground outside of school hours while ensuring their safety and adequate supervision. In addition to providing a shared recreational space, allowing access to the playground outside of school hours fosters active community participation, promotes inclusivity, and encourages meaningful interactions among students, families, and community members. By leveraging the resources and expertise of local organizations and community centers, the superintendent can optimize the potential of the playground and create an inviting environment for community engagement and enjoyment beyond school hours. Although opening the playground for extended hours while utilizing surveillance measures (Choice A) would likely also benefit the students, families, and community to an extent, it would not have as positive an impact as collaborating with local organizations would because it would not actively involve the community at large.

74. D: Understanding the perspectives of teachers in the district regarding evaluation methods is essential for fostering buy-in and establishing a system that genuinely facilitates professional growth. In this situation, collaborating with teachers during the initial phase of implementation benefits the development process by bringing their firsthand expertise into the process. Engaging teachers in the design and piloting of the evaluation system means the superintendent can ensure that the system reflects the real challenges, needs, and nuances of the classroom environment. This collaborative approach demonstrates respect for teachers' professional knowledge while increasing their investment in the system's success. When teachers are active participants in designing the evaluation process, they become more likely to find it relevant, fair, and supportive of their growth. Including their perspectives in the pilot phase allows for more practical adjustments to be made based on their feedback, thus leading to a more accurate and effective evaluation system. Ultimately, this process would foster a sense of ownership and accountability among teachers, making them more likely to accept the evaluation system and its outcomes.

75. C, D: Deficit-based education refers to the implicit belief that students from marginalized groups, such as those from low socioeconomic backgrounds or different ethnicities, are inherently less academically capable than their non-marginalized peers. This perception can unconsciously influence educators' attitudes toward these students, leading to lowered expectations and ineffective instruction, and therefore must be addressed explicitly and comprehensively. One effective strategy to address this issue would be to adopt a strengths-based approach to instruction in which educators recognize and appreciate the unique talents, capabilities, and potentials of students from marginalized backgrounds. Rather than focusing on perceived deficits, a strengths-based approach emphasizes the diverse strengths and assets that students bring to the classroom. Strengths-based learning involves providing opportunities for students to demonstrate their abilities, talents, and interests while adapting instruction to build upon their existing strengths. Through this approach, educators foster a more empowering and inclusive learning environment where each student is valued and viewed as academically capable. To strengthen the effectiveness of this initiative, the superintendent should provide professional development opportunities for educators to develop cultural competence. Doing so would equip teachers and staff with the fundamental knowledge and skills necessary to recognize and eliminate their own implicit biases, thus creating a more equitable, supportive, and culturally responsive classroom environment. By implementing both of these strategies, the superintendent can actively make progress toward mitigating the detrimental effects of deficit-based education to ensure fair treatment and high expectations for all students.

76. A: Developing students' social-emotional skills is a fundamental aspect of fostering comprehensive whole-child learning and development (which encompasses academic progress, social interactions, and emotional well-being). In a middle school where students face challenges in their social interactions and struggle to form positive relationships, a superintendent could best demonstrate commitment to this notion by implementing a comprehensive social-emotional learning (SEL) curriculum. Doing so would equip students with the necessary skills to navigate social interactions, build empathy, and develop meaningful connections. Focusing on students' social and emotional development helps them learn to understand and respect one another, communicate more effectively, and cultivate positive relationships. This holistic approach creates an inclusive and supportive school environment that enhances overall well-being and student achievement.

77. B, C, E, G: Multifaceted challenges within a school district require a nuanced approach that encompasses various strategies, from major changes to adaptive adjustments. This style of approach simultaneously accounts for the complexities of the issues at hand and the need to engage stakeholders and leverage their insights. A layered approach ensures that the superintendent can address challenges comprehensively, ultimately fostering a more effective solution. In this scenario, the new superintendent must devise solutions related to student test scores, teacher turnover, and community involvement. By developing a comprehensive five-year plan, the superintendent can implement a transformational approach that advocates for a complete overhaul of the curriculum, innovative teaching methods, and administrative restructuring. This approach would address root causes head-on for substantial and lasting change. Introducing small, targeted changes is an incremental problem-solving approach, facilitating steady progress while minimizing disruption. This strategy acknowledges that complex issues may require gradual improvements to yield consistent results. Holding regular town hall meetings would show that the superintendent recognizes the importance of community involvement in addressing multifaceted challenges and would allow for an adaptive approach, incorporating stakeholders' insights to refine improvement strategies over time. Lastly, establishing a cross-functional task force comprising district officials, teachers, and community members is beneficial in leveraging a range of perspectives to facilitate ongoing adaptation. By implementing these diverse strategies, the superintendent can effectively address complex issues, leverage stakeholder perspectives, and ensure a well-rounded response that maximizes the potential for lasting positive change in the district.

78. A, D: A multifaceted approach to developing curriculum and instruction systems is essential to ensure that learning experiences align with academic standards, reflect high expectations for student learning, and promote cultural responsiveness. In this scenario, the superintendent works with a committee of administrators and teachers to gather multiple perspectives from individuals attuned to students' needs, thus allowing for an effective review and revision of the current English Language Arts (ELA) curriculum and instructional practices. Throughout this collaboration, the superintendent and committee should prioritize researching various ELA textbooks and learning materials that best align with academic standards and offer rigorous, culturally responsive content. Carefully choosing materials that reflect students' backgrounds helps to ensure that learning experiences are relevant and meaningful, therefore promoting active engagement in learning within a culturally relevant context. Further, the superintendent and committee should focus on creating professional development workshops focused on culturally responsive teaching methods. Doing so would empower teachers with the necessary knowledge and skills for integrating these practices into ELA instruction to foster an inclusive, respectful atmosphere that enhances student engagement and improves learning outcomes. Through this comprehensive approach, the superintendent and curriculum committee can develop an effective system of curriculum instruction that embraces cultural diversity, aligns with high academic standards, and improves student success in English Language Arts.

79. A: A systematic approach is integral when devising strategic plans for district and school improvement efforts. In this scenario, the superintendent's comprehensive review of the mathematics education goals and identification of the proficiency gap establish a foundational understanding of the existing shortcomings. By subsequently conducting a needs assessment, the superintendent can delve deeper into the specific areas that require intervention. This entails gathering data and insights to pinpoint the high-leverage areas of need within mathematics education. With this data, the superintendent can then craft targeted strategies that align with the identified gaps, ensuring a focused, systematic, and effective approach to improving mathematics proficiency skills throughout the district.

80. B, C: Employing multiple approaches to evaluate assessment practices in the classroom is beneficial in providing the feedback necessary for a comprehensive analysis of the validity and overall effectiveness of the assessments. In this scenario, regular classroom visits would allow the superintendent to observe the implementation of the new formative assessment strategy in action. The superintendent can witness how the strategy is applied in daily instruction, the level of student engagement, and the strategy's alignment with learning targets, thus gaining valuable insight into the strategy's validity and effect on student learning. Pairing this approach with analyzing student work samples and portfolios would allow the superintendent to assess students' growth and development over time after the implementation of the new formative assessment strategy. This would help the superintendent gauge the extent to which the new strategy aligns with the curriculum, standards, and instructional practices while providing relevant and meaningful feedback regarding student progress. In combination, the approaches described in choices B and C would allow the superintendent to evaluate both the implementation of the new formative assessment strategy in the classroom and the long-term effect on student learning. Through this approach, the superintendent can identify strengths and areas for improvement to continuously enhance the learning experience for students.

81. C: Translating a district's vision into tangible outcomes requires the development of a strategic plan. Such a plan serves as a framework that guides the execution of the vision and ensures the alignment of actions toward a common goal. The process involves careful consideration of the necessary resources that will support the plan's implementation. This is especially true in a diverse educational environment, where promoting cultural awareness is essential for creating an inclusive learning environment. In this situation, establishing a team of culturally knowledgeable educators, including bilingual instructors, to design and deliver a new cultural awareness curriculum would be most strategic in acquiring the essential human resources needed to support the superintendent's vision. This team of culturally knowledgeable educators would possess the expertise necessary to deliver the curriculum in a culturally sensitive fashion to align with the district's goal of integrating cultural diversity into daily learning experiences. Culturally knowledgeable educators can authentically incorporate diverse perspectives, experiences, and traditions into the curriculum, fostering an inclusive and enriching educational environment for all students.

82. B, D: Efficient organizational structures are essential in a school district to ensure smooth daily operations and effective management. In this scenario, the recent increase in student enrollment has put a strain on these systems, leading to challenges in coordinating resources and timely decision-making for administrators and staff members. To adequately address these issues and prevent disruptions to teaching and learning, it is important that the superintendent employ a variety of approaches to increase the efficiency of daily responsibilities. By first engaging in a comprehensive analysis of existing organizational structures, the superintendent can identify areas that need improvement and streamline administrative tasks. This approach would allow administrators and staff to make targeted improvements for optimizing workflow and enhancing overall efficiency, thus better aligning the district with its growing needs. By also implementing a task management system, administrators and staff can track their responsibilities efficiently, practice better time management, and improve daily productivity. This strategy would help ensure that tasks are organized, deadlines are met, and essential matters receive appropriate and timely attention. By adopting both of these strategies, the superintendent can help the district successfully navigate the challenges of increased student enrollment, therefore safeguarding the quality of teaching and learning while ensuring that resources are coordinated effectively and decisions are made in a timely manner.

83. A: Developmentally Appropriate Practice (DAP) refers to an approach to education that recognizes the unique qualities of each child and acknowledges that children learn and develop at their own pace. According to this framework, effective early childhood education should be tailored to the developmental needs, interests, and abilities of young learners. The principles described in the prompt align closely with the core principles of DAP. DAP emphasizes active engagement with the environment, sensory exploration, and play as essential elements of effective learning for young children. By incorporating these principles into curriculum planning and instruction, the superintendent and educators can create an environment that is tailored to the individual needs and developmental stages of each child, fostering a more meaningful and successful learning experience. DAP also emphasizes the interrelation of cognitive, physical, social, and emotional development, promoting a holistic approach to education that supports whole-child growth and well-being. By adopting DAP as a curriculum planning framework, the district can create a more developmentally appropriate and enriching learning environment for its young students.

84. C: A key responsibility of the superintendent is securing funding to support district goals and enhance the learning experience for students and then ensuring ethical practice and accountability in managing these funds. Doing so promotes a sense of transparency and trust while ensuring that funds are utilized responsibly to benefit the school community. In this scenario, the superintendent is seeking to secure newly added funds to the district's budget with the intention of providing the infrastructure and resources necessary to improve digital literacy and technological competency among students in the district. To achieve this, the superintendent should begin by identifying federal, state, and local grants that are explicitly designated for this purpose. Seeking out grants specifically intended for technology enhancements would allow the superintendent to allocate funds to support the district's vision without diverting resources from other programs. These grants would provide targeted support for the intended goal, therefore ensuring that the funds are used efficiently and transparently. Further, leveraging such grants would support responsible fiscal management, as it would enable the district to provide the necessary infrastructure and resources to enhance students' technological skills and learning experiences without overburdening the existing budget or compromising other initiatives.

85. D: Highly skilled and experienced educators play a significant role in driving student achievement and overall school success. As such, retaining effective administrators and staff members is essential for any school district to maintain continuity and foster a positive, productive learning environment. By implementing effective retention strategies, such as mentorship programs for new administrators and staff, the superintendent can create a supportive, collaborative environment that encourages professional growth and job satisfaction. Mentorship programs offer invaluable benefits for new educators—they provide guidance and support during the potentially overwhelming initial phase of employment. New administrators and staff members often face challenges when acclimating to a new environment, and having experienced mentors can ease their transition, increase confidence, and ensure a smoother integration into the school community. Additionally, mentorship fosters relationships between experienced and new educators, leading to increased collaboration and knowledge-sharing. This promotes a positive working environment and enhances job satisfaction, making educators more likely to remain with the district for the long term. Ultimately, prioritizing effective mentoring and retention strategies helps to ensure an efficient and stable staffing management system that benefits both educators and students.

86. A: Effectively managing staffing needs, including planning for the future, is an important component of ensuring a stable, well-functioning school district. In this scenario, an efficient recruitment system is necessary to address the historically high turnover rate among educators and staff in the district. The superintendent can proactively plan for future staffing needs by establishing internship programs through partnerships with local colleges and universities. These internship programs would provide aspiring educators with hands-on experience in the field while creating a candidate pool for future hiring needs in the district. This would make the recruitment process more efficient while increasing the likelihood of finding highly qualified educators who are already familiar with the district's values. By establishing an internship program as part of the district's recruitment process, the superintendent can effectively address staffing needs, foster a supportive work environment, reduce the turnover rate, and ensure continuity throughout the school district.

87. C: Ensuring due process procedures are followed in a school district is integral when handling situations that may involve disciplinary action or dismissal. Upholding these procedures protects the rights of all employees and promotes a fair and equitable work environment. In this scenario, the superintendent should first provide the accused employee with written notice of the allegations against him or her and the evidence supporting the claims. By doing so, the superintendent demonstrates transparency and respect for the employee's due process rights. This initial notification allows the employee to understand the claims against him or her and prepare a meaningful defense. Following this procedure mitigates the risk of arbitrary decisions, reduces the potential for legal challenges, and fosters a culture of accountability and fairness within the district.

88. A: Distinguishing between and utilizing different evaluation systems is necessary to effectively support teacher professional growth, as different contexts warrant varying approaches to observation and feedback. In the given scenario, the Peer Collaboration Evaluation (PCE) emphasizes self-reflection and self-assessment through its collaborative nature, where teachers actively engage in reviewing their own and one another's teaching practices. Conversely, the Classroom Observation Feedback (COF) system focuses on the expertise of instructional coaches to provide external observations and coaching, therefore offering outside perspectives and support for teachers. By understanding the distinct characteristics of each system, the superintendent can strategically implement these evaluation approaches based on specific teacher development needs. The PCE system facilitates introspection and collaboration among teachers, promoting a deeper understanding of their instructional strategies. The COF system harnesses the expertise of instructional coaches to offer valuable insights and guidance for improvement. The duality in evaluation methods enables the district to cater to diverse teaching scenarios and objectives, fostering a comprehensive and tailored approach to professional development.

89. C: Engaging stakeholders in developing strategies for continuous improvement through evidence-based inquiry helps foster a collaborative and overall effective educational environment. Doing so allows for a comprehensive decision-making process, leveraging stakeholders' diverse perspectives and insights. Such an approach fosters a sense of ownership among stakeholders, thus increasing engagement while ensuring that improvement strategies are based upon concrete, reliable data and informed by current practices and ideologies. In this scenario, the superintendent can most effectively achieve their goal by holding regular quarterly meetings with math teachers, curriculum experts, parents, and researchers where the collective of stakeholders can review student assessment data, identify patterns, and work together to develop strategies for improvement. This approach would encourage stakeholders to examine quantitative data to drive decision-making. Further, the collaborative nature of these meetings would allow stakeholders to bring forth their observations and experiences, thus facilitating constructive dialogue that supplements the data-driven approach. The strategies developed through this combined effort not only result from evidence but also reflect a nuanced understanding of the district's educational needs. This ultimately contributes to the development of effective strategies that target specific areas for improvement, thus enhancing student assessment scores in mathematics across the district.

90. B: To accurately measure student achievement and gather meaningful feedback on the effectiveness of a curriculum, it is important to ensure that both instructional practices and assessment methods are reflective of the curriculum's performance indicators. As such, when a new curriculum is adopted, the superintendent should review and revise existing assessment methods to ensure they are in alignment. Doing so provides the district with accurate, reliable, and relevant information about student learning and progress by directly assessing the knowledge and skills outlined in the new framework. This allows teachers to provide meaningful feedback to students and make informed instructional decisions based on assessment data. Ensuring that assessment methods align with the new curriculum provides insight into its effectiveness and areas for improvement, allowing for continuous adjustments to enhance the overall quality of the curriculum.

91. B: To foster an environment of equity, it is important that educators demonstrate a strong understanding and consideration of each student's unique circumstances, including his or her socioeconomic background. In this situation, the socioeconomic status of many students poses a significant barrier to their participation in school athletics, thus hindering the creation of a truly equitable educational experience. By implementing a tiered fee structure based on family income, the district acknowledges the diverse financial circumstances of its student population and recognizes that some families may be unable to pay due to economic challenges. With a tiered fee structure, low-income students can benefit from reduced or waived participation fees according to their level of need. This approach ensures that financial constraints do not prevent students from participating in school activities, therefore promoting inclusivity and equal opportunities for all. By reducing or eliminating the financial burden, the district ensures that students from economically disadvantaged backgrounds have the same opportunities to participate in extracurricular activities as their more financially privileged peers.

92. D: In order for assessments to provide valid and reliable feedback on student achievement, they must align explicitly with specific learning outcomes outlined in the curriculum. This alignment ensures that assessments accurately measure student understanding and progress, enabling teachers to make informed decisions about future instruction and ultimately improve student learning outcomes. By conducting a thorough analysis of the curriculum, the superintendent, along with a team of administrators and teachers, can identify the essential knowledge and skills that students need to acquire to succeed in mathematics. This analysis ensures a clear understanding of the learning objectives and allows for the alignment of assessment methods with instructional practices. By identifying the specific learning outcomes that need to be assessed, the district can develop assessments that directly measure student progress in those areas. This ensures that assessments provide accurate and meaningful information about students' understanding and mastery in relation to the intended learning outcomes. Further, aligning assessments with the curriculum allows teachers to focus instructional practices on addressing specific learning objectives, thus resulting in more targeted and effective teaching strategies. Through the analysis of the mathematics curriculum and identification of specific learning outcomes, the superintendent, teachers, and administrators establish a cohesive approach to assessment that aligns with the district's goals. This approach allows teachers to accurately monitor student progress, provide targeted feedback, and make informed instructional decisions to improve student learning outcomes in mathematics.

93. D: A superintendent must demonstrate a strong understanding of the unique needs of diverse student populations in order to facilitate and safeguard an equitable educational environment. This includes ensuring programs are in place to provide every student with the necessary resources and support to succeed academically. In this scenario, implementing a comprehensive English as a Second Language (ESL) program would be the most effective strategy for ensuring equity across schools in the district in that it would address the specific language learning needs of English Language Learner (ELL) students. An ESL program would offer targeted English language instruction tailored to the individual students' levels of proficiency. This would provide ELLs with the specialized assistance, support, and resources necessary to overcome language barriers, build English proficiency skills, and achieve learning targets, thus fostering an inclusive learning environment that promotes equity for all students.

94. B: In a continuously evolving educational landscape, it is essential for school districts to remain adaptable and responsive to the changing expectations and needs of students and stakeholders. In this scenario, the superintendent's approach of conducting town hall meetings, surveys, and focus groups demonstrates a proactive effort to involve all stakeholders in the process of shaping the district's mission, vision, and core values. By engaging parents, teachers, students, and community members, the superintendent gains insights into their perspectives, concerns, and expectations. This approach fosters a sense of ownership within the community while ensuring that the district's educational goals and values are aligned with the actual needs of its constituents. Through this collaborative process, the district can make informed adjustments, ensuring that its mission and values resonate with the diverse and dynamic needs of both present and future students, ultimately contributing to a more effective and inclusive learning environment.

95. B: As the leader of the school district, the superintendent is responsible for fostering an environment characterized by ethical and professional behavior. As such, after discovering that an administrator in the district has manipulated student attendance records to improve the school's Average Daily Attendance rate, the superintendent must take prompt and decisive action to maintain the ethical standards of the district. This includes immediately addressing the issue with the administrator in question and initiating appropriate disciplinary actions according to the district's policies. The superintendent upholds honesty, legality, and ethical conduct within the district by holding the administrator accountable for their actions and sending a clear message that such behavior is unacceptable. This approach also serves to cultivate a culture of professional and ethical behavior by deterring others in the district that may have considered engaging in similar misconduct.

96. C: Establishing a system for peer observation and feedback is an effective strategy for promoting mutual accountability among staff members for the success of each student and of the school as a whole. Implementing such a system gives staff members the opportunity to observe their colleagues, provide and receive constructive feedback, and participate in professional dialogue. This strategy encourages collaboration and fosters a sense of shared responsibility toward students and the school. It also promotes continuous professional growth as staff members learn from one another, share ideas, and work together to improve instructional practices and student achievement.

97. C: Developing a strategic plan for improvement in a school district requires not only a clear vision but also effective communication and alignment among stakeholders. This ensures that everyone involved is working collectively towards the common goal. One aspect of this process involves preparing stakeholders and fostering shared understanding to drive commitment. In this scenario, the common goal is to enhance academic performance and bridge classroom learning with real-world applications. The superintendent can establish alignment between teachers, parents, and local business leaders regarding this goal by holding regular collaborative meetings, workshops, and projects. Regular meetings would provide a platform for open dialogue, enabling stakeholders to exchange insights, perspectives, and concerns. Further, workshops and joint projects would facilitate hands-on collaboration among stakeholders, enabling participants to contribute their expertise and collectively shape the initiative's direction. This process would cultivate a sense of shared ownership and commitment, ensuring that stakeholders understand the vision, feel valued, and actively contribute to its success. By fostering alignment through shared understanding, the superintendent can effectively lead the district towards achieving the overarching goal of preparing students for the evolving job market.

98. A: Implementing a comprehensive equity policy across the school district is a significant first step in ensuring that all students have access to a high-quality education. To strengthen this initiative, school leaders, teachers, and staff should be provided with training opportunities focused on cultural responsiveness and implicit bias to ensure that the policy is properly implemented district wide. These training opportunities would promote awareness of cultural differences, help educators recognize and eliminate personal biases, and foster culturally responsive teaching practices. This includes providing the fundamental knowledge and skills necessary to adapt curriculum and instructional strategies according to students' diverse needs, fostering open communication by eliciting and responding to student feedback, and establishing partnerships with community organizations that can provide support and resources to promote student success.

99. B: Fostering transparency among staff, parents, and community members within a school district establishes the foundation of trust necessary to build positive, productive, and collaborative relationships that ultimately benefit student learning. When stakeholders have a clear understanding of the decision-making processes within a school district, they develop a greater sense of trust and are more inclined to become active participants in the education program. In this situation, establishing a committee of staff, parents, students, and community members to review and provide input on fund allocation for technology resources across schools would effectively promote such transparency and build trust among stakeholders. Doing so would actively involve individuals from different stakeholder groups in the decision-making process and foster open dialogue regarding the equitable distribution of technology funds across schools. This collaborative approach would foster a sense of inclusivity, openness, and trust among staff, parents, and community members, thus leading to better decision outcomes and increased confidence in the district's handling of technology resource funding allocation.

100. B: Curriculum mapping is a systematic process that involves identifying and aligning the scope and sequence of curriculum content, instructional strategies, and assessments across grade levels or subjects. This strategy allows teachers to create a comprehensive overview of the curriculum and facilitate a seamless transition from one grade level to another for students. By providing a clear roadmap for teachers, curriculum mapping promotes collaboration and consistency in instruction. It also ensures that academic standards are effectively addressed, thus leading to improved student learning outcomes. In this scenario, by engaging teachers, curriculum specialists, and administrators in a curriculum mapping process, the superintendent can foster collaboration and shared understanding of the curriculum's strengths and areas for improvement. Through this collaborative effort, educators can identify where adjustments are necessary to ensure alignment with academic standards, close content gaps, and improve instructional coherence. This approach would allow the district to make informed decisions about curriculum development and instructional practices to support student learning outcomes more effectively.

101. B: Promoting a shared understanding of a school district's core values throughout the educational community requires concrete actions that resonate with all key stakeholders. An integral component of the superintendent's role as a leader is modeling the district's core values in his or her daily life and practices. By doing so, the superintendent sets a powerful example for students, teachers, administrators, and community members, demonstrating the practical application of the values in real-life contexts. In this scenario, the superintendent can best model the district's core values of compassion, collaboration, and social responsibility by organizing a series of district-wide community service events. Such events would showcase the district's core values while bringing together various stakeholders to collectively contribute to the betterment of the local community. By actively participating in these events, the superintendent can show the district's values in action, thus cultivating a deeper understanding and appreciation for these values among members of the educational community.

102. B: Having a well-defined change model is beneficial when introducing significant educational changes, such as integrating a social and emotional learning (SEL) component into an existing curriculum. These models offer structured frameworks that guide the transition process, ensuring that the change is implemented effectively and minimizes disruption. In this scenario, the superintendent can best mitigate uncertainty and risk while integrating the new curriculum by choosing a change management model that ensures that the transition is gradual and well-managed. A carefully chosen model would provide step-by-step guidelines for introducing the SEL component. This approach allows for stakeholder engagement, clear communication, and systematic adjustments based on feedback and emerging needs. Ultimately, a well-defined change model would enable the superintendent to navigate uncertainty and risk more effectively by fostering collaboration, addressing challenges incrementally, and providing a stable framework for teachers and students during the implementation process.

103. B: An important part of the superintendent's role includes navigating challenges when implementing new educational initiatives. The introduction of a novel curriculum, such as a social and emotional learning (SEL) program, may encounter resistance from stakeholders, including teachers and parents, who voice concerns about potential disruptions. Responding appropriately is essential to address stakeholders' concerns and ensure that the change process aligns with the district's overarching goals of providing a comprehensive education that addresses students' diverse needs. Establishing a committee of teachers, parents, and administrators to collaborate in addressing concerns, sharing insights, and co-creating solutions would demonstrate a comprehensive approach to stakeholder engagement and problem-solving. This inclusive approach would foster an open exchange of ideas and dialogue, thus ensuring that the change process becomes a collective effort that is informed by the diverse insights of all involved. By holding these meetings, the superintendent can directly address concerns while promoting a shared sense of ownership and commitment to the district's overarching goals.

104. B: Addressing the achievement gap and promoting equitable access to learning opportunities requires a systemic approach that would reach all students across the school district. In this situation, the superintendent can achieve this goal by implementing a comprehensive district-wide mathematics review and revision process to ensure that the curriculum is aligned with best practices and tailored to support the learning needs of underperforming students. Such an initiative would involve a thorough evaluation of the existing curriculum, identifying components that may contribute to the achievement gap, and revising it to provide targeted support for the identified group of underperforming students. This would allow for the incorporation of research-based instructional strategies, differentiated learning materials, and resources that specifically address the learning needs of these students. By reviewing and aligning the mathematics curriculum district-wide, the superintendent can ensure consistency in instruction and equal access to resources and materials across all schools. This would ultimately help eliminate potential disparities between schools and classrooms, thus promoting equitable opportunities for all students to succeed in mathematics.

105. D: In order to create a culture in which staff are committed to assuming responsibility for student success and wellbeing, it is important to prepare them with knowledge and strategies for meeting a diverse range of needs. This can be achieved by establishing collaborative professional learning communities within schools and providing ample professional development opportunities focused on meeting students' holistic needs. By establishing professional learning communities, the superintendent promotes collaboration among staff and fosters a collective commitment to student success. In this space, educators can regularly share ideas, learn from one another, discuss student needs, and develop effective strategies for meeting them. Further, providing ample professional development opportunities equips educators with the necessary knowledge, skills, and strategies to effectively support students in their academic, social, emotional, and physical development. This ultimately empowers teachers to take action in addressing varying student needs.

106. B: Developing productive relationships with local colleges and universities is a powerful strategy for expanding learning opportunities for students throughout the district. Such collaboration can lead to the development of programs that enrich the overall learning experience, such as guest lectures, internships, and dual enrollment opportunities. For high school students specifically, partnering with local colleges and universities is beneficial in encouraging them to pursue post-secondary education and preparing them to do so. In this scenario, establishing a dual enrollment program with the local community college would allow high school students in the district to enroll in college-level courses, earn credits, and broaden their academic experiences. Dual enrollment programs prepare students for college rigor, help facilitate a seamless transition from high school to college, and boost students' readiness and confidence to pursue higher education. Additionally, earning college credits while in high school further incentivizes students to attend a higher education institution by reducing the time and cost associated with obtaining a degree. By partnering with the local community college to offer dual enrollment opportunities, the superintendent can enhance student learning opportunities, foster academic growth, and cultivate a college-bound culture within the district.

107. B: The Family and Medical Leave Act (FMLA) is a federal law that allows employees to take up to 12 unpaid weeks of leave for family and medical reasons while maintaining their employment status. This includes the ability to take leave for their own health conditions, caring for an immediate family member, or for the birth, adoption, or foster care placement of a child. In this scenario, the superintendent must grant the teacher's request for extended medical leave according to the FMLA, as the teacher has submitted the appropriate documentation and meets eligibility requirements. By granting the teacher's request for extended leave, the superintendent ensures compliance with the FMLA, protects the teacher's job during her absence, and demonstrates commitment to supporting employees in the district during medical leave by providing the appropriate accommodations and benefits.

108. D: Analyzing and interpreting data from professional development programs helps the superintendent make informed decisions about strategies that can effectively motivate staff for continuous learning and growth. Empowering educators through targeted professional development initiatives can enhance teaching practices, which ultimately improves student learning outcomes. In the given chart, the superintendent can observe the improvement scores, which represent the growth made by staff in each professional development area. Among the options provided, Classroom Management Strategies demonstrated the lowest improvement score of 10. As the other professional development programs show higher growth percentages, it is evident that the Classroom Management Strategies program requires more attention and support to foster continuous learning and improvement for staff. By prioritizing this area, the superintendent can implement tailored strategies and support systems to empower educators and enhance classroom management techniques. Motivated and skilled educators in this domain can positively influence student behavior, engagement, and academic achievement, ultimately contributing to an improved learning environment within the district.

109. C: Using data from professional development programs, the superintendent can identify strengths, areas for improvement, and trends to implement research-based approaches and foster continuous growth for staff members. In the given chart, the superintendent can analyze and interpret improvement scores between pre-assessments and post-assessments, which represent the growth made by staff in each professional development area. Among the options provided, the Culturally Responsive Teaching program stands out as the most impactful. This is indicated by its improvement score of 20, a 40 percent increase in participant score from pre-assessment to post-assessment. This score shows that participants in this program experienced significant growth in knowledge and skills related to culturally responsive teaching practices. By focusing on research-based strategies, the superintendent can ensure that the staff receives high-quality training and support, leading to positive outcomes in student learning and overall school performance. Furthermore, by studying this data, the superintendent can uncover insights into the program's efficacy, which can be utilized to enhance other professional learning programs, thus supporting the continuous growth and development of staff members.

110. A: Providing professional development opportunities that align with staff interests and needs is essential in promoting motivation for continuous learning and growth. Offering workshops and training programs that resonate with staff members creates an environment where educators feel valued, supported, and eager to enhance their skills and knowledge. In this scenario, the data provided in terms of staff participation for each program serves as a valuable tool for the superintendent to assess the effectiveness of and staff engagement in different professional development offerings. Based on the data presented in the given chart, "Equity and Access for All: Empowering Diverse Learners," would likely be the most engaging and sought-after future professional development opportunity. The significant number of participants (50) in the "Culturally Responsive Teaching" program illustrates staff members' interest in cultivating an inclusive learning environment that meets the diverse needs of their students. By offering this workshop, the superintendent can take a proactive approach to address student diversity while aligning professional development with staff interests and growth objectives. By recognizing the impact of well-tailored professional development, the superintendent can plan future opportunities that continue to promote staff motivation for ongoing learning and growth. Through data-driven decision-making, educators can be offered targeted training sessions that empower them with research-based strategies, fostering a collective commitment to creating equitable, effective, and innovative learning experiences for all students.

111. D: An efficient and well-organized transportation system is essential for the smooth functioning of a school district, as it directly affects student attendance, punctuality, and overall learning experience. Inconsistency in bus timings and delays can significantly disrupt teaching and learning, as students arriving late to school may miss important instruction. To address these issues and optimize the district transportation system, the superintendent should begin by reviewing and rearranging existing bus routes to improve efficiency. Reviewing existing bus routes would allow the superintendent to gather information and identify routes that may be inefficient or prone to delays. With this information, the superintendent can make necessary adjustments to routes and can conduct further investigations to identify specific delays and continue improving the overall efficiency of the transportation system, thus reducing interruptions to teaching and learning.

112. C: Integrating community resources into student learning experiences enriches the educational program by aligning the curriculum with students' diverse cultural backgrounds. Doing so fosters personal connections to learning and promotes a greater sense of inclusivity, cultural awareness, engagement, and, ultimately, academic achievement. By collaborating with local artists, musicians, and performers to offer workshops and performances at schools in the district, the superintendent can effectively tap into the community's resources to enrich student learning. Providing interactive and immersive experiences that go beyond traditional classroom settings will expose students to diverse cultures and traditions, thus helping them develop a deeper understanding and appreciation for cultural diversity while promoting inclusivity within the educational environment. Implementing these workshops and performances during school hours would ensure that all students have access to a range of cultural experiences, whereas an after-school program may limit students' ability to attend and make students more inclined to choose workshops and performances aligned with their own backgrounds. Further, these workshops would strengthen the connection between the school and community and promote a greater sense of pride and belonging among students as they see their own cultural heritage represented and celebrated.

113. D: Cultivating an educational environment that promotes success for all students requires the superintendent to possess a deep understanding of the community's strengths and needs. This understanding allows the superintendent to align curriculum, learning targets, and educational experiences with the diverse backgrounds of the district's students. To achieve this, the superintendent should actively engage and involve all stakeholders within the school community, seeking their perspectives and insights on decisions pertaining to the education program. By forming an advisory council comprising a diverse range of stakeholders—including educators, parents, and community members—the superintendent can gain valuable insights into the community's strengths and needs while simultaneously establishing and maintaining a strong presence within the community. This approach would allow the superintendent to gather multiple perspectives while allowing stakeholders to directly influence decisions related to the education program, thus promoting open dialogue and productive collaboration. Further, through regular engagement with council members, the superintendent can remain connected to the community and stay attuned to its evolving strengths, needs, and goals while fostering a sense of trust, inclusivity, and transparency within the district. By harnessing the diverse perspectives of the advisory council, the superintendent can ensure that decisions authentically reflect the values, goals, and cultural nuances of the community, thus leading to an improved school environment and enhanced student learning outcomes.

114. B: When developing a school district's mission, vision, and core values, involving stakeholders from various backgrounds—such as parents, educators, community members, students, and representatives from cultural organizations—is beneficial in helping to ensure that these guiding principles are comprehensive and reflect inclusivity. In this scenario, the superintendent has a goal of creating an educational framework that supports the academic success and well-being of all students. In a diverse school district specifically, achieving this requires that the superintendent involve relevant stakeholders to ensure that the district's mission, vision, and core values reflect the experiences of those directly affected. Engaging parents, students, educators, community members, and representatives from cultural organizations in collaborative discussions would allow for a wide range of perspectives to be integrated into the overarching goals of the district. Through this approach, each stakeholder group can contribute valuable insights that allow for more well-rounded and nuanced outcomes. For example, involving parents can provide an understanding of the community's expectations for education and the specific needs of students. Engaging students ensures that their voices are heard and that their perspectives are integrated into decisions. Additionally, including representatives from cultural organizations can help ensure that cultural diversity and inclusivity are central to the district's guiding principles. By embracing the input of multiple stakeholders, the superintendent can create a mission, vision, and core values that reflect the school community and allow for a more inclusive and culturally sensitive learning environment where the diverse needs of all students are acknowledged and addressed.

115. C: Engaging a diverse array of stakeholders is a vital component in the process of redefining a school district's mission, vision, and core values. These stakeholders—including teachers, parents, students, and community representatives—possess a wealth of distinct experiences, insights, and ideas that can be leveraged to guide decision-making processes. Convening focus-group sessions with these stakeholders would allow the superintendent to pose critical questions and harness their collective insights, concerns, and perspectives. Focus groups offer an interactive and comprehensive platform for effective decision-making, as they allow for meaningful exchanges and encourage participants to openly share their viewpoints. This would enable the superintendent to consider a diverse range of perspectives and make well-informed decisions that accurately represent the values and needs of the entire school community, ultimately contributing to a more comprehensive, inclusive, and effective mission, vision, and set of core values.

116. A: Recognizing the contributions of stakeholders in the process of reshaping a district's mission, vision, and core values is beneficial in fostering a sense of ownership and shared commitment to the outcomes. By acknowledging the efforts and insights of parents, students, teachers, and community members, the superintendent reinforces the message that their perspectives are valued and integral to the decision-making process. This recognition instills a sense of pride among stakeholders while demonstrating an inclusive approach that promotes collaboration and engagement. In this scenario, the superintendent can best demonstrate the district's gratitude by publicly acknowledging the valuable insights of key stakeholders during town hall meetings and district-wide events. Publicly recognizing contributions in such settings ensures that all stakeholders are visibly acknowledged for their roles. This inclusive approach fosters transparency, mutual respect, and a sense of unity among the school community.

117. C: Facilitating open, meaningful, and accessible communication is an important component in fostering engagement among students' families and the community. This includes ensuring that families and community members are informed about the school district's academic programs and initiatives and how the community can contribute to the programs' success. In this scenario, families and community members in a rural school district may face challenges in accessing the internet or may have limited internet connectivity. This can hinder their ability to stay informed about the district's academic programs and initiatives through online platforms. By sending out printed brochures and pamphlets, the superintendent can ensure that information reaches these families and community members directly despite potentially limited internet access. Printed materials would provide tangible and accessible resources that can easily be shared and referred to at any time. Further, this approach would allow for a comprehensive presentation of the district's offerings, with detailed information about academic programs, initiatives, and the district's goals. This approach promotes transparency and supports family and community engagement by ensuring all individuals have access to relevant and comprehensive information.

118. B: Recognizing the importance of students' cultures, backgrounds, and languages as assets to teaching and learning is integral for creating an inclusive and enriching educational environment. Students' diverse backgrounds offer a wide range of knowledge, perspectives, and experiences that enhance overall learning. A superintendent can best exemplify this educational philosophy by prioritizing collaboration with teachers and language specialists to develop culturally responsive and linguistically appropriate learning materials in the curriculum. Doing so would help ensure that students feel culturally and linguistically represented in learning materials as well as provide the support necessary to facilitate meaningful connections to academic content while promoting language acquisition. Through this approach, the superintendent acknowledges students' cultures and languages as assets in the classroom, thus promoting a greater sense of inclusivity, engagement, and motivation for learning.

119. B: Properly addressing student misbehavior is essential in fostering a positive and productive school culture. This includes ensuring that instances of misconduct are handled fairly, appropriately, and consistently. By having the students responsible for the vandalism incident participate in a restorative justice program, the superintendent can ensure that they are held accountable while simultaneously providing opportunities for growth, learning, and repair. This approach would include having the students repair the damage they caused, engage in discussion with affected staff members, such as building service workers, and reflect upon the impact of their misconduct as well as ways in which they can make amends. By individualizing the consequence based on the specific circumstances, the superintendent promotes accountability and provides a fair, consistent, and meaningful resolution for the incident. Restorative practices such as this give students the opportunity to learn from their actions, develop empathy, and take personal responsibility to repair and make amends for the damage caused.

120. A: By offering regular and comprehensive professional development opportunities, a superintendent creates an environment in which teachers and staff can continuously improve their instructional practice. Regular professional development helps staff to build upon pedagogical knowledge and skills, stay current with new teaching methodologies, and develop strategies to effectively address the diverse learning needs of students. This ultimately benefits student learning by ensuring teachers and staff are equipped with the knowledge and tools necessary for designing and implementing quality instruction. Further, by providing regular professional development opportunities, a superintendent demonstrates a commitment to supporting the personal and professional growth of staff members. This contributes to their overall well-being and promotes a positive work-life balance by fostering a sense of fulfillment, growth, and overall job satisfaction.

OSAT Practice Test #2

To take this additional practice test, visit our online resources page:
mometrix.com/resources719/osatsuper248

Online Resources

Due to our efforts to try to keep this book to a manageable length, we've created a link that will give you access to all of your online resources:

mometrix.com/resources719/osatsuper248

It's Your Moment, Let's Celebrate It!

Share your story @mometrixtestpreparation